D0005304

# Reading and Writing in the Global Workplace

## *Gender, Literacy, and Outsourcing in Ghana*

Beatrice Quarshie Smith

LEXINGTON BOOKS
Lanham • Boulder • New York • Toronto • Plymouth, UK

Published by Lexington Books
A wholly owned subsidary of The Rowman & Littlefield Publishing Group, Inc.
4501 Forbes Boulevard, Suite 200, Lanham, Maryland 20706
www.rowman.com

10 Thornbury Road, Plymouth PL6 7PP, United Kingdom

Copyright © 2012 by Lexington Books

*All rights reserved.* No part of this book may be reproduced in any form or by any
electronic or mechanical means, including information storage and retrieval systems,
without written permission from the publisher, except by a reviewer who may quote
passages in a review.

British Library Cataloguing in Publication Information Available

**Library of Congress Cataloging-in-Publication Data**

Smith, Beatrice Quarshie, 1958-
Reading and writing in the global workplace : gender, literacy, and outsourcing in Ghana / Beatrice
Quarshie Smith.
p. cm.
Includes bibliographical references and index.
ISBN 978-0-7391-3784-0 (cloth : alk. paper)• —ISBN 978-0-7391-3786-4 (ebook)
1. Women• —Employment• —Effect of technological innovations on• —Ghana. 2. Offshore out-
sourcing• —Ghana. 3. Information technology• —Economic aspects--Ghana. 4. Globalization• —
Economic aspects• —Ghana. I. Title.
HD6218.3.S65 2012
331.48165109667• —dc23
2012011440

♾™  The paper used in this publication meets the minimum requirements of American
National Standard for Information Sciences Permanence of Paper for Printed Library
Materials, ANSI/NISO Z39.48-1992.

Printed in the United States of America

For my mother (Theodora O. Quarshie) and in memory of my father
(Dr. Reginald A. A. Quarshie)

This project was funded in part by a grant from the American Association of University Women and by a Jeanne Campbell Research Fellowship from the Center for the Education of Women at the University of Michigan.

# Contents

# Acknowledgments

Many people supported me while I worked on this project. While I cannot thank them all by name here, I am nonetheless really appreciative of the help I got. None of the work I report in this book would even be possible without the many women and men who work in the offshore sites of CTI and CDN. They took me in, gave their time, shared their work and offered their friendship and their trust. To the focal women and their network of friends I am profoundly grateful. I hope this book does justice to your experiences.

I am grateful to Ron Strickland and Patty Sotirin for reading and commenting on the manuscript at various stages and to my colleagues at the Center for the Education of Women at the University of Michigan for hosting me and providing me with a community within which to work, explore and receive feedback on my ideas.

This project would have been impossible without the financial support of the American Association of University Women (AAUW). An AAUW's American Fellowship grant enabled me to do field work in Ghana and for that I am profoundly grateful.

Deborah Curtis, the Dean of the College of Education at Illinois State University where I taught from 2000–2008 provided me with resource support and for that I wish to express my profound gratitude.

I want to thank Ron Strickland, my best friend and partner, for his support, understanding, and sacrifice; the months I spent doing fieldwork could only happen because you held things together at home. I truly appreciate all you do and all you have done.

Lastly, I want to thank the anonymous reviewers for their thoughtful suggestions to the manuscript and Amy King for her guidance and support.

Any errors, shortcomings, and omissions are entirely mine alone.

*Copyright Acknowledgments*

I am grateful to the International Reading Association for permission to reuse parts of my 2006 piece "Outsourcing and digitized work spaces: Some implications of the intersections of globalization, development and work practices." *Journal of Adolescent and Adult Literacy*, 48, 596–607; and to Hampton Press for permission to reuse my 2007 book chapter "Researching hybrid literacies: Methodological explorations of "ethnogra-phy" and the practices of the "cybertariat" in DeVoss, D. & Mckee, H. *Digital writing research: Technologies, methodologies, and ethical issues.*

# Tables and Photographs

# Acronyms

Canadian International Development Agency (CIDA)
US Agency for International Development (USAID)
International Monetary Fund (IMF)
United Nations Development Programme (UNDP)
Food and Agricultural Organization (FAO)
International Labour Organization (ILO)
Client Technological Industries (CTI)
Client Data Network (CDN)
Business Process Outsourcing (BPO)
Information Technology Process Outsourcing (ITO)
Non-Governmental Organization (NGO)
31st December Women's Movement (DWM)
Client Computing Services Department (CCSD–CDN)
Selective Data Solutions Department (SDSD–CDN)
Quality Option Solutions Department (QOSD–CDN)
Export Processing Zone (EPZ)
Association of African Women for Research and Development (AA-WORD)
Women and Development (WAD)
Gender and Development (GAD)
Women in Development (WID)
Development Alternatives with Women for a New Era (DAWN)
Ministry of Women's and Children's Affairs (MOWAC)
December 31st Women's Movement (DWM)
Economic Recovery Program (ERP)
Structural Adjustment Program (SAP)
Central Intelligence Agency (CIA)
Knowledge Management (KM)
Program of Action to Mitigate the Social Costs of Adjustment (PAM-SCAD)
Women's Empowerment Research Project Consortium (WERPC)
Organization for Economic Co-operation and Development (OECD)
Structural Adjustment Participatory Review International Network (SAPRIN)
Health Insurance Portability and Accountability Act (HIPPA)

# Gender, Biography, and the Researcher: Locating the "Self" in the Study of "New" Workspaces

"Are you going to write about us?" — A simple question posed by Nola Addy,[1] a woman who works in a data-processing outsourcing facility in Ghana, opens a floodgate of critical issues related to researching and writing about other people's experience. What does that process mean, or what should it mean? I have frequently wondered what concerns might be lurking beneath the polite surface of that question. Could she have been asking about what I stand to gain in my desire to "write" about them? Could she have been wondering about my motives, interests and whose side I am on? Could she have been wondering about how what I have been told will be represented as I "write"? Could she have been concerned about what that writing might mean for her and her co-workers? Nola's question, examined from different angles, is ever-present in the writing of this book, for in attempting to answer the question, I confront my own biography as an academic, a woman, an African immigrant in the United States, and a researcher who has chosen to study two work sites in a country with which I continue to maintain intimate ties. In this preface to the volume I situate myself as a researcher and offer brief discussions on the issues that frame my experience and the work I have done.

This book and the process of generating it have been heavily influenced by my biography on several fronts; fronts that capture the complex cross currents of what Arjun Appadurai describes as "resources for experiments with self-making" in the "global now" (1997, 3). There is the dimension of my identity as a woman. There is the dimension of my identity as an African immigrant in the United States who opted for naturalized citizenship even while maintaining my Ghanaian ties. There is the dimension of my development as an academic through higher education in Ghana, the United Kingdom and the United States. There is the dimension of my itinerant sojourns in multiple places around the world, from teaching stints in Saudi Arabia, Qatar and Thailand to consulting work in Tanzania. And finally there are the unique intersections that these influences produce. The various strands of my biography have shaped how I came to be a researcher and how I came to conduct the research that is the subject of this book. Of course, biography, however layered and complex, only partially answers Nola's question. But to situate the "self" and the research process, this preface uses my biographical stories to frame the project while foregrounding the methodological implications of Nola's question and its influence on my practices.

## BIOGRAPHY AND THE RESEARCH PROCESS

My research training was begun in the manner of the traditional doctoral apprenticeship process; it was inaugurated under what can best be described as a patriarchal model. But this smooth path to a calm destination was interrupted by the exceptionally powerful experience of shifting research orientations from a positivist/foundational paradigm to a qualitative one *in situ* and as a result, of breaking with a mentor. My dissertation project began as a straight-forward quantitative study of the reading practices of English for Business Purposes second language learners at a university in the Persian Gulf. But during my data-collection period conditions changed dramatically after the Iraqi invasion of Kuwait in the summer of 1990. As the build-up to war commenced it became clear that a linguistics-based study alone would not do justice to the intricate human dramas that confronted the Qatari, Palestinian and Kuwaiti English language students whom I taught. For example, there were some painful conversations, emotions, and messy human relations that the Kuwaiti, Qatari, and the few Palestinian students were navigating that quantitative data and a discussion of that data alone could not adequately capture. Far from a matter of simply reporting what was easily reportable, I recognized the potential political implications of my research and the potential consequences of not engaging the messy stuff in the research process. I had a conversion, but, given the very structure of the dissertation supervision process, it was not going to be my conversion alone—since my dissertation director rejected my shift of focus, I chose to form a new committee. With the support of the new committee, I redesigned my project using mixed methods. This experience has made me ever so alert to questions about whether the research processes I use can ever adequately capture the messiness of the experiences I attempt to capture. This initiation into the research process has framed the choices I make in research paradigms. It is also this experience that encapsulates for me the seriousness with which Nola's question ought to be addressed in the process of crafting this book.

Conversations in the qualitative research community recognize the messiness, the mixed emotions, and at times the sheer paralysis that the research process can provoke. I have often attributed the emotions and feelings I secretly harbor about the research process to my inexperience. But other researchers have noted the critical triple crises of representation, legitimization, and praxis in qualitative research over the last two decades (see, for example, Denzin and Lincoln 2003; Saukko 2003). These research issues, taken in the context of Nola's question, are serious concerns for me. Prominently entangled in these crises is the location of researcher "self." Nola's question gets at my values as a person, and, by default, as a researcher. Certainly my values are heavily imbricated in my choice of a researchable "problem," the paradigm that guides my inquiry, my theoretical framework, my data-gathering and data-analysis methods, the choice of research sites and how the values of the research sites are represented as I analyze and report the research.

New media and migration and their effects on the imagination have been theorized as critical dimensions to globalization by Appadurai and others. Media and migration frame this project on two levels. My personal stake in the research is affected by the conditions of ethnicity, citizenship, gender, and race and how they are shot through by the peculiarities of diasporic nationalist identification, and by race and gender relations in the "new" communities I have come to embrace. These strands of commitment and influence cannot be easily disentangled. The result is an amalgam that is constitutive of my subjectivities. On a professional level, the fieldwork that generated data for this book began in 2004 and was completed in 2005. The field was two "outsourcing" workspaces in Ghana—spaces made possible by the relocation of labor processes offshore and the construction and representation of such labor practices in American political and economic discourse. For my purposes I have named the two sites "Client Technological Industries" (CTI from hence) and "Client Data Network" (CDN from hence). My interest in gender, knowledge and work focused my attention on a *New York Times* article about outsourcing work in Ghana (July 22, 2002, A4). In the *Times* piece women who worked at a company that processed New York City ordinance violation tickets jokingly referred to their workplace as "an electronic sweatshop," but they also revealed an almost half-serious hope that working for an American company might give them access to the "American dream," in some vague undefined way. One woman interviewed in the article joked that if she were to move to New York, she would know where not to park her car. Shortly thereafter, Thomas Freidman wrote about other business process-outsourcing operations in Ghana in his *New York Times* column and later in his bestselling book *The World is Flat* (2006).These discussions of outsourced work in Ghana raised a host of questions for me: Why Ghana? What larger social, cultural, political and economic processes are at play in the relocation of work to Ghana?

A convergence of cultural, political and economic forces has contributed to the offshore relocation of U.S. business processing services. Companies engaged in data-processing services take advantage of the postmodern diffusion of technology, the global restructuring of capital markets and the easing of restrictions on foreign direct investment in countries like Ghana. Ghana's favorable political climate and the availability of a well-educated English speaking labor force are further attractions. For almost twenty-five years now, Ghana has been the "model" tutee of the International Monetary Fund (IMF) and the World Bank as its leaders follow economic reform plans and directives attached to aid programs from the two bodies. Adopting an indigenized version of western concepts of democratic processes coupled with neoliberal-inspired free enterprise philosophy, Ghana's leaders are spear-heading fundamental changes to society (Boafo-Arthur 2007). Ghana therefore provides a location where the intersections of the patterns brought on by the global political, economic and cultural restructuring, and their effect on gender, development, technology and literacy can be explored in microcosm. My analysis of outsourcing in Ghana is concerned with the particular ways in which these dynamics interconnect in particular places at particular times. What, for example, is the nature of work in these spaces? How do media and popular-culture representations of American society shape the expectations of outsourcing workers? Historically, Sub-Saharan Africa has lagged behind in the march toward modernization. What work-related literacies and practices enable services to be provided for western companies in spaces powered by information communication technologies in a part of the planet that even the most astute observers assumed would be irrelevant to the new global economy?[2] Why are these spaces so heavily populated by women? What are the effects of the presence of so many women in wage labor on family and community?[3]

It is clear that even societies that are supposedly "irrelevant" in the globalizing dynamic are undergoing radical change. This project is a way of understanding a specific instance of this change at a particular place at a particular time.

## NOTES

1. All participant names and company names are pseudonyms. I use Nola for Nola Addy. Except for a few occasions, I have elected to use the first names of all participants. Elsewhere, Quarshie Smith (2005 & 2007), I have used CCS as a pseudonym for CTI. Company names and participant names have been changed to preserve confidentiality.
2. I have written about this elsewhere—see Quarshie Smith (2005 & 2007)
3. The questions that guided my fieldwork and which frame the research are

- In what ways and for what purposes do women in process outsourcing use digital and information communications technologies in their literacy practices in the workplace?
- In what ways and for what purposes do women enact gender and culturally specific literacy practices in their online and offline workspaces?
- How are constructions of gender implicated in the women's technology-mediated literacy practices within their online work communities?

- How do the local and the global intersect? That is to say, what are the global economic conditions that make this arrangement proliferate for outsourcing companies?
- What are the current and potential future political implications of such arrangements? How are these economic and political issues perceived by Ghanaians?

# ONE

## Gender, Globalization, and "New" Workspaces

Feminist scholars insist that globalization is a gendered process and that its effects on women and men are radically different (Hawkesworth 2006). For feminists, a critical issue in the ongoing debate about characteristics of globalization is the absence of gender-focused analyses in mainstream social and political science research and theory-building. The task has been to demonstrate the "thoroughly gendered" nature of globalizing processes and thus to make visible what other analyses leave unarticulated (Hawkesworth 2006, 11). This book seeks to contribute to this project by examining the effects of globalized workplaces in relation to traditionally gendered institutions in Ghana. The places where people work are changing. Specific workplace literacies and other production practices that workers use have been changing (Farrell and Fenwick 2007). In many areas of the global South these ongoing cultural, economic and political transformations have resulted in unprecedented numbers of women entering the official wage labor economy. As Leys notes in his forward to Huws (2003), since the middle of the twentieth century most office work in advanced industrial societies has been done by women (xi). Now, at the beginning of the twenty-first century, this feminization of office work and information processing is taking place in emerging economies such as Ghana's.

Technological innovation is the main gateway to participation in the global economy. Various technologies offer the infrastructure for the fluid movement of capital, data, images, and labor around the world. This has made the infusion/diffusion of technologies into countries in the global South critical to their access to the global economy. Connectivity to the global information technology grid fuels the relocation of work from the North to the South as capital relentlessly searches for cheap, efficient

1

labor. The application of information communication technologies (ICT's) to labor processes has meant that any work that can be digitized may be outsourced offshore (Huws 2003). These outsourcing processes have largely (though not exclusively) affected women because as capitalism assigned office work to women during the twentieth century it also located them at the vanguard of workplace technology adoption in the twenty-first century. In the western economies therefore women largely bore the social costs of the use of workplace technologies and the subsequent degradation of work that these technologies created. Women also ultimately lost their jobs as that work shifted offshore (Huws 2003).

Outsourcing—the practice whereby companies use sub-contractors to perform non-core functions—is a common labor arrangement. Companies that offer outsourcing services have proliferated to meet the demands of the market for these services. Some of these companies exist for the sole purpose of providing third- and fourth-tier contract services. While the focus of outsourced functions can be narrow—such as payroll, billing, data entry, indexing, and transcription—they can also be extensive and substantive. These expansive practices can generally be grouped under business process outsourcing (BPO) functions or information technology process outsourcing (ITO) functions. BPO services cover call center support, human resources, finance and accounting, claims processing, quality assurance, etc. Examples of ITO services may be telecommunications, "voice over internet protocol" (VOIP), software development and testing, network security, etc. Offshore outsourcing refers to the practice of doing outsourced work off the shores of the country where that work originated. American companies depend on sub-contractors in India, Ireland, the Philippines, Ghana, and South Africa, to name a few, to meet some of their non-core, non-revenue generating functions. While cheap labor is often the logic for these arrangements, some companies argue that the delegation of functions give them a foothold into new markets for the sale of their products or services.

Gender-focused analyses of labor practices in business processes and information technology outsourcing are necessary not only because women tend to do this work but also because examining these practices may shed light on the precise mechanisms by which various modes of feminization occur in specific contexts. While there is no question that a different kind of workplace is emerging in societies in the global North, we are only beginning to learn about the particular situational inflections workplaces take on as "new" work migrates to the global South.[1] As I argue in later chapters, the cycle of work degradation and loss shifts offshore with outsourced work where a new labor corps starts yet another round of culturally grounded pioneering of workplace transformations whose end result is as yet unknown but which historical analyses render all too predictable.

## "KNOWLEDGE" WORK AND "DEVELOPMENT"

Business process and information process outsourced work fits into what is now commonly labeled "knowledge" work. The global economy is often described as the "knowledge economy." I use the quotation marks to signal the need to unpack these labels (Farrell and Fenwick, 2007). Outsourced work that is knowledge-based in the global South is only accessible to these locations via a technology infrastructure and a political climate that supports their growth. It is a dynamic that links globalizing processes to the development agenda of nations in the global South and donor agencies of the North. The ideological underpinnings of the gap between North and South are underscored by the terminology adopted to describe the two over the last forty years.[2] Wherever one locates development in contemporary discussions, it is clear that access and participation in the global economy has become critical to the agenda and aspirations of many in the "less developed" world. Technology infusion and diffusion and the rate at which "less developed" economies absorb these technologies is critical to bridging the gap between rich and poor nations (World Bank, 2008). Access to the versions of knowledge needed to participate in the global economy has become critical to nations like Ghana as they seek to secure the benefits of the ICT revolution. The United Nations Commission on Science and Technology has called on member states to evaluate the social and economic impacts of ICTs and to create opportunities for capacity building that will ensure their beneficial use and absorption within national economies and civil society. In relation to ICTs and development the commission notes:

> Government innovation policies should promote national knowledge systems that support the development and increase the competitiveness of national economies. Special emphasis should be put on human capital formation and education. Measures such as the establishment of development-friendly intellectual property regimes and competition policies, reinforcement of research systems, development of ICT infrastructures, and the creation of a trustful environment for ICT use, need to be integrated within general national economic development strategies. (UNCST 2008)

Ghana has adopted various development agendas since independence, but a consistent set of policies adopted since the early nineties make apparent the ways in which the country is navigating the tension between social and cultural disintegration and economic capacity-building as it attempts to build the infrastructure that will sustain development projects, particularly in the area of job creation. As I demonstrate in later chapters, it is also this tension that situates Ghana in global flows of production and development.

The development debate invariably draws attention to inequalities in global political economy. The core of the world economy is managed on a decentralized international scale, yet until recently the gross differences in income and wealth between nations in the North and South had not been considered problematic. In the emerging paradigm discourses of superiority and morality are replaced by models of 'development' advocated for by Non-Governmental Organizations (NGOs) and activists. Donor nations and organizations have sought to go beyond providing mere band-aids to seeking ways to support more sustainable development (see Waters 2001, 112). As Manuel Castells points out, however, even aid to Africa that is ostensibly motivated by altruism serves the self-interest of the global North. Aid is an approach to prevent massive famine and therefore a strategy to forestall potential mass migration to the North (1996, 135). The development debate pits activists against the IMF and the World Bank. These transnational organizations are criticized by anti-globalization activists for their lending practices and prescriptions to economies in the South. The two bodies have been providing considerable resources to nations like Ghana to support economic and technological infrastructure development (I examine the role of the IMF and World Bank in Ghana in chapter 2). The Ghanaian government's apparent ability to use resources while adhering to IMF and World Bank recommendations has made Ghana a "model" economy. The IMF and World Bank imprimatur has constructed a favorable investment climate that has set in motion the relocation of outsourced work to the country. The outsourcing economy in Ghana, I contend, presents a uniquely interesting confluence of the complex and contradictory economic, cultural and political changes brought on by global restructuring.

## THE SITES, RESEARCH PARADIGMS AND ISSUES

In my research, I use a multi-sited design that enacts an adapted form of ethnographic research practices. Situated ethnographic research accommodates a theoretical orientation incorporating Appadurai's (1997) idea of "scapes" and "flows."[3] Appadurai's concept of "scapes" (as in ideoscapes, technoscapes, financescapes, mediascapes, ethnoscapes, etc.) refers to spheres of existence that layer social reality—for example, media, ideology, and technology. Appadurai argues that "flows" can connect two physically disconnected locations such as the United States and Ghana. In my case "flows" connect the two sites, Client Technological Industries (CTI) and Client Data Network (CDN), to the discursive "scapes" that traverse them as well as to the Unites States, where their work originates and ultimately returns. These scapes are not static; they are suffused by the flows of capital, commodities, images, texts, and people's aspirations, imaginations, and desires. These flows connect different places and people. Appadurai's notion of "scapes" is critical since it allows me to take full account of the fluid relationships between the "virtual," physical, and structural conditions of labor at CTI and CDN. Appadurai's conceptualization enables me to situate the experiences of women working at the two locations in the larger context of a country navigating the tensions between social dislocation and capacity building.

Using ethnographic practices at the two sites, my goal was to generate a comprehensive understanding of the behaviors, social interactions, values and beliefs of the work communities of CTI and CDN. A multi-sited study of these social communities enables me to paint "a picture" by capturing practices in them at a particular historical moment. My principal goal is to describe the relationships among literacies and work at CTI and CDN, fully cognizant of Nola's question and all that may be implied by it. As Florio-Ruane and McVee (2002) point out, contemporary ethnographers have to grapple with how they address the ever-present danger of constructing descriptions of others that freeze or stereotype their realities and in the process leave them voiceless. Through the examination of ordinary daily routines, practices and observances at CTI and CDN, I have worked self-consciously to create accessibility to the communities under study while being self-reflexive about my situation as a researcher.

## WORKPLACE LITERACIES AND "NEW" WORK

This book situates workplace literacy and work-related knowledge as social practices better understood in the context of larger social, economic, cultural, and political dynamics. Barton, Hamilton & Ivanič (2000) begin the introduction to their edited collection *Situated Literacies: Reading and Writing in Context* with the following observation: "Literacies are situated. All uses of written language can be seen as located in particular times and places. Equally, all literate activity is indicative of broader social practices"(1). Understanding literacy as social practice is, however, merely the foundation of analyses, not an end point. Treating such understanding as an end in itself does not take us far. As Alastair Pennycook argues in *Language as Local Practice,* moving beyond this starting point into broader analyses requires substantively rigorous grounding of the terms "social" and "practice" (2010) in ways that focus attention on the material implications of language use. Pennycook reclaims practice not as an add-on to theories of language, literacy or discourse but as "repeated, social and meso-political practices that mediate between social structures and individual action" (32). Understanding literacy as social practice is to move beyond descriptive analyses into understanding the "material and political consequences of language use" (32). Indeed what is foregrounded in this approach is understanding the ideological bases of literate practices as well as the contexts in which practices occur; it is a move that examines epistemologies of practice and contexts. These contexts are local/global and they blur the boundaries of orality, literacy and multimodality. The Workplace Ethnography Project (1944–2002) and the numerous publications based on it, for example (Hodson, 1999, 2001; 2002), provide rich data on ethnographies of workplaces in eighteen countries.[4] In the global North these studies have generated insights into workplace dynamics, organizational leadership, workplace education and training as well as change. As certain work functions began migrating to the global South, researchers have followed. Researchers hope to document, interrogate, analyze and in the process understand the social contexts of work and the practices that make doing work possible. In these contexts, local ways of doing work do not exists as "autonomous" essentialized practices; rather even the local is shaped by participant immersion in other local literacy practices. Thus practices such school, religious, bureaucratic and family literacies complicate the local, and my later chapters illustrate this. Further, to interface literacy with the global is to grapple with the fundamental construct of the hybrid (Street, 2007). There is no pure global literate practice; rather there is the layered construct that is practiced by participants in spaces that are shaped by multiple but complex influences at particular moments.

In an influential book on the emergence of digital environments from the early 1990s, Jay Bolter argued that in postmodern society "print will no longer define the organization and presentation of knowledge, as it has for the past five centuries." But this does not mean that literacy will die, he concludes: "What will be lost is not literacy itself, but the literacy of print, for electronic technology offers us a new kind of book and new ways to read and write"(Bolter, 2). Yet we have lacked research that explores these new ways to read and write in the workplace; research that grounds the specific demands of literate workplace culture in networked environments. To date there has not been any significant examination of the many outsourcing sites that are appearing in places such as Ghana. Yet it is clear that work and work practices have undergone radical transformation as a result of globalization and the uses of Information Communication Technologies (ICTs). Outsourced process work such as processing insurance claims, data processing, and product servicing is almost always performed in environments powered by ICTs. These workspaces are digitized, fluid and immaterial in societies that are often dealing with the infrastructure development of modernization and globalization at the same time.

I use the montages of CTI and CDN to understand the literate practices of these sites, the questions they raise about the uses of Information Communication Technologies (ICTs) in these "new" workspaces, the feminization of labor, the implications of ICTs for workforce development for women in global South locations such as Ghana and the place of the imagination in the "hybrid" workspaces that now cross national boundaries because of the virtual and transnational character of the work people do. The montage offers a nuanced understanding of the literacies of outsourcing and how these intersect with gender, technology, globalization, and development. It offers a way of understanding the contested meanings, practices and spaces in which outsourcing work gets done and thus the impact of global economic restructuring on knowledge, work, gender, family and community at a particular place and at a particular historical moment.

Economists from the time of Adam Smith and David Ricardo have acknowledged the indispensable role of labor in the creation of wealth, and Karl Marx famously pointed out the contradictory way in which capital both needs labor and needs to de-emphasize the importance of labor in the creation of wealth. Outsourcing can be seen as a strategy to de-emphasize labor's contribution. But in *Multitude*, the second installment of their three-volume study of the shifting political and economic conditions of postmodern globalization, Antonio Negri and Michael Hardt take this insight a step further. Labor creates wealth both directly—through organized production and through the resistance of labor to exploitation by capital, which prompts innovation. At the end of *Multitude*, Negri and Hardt present this case in order to argue against the association of innovation, key to the creation of wealth, with the individual-subject-as-manager. Innovation, they argue, occurs in all sorts of collective forms—such as the development of folk medicines by traditional societies (336–40). But, more to the point for my study, the outsourcing that is happening as a result of the inherent conflict of interest between labor and management is both enabling and being enabled by technological innovation. For this reason, among others, Negri and Hardt see such aspects of globalization as opportunities for democratic change.

My multi-sited study offers an opportunity to explore these tensions between labor and capital in a local setting. I propose that the Information Technology and Business Process outsourcing workspaces in "less developed" economies offer sites to contest the apparent mass transfer of notions of workplace literacy as functional, skill-based and thus somehow neutral and unproblematic onto other contexts. I also propose that an examination of particular workspaces offers feminist scholars exemplars for examining the specific conditions under which labor gets feminized. I argue that the tensions among the push for development, for access to the "benefits" of globalization, and the literacies that enable participation in these locations have damaging consequences for individuals, particularly women, and communities when work and the language-mediated practices associated with dominant economies are unproblematically transferred into these settings. Highlighting the implications of these tensions for workplace literacy studies, I argue, offers an opportunity for the subfield to engage in research and advocate for work-

place education practices that may mitigate some of the damaging consequences of globalization, particularly for women.

My purpose in writing this book is not to evaluate outsourcing per se:
in fact I would argue that outsourcing is not universally bad. Rather my
interest is in understanding the contested meanings, practices and spaces
in which outsourcing work gets done. I want to understand the particu-
larity of the impact of global economic restructuring on work, and on
gender relations at a particular place and at a particular historical moment. I argue that cyber-work raises complex social, cultural and political
concerns for workplace studies and for scholars in the subfield who work
from a feminist orientation. I argue that these concerns need to be confronted if globalization is going to translate into workplace practices that
are humane and facilitative of the kinds of aspirations that host communities have. IT and BP outsourcing and other forms of cyber work offer
opportunities to begin examining the new work that is being done by
new workers in the new places. For the emerging subfield of workplace
literacy studies, I argue, these new times require new approaches as we
cannot only focus on how technologies are shaping work in the global
North—research in offshore settings will be critical to how we come to
understand work, gender, literate practices and knowledge in the workplace in the twenty-first century.

## OVERVIEW OF THE BOOK

I use montages of the two establishments to understand the literate practices at these sites, the questions they raise about the uses of Information
Communication Technologies (ICTs) in these "new" workspaces, the feminization of labor, the implications of ICTs for workforce development
for women in global South locations such as Ghana and the place of the
imagination in the "hybrid" workspaces that now cross national boundaries because of the virtual and transnational character of the work
people do.

*Part One: Introduction and Background*

The next chapter, "The Ethnographic Context: Ghana 50 Years after
Independence," discusses the political and economic history of Ghana as
well its education system and labor market. The chapter constructs a
larger context for the country's contemporary circumstances by locating
its economic infrastructure development in the context of larger global
economic and political changes. The chapter discusses the relationship
between Ghana and the IMF and World Bank over the last five decades.

# TWO

## The Ethnographic Context: Ghana Fifty Years after Independence

Outsourcing operations in Ghana are embedded in a complex environment of historical, political, economic, and social relations. Untangling these threads is important to understanding practices in workspaces using Information Communication Technology (ICT). Wage labor and the literacies that go with it offer one means to individual and community sustainability. For many nations in sub-Saharan Africa, the conditions for job creation and community sustainability have always been conflicted, and this has been particularly so in the post-colonial era. In chapter 1 I briefly introduced the theoretical orientation of the book as working with a conception of literacy as social practice. This chapter provides a historical overview with particular attention to politics, the economy, and sociocultural dynamics in order to contextualize the policies and practices of the two companies under study. The overview is mostly chronological though the chronology is interrupted as some important issues are extensively explored.

Outsourcing companies and donor agencies assert the importance of a highly skilled labor force; here I will discuss Ghana's educational system and attempts to reform it in the effort to meet these expectations. I draw attention to the alphabetic focus of school-based literacies in the education reform process, the high population rate, and number of unemployed/underemployed. I discuss the literacies related to outsourcing work in the contemporary context of globalization. The final section of this chapter shares information about the companies, their management personnel, focal participants and their immediate networks of friends with whom I interacted during the research process.

# THE NATION-STATE: A POLITICAL, SOCIAL AND ECONOMIC EVOLUTION

At independence from Britain in 1957 and under the charismatic leader-ship of Kwame Nkrumah, the new Ghanaian state was a symbol of hope for African nations still under colonial domination. The post-indepen-dence euphoria was short-lived, however, as Nkrumah's ambitious pro-jects depleted the nation's financial reserves rather rapidly (Konadu-Ag-yemang, 2001). Nkrumah was deposed in a military coup while en route to Peking in 1966.[1] A new civilian ruler, Kofi Abrefa Busia, emerged in 1969 as the coup leaders lifted a ban on politics and allowed new elec-tions. But this first coup d'état began a cycle of coup d'états, interspersed with attempts at democratic rule and the return of various military per-sonalities until the early 1990s. From 1966-1987 Ghana went through a protracted period of political instability with the Second Republic, the coup of 1972, and the 1979 coup by junior officers that deposed the coup leaders of 1972. Flight Lieutenant Jerry Rawlings, the leader of the 1979 coup, vowed to return the country to civilian rule as soon as possible. He kept this promise, handing over power to a civilian government after a few months, only to return in yet another coup in 1981. The 1981 coup toppled the democratically-elected government of Dr. Hilla Liman and the Third Republic. A significant outcome of this political instability was economic stagnation and deepening crises as standards of living fell pre-cipitously and job creation fizzled. In January 1993, Ghana started yet another democratic experiment under a liberal democracy implementing neoliberal economic policies. The current influx of transnational compa-nies, foreign direct investment, outsourcing-related work and other workplace practices are best understood through the lenses of these polit-ical and economic developments.

## SECOND, THIRD, AND FOURTH REPUBLICS

Ghana's protracted period of post-independence political instability has had both social and economic consequences that are still prevalent today. While by the 1980s it was clear that the independence movement had failed at creating and sustaining political institutions, it is still the case that current political and economic frameworks can be traced to the Nkrumah and Busia regimes. These regimes laid the foundation for the economic and political infrastructure of the country. For foreign ex-change Ghana's economy is largely dependent on the exportation of cash crops—particularly cocoa, timber and minerals, especially gold. Agricul-ture provides employment for the majority of citizens. Cash crops such as cocoa are mainly cultivated by men while women engage in subsistence farming. Cocoa exports have normally provided about half of the country's hard currency earnings but commodity prices have always been volatile. In the early 1960s a combination of factors—including free market competition, the mismanagement of the industry and corruption—contributed to a severe decline in cocoa income. Under pressure from the International Monetary Fund (IMF), the Busia government acquiesced to structural adjustment measures. The policy was met with resistance and protests by the middle class and the salaried work force, both of which faced wage freezes, tax increases, currency devaluations and rising costs of living. This Busia-era IMF-sanctioned structural adjustment also marks the beginning of the country's relationship to the Bretton Woods institutions. The pressures on the government opened the space for a coup that ended the Second Republic in 1972. As Boafor-Arthur (2007) notes, by the end of the Second Republic, Ghana had tried both left-leaning and conservative governing processes and failed.[2]

In 1972 a new military regime repudiated some of the structural adjustment measures the Busia government had put in place and re-valued the currency upward. It reduced the burden of the national debt by the repudiation of US $90 million in debt to British companies; most of these were incurred during the Nkrumah government. Additionally, the military regime unilaterally rescheduled the rest of the country's debts while also nationalizing all large foreign-owned companies. While these moves had populist appeal among Ghanaians they further aggravated the problem of capital flow.

The uncertain global economic outlook of the early 1980s did not help matters, either. In the global North the crisis of capitalism and the corrective restructuring that resulted from it took on different manifestations in different countries (Castells 1996). For sub-Saharan Africa and Latin America it resulted in cuts in IMF money supply which suppressed wages and imports. Ghana's economy declined even further as a result. Thus, for example, the Liman government's first budget (fiscal 1981) projected the inflation rate at 70 percent. The budget deficit for fiscal 1981 amounted to 30 percent of the gross national product. When Rawlings returned via another coup on December 31, 1981 the economy was on the verge of collapsing (Konadu-Agyemang 2001). In the next section I look at the Economic Recovery Program (ERP) across various Ghanaian regimes.

## THE ECONOMIC RECOVERY PROGRAM (ERP)

Though Rawlings came into power professing a leftist orientation, global economic pressures forced his left-leaning government to reposition itself and embrace neoliberal economics. By 1983 Rawlings' government had announced a program of economic austerity and sacrifice. Economic recovery, the government asserted, required a significant injection of capital that could only be obtained from the Bretton Woods institutions. With IMF and World Bank assistance and over the objections of the left wing of the government, the Rawlings regime began implementing a multi-phased Economic Recovery Program (ERP)/Structural Adjustment Program (SAP) whose logic was very much the tenets of the "Washington Consensus."[3] In 1983 the then secretary for finance and economic planning, Kwesi Botchwey, publicly defended World Bank assistance to Ghana thus:

> It would be naive and unrealistic for certain sections of the Ghanaian society to think that the request for economic assistance from the World Bank and its affiliates means a sellout of the aims and objectives of the Ghanaian revolution to the international community. . . . It does not make sense for the country to become a member of the bank and the IMF and continue to pay its dues only to decline to utilize the resources of these two institutions. (Ghana Country Guide 2012, 68)

Economic stability was urgently needed if other systemic issues in the economy were to be tackled. The multi-phased ERP set up benchmarks for each phase of implementation. Phase one (1983–1986) sought to lay the groundwork for economic stability. Economic stability would in turn create a climate conducive for the generation of capital that would allow policy makers to reduce and or control inflationary pressures. Ultimately, the goal was to create confidence in the nation's economic recovery potential. Evidence that these measures were beginning to work by IMF/World Bank standards started appearing in 1987. The inflation rate dropped to 20 percent, and for the first time the economy grew between 1983 and 1987. Of course, these indicators do not foreground the costs of ERP to the masses of ordinary citizens.

During Phase Two, from 1987 to 1989, the government began a process to divest itself of assets by privatization. It also put in place radical foreign exchange reforms that resulted in devaluing the currency, the cedi. By some estimates Ghana's economy grew at 6 percent per year during this period (Konadu-Agyemang & Takyi, 2001, 25). The overarching goal of the ERP was to reduce Ghana's debts and to improve its trading position in the global economy. The strategy was to restore economic productivity at minimum cost to the government by instituting stringent fiscal, monetary and trade policies to lower inflation, increasing foreign exchange, restructuring economic institutions, restoring production incentives, rehabilitating infrastructure (such as roads and harbors) to enhance conditions for the production and export of goods, and increasing the availability of consumer goods (see http://countrystudies.us/ghana/70.htm). Notably, these reforms opened up the country for fuller participation in the production and consumption regimes of the industrialized West.

As the country followed these World Bank and IMF "guidelines," it was "rewarded." Assistance from donor countries to Ghana's recovery program averaged US $430 million in 1987 and the military regime made a payment of more than US $500 million in loan arrears dating to before 1966. As a further reward for meeting these actions, international agencies pledged more than US $575 million to the country's future programs by May 1987. Missing in these macroeconomic success stories, however, is an account of the hidden costs of ERP on citizens. As critics point out, growth in GNP and GDP, the drop in inflation, increase in industrial production and the credibility Ghana had created to attract foreign direct investment did not qualitatively enhance conditions of living of ordinary citizens (Konadu-Agyemang, 2001; Panford, 2001). Critics argue that these gains are not engendering development substantively. Massive unemployment and underemployment, for example, has persisted.

As macroeconomic processes froze citizens out of wage labor and in the absence of a social safety net people began exploring both legal and illegal approaches to survival.[4] Cross-border circuits in human trafficking, prostitution, the drug trade and money-laundering have become more prevalent; the CIA Fact Book now describes the country as a source of cannabis for the international drug trade and a major transit hub for heroin from Asia and cocaine from South America, all destined for Europe and the United States (https://www.cia.gov/library/publications/the-world-factbook/geos/gh.html).

Phase Three (1990–1993) of the ERP further demonstrates the pervasiveness of the neoliberal ideology of allowing the "invisible hand of the market" to regulate the economy with little or no government regulation. During the third phase of the ERP the government strengthened monetary reforms, cut private corporate taxes to boost private-sector growth and further removed itself from investments in entities it had held for the collective good since independence. Privatization, according to neoliberals, creates private wealth which will in turn eventually lead to social benefits. The government under IMF/World Bank mandates also agreed to extensive banking reforms; it agreed to liberalize its administrative structure; and agreed to strengthen the management of the public sector. These conditions are clearly in large measure responsible for the increase in private sector investment in the country and the emergence of outsourcing entities. By the early 1990s, ERP had successfully rehabilitated Ghana's international financial reputation mainly based on its ability to make loan repayments. The result was that Ghana could make an entry onto the international capital market for the first time in almost two decades. The social costs of structural adjustment notwithstanding, Ghana had become a model client of the powerful transnational institutions—the IMF and World Bank (Konadu-Agyemang, 2001).

The country still had a huge debt burden and critics argued that the ERP had failed to bring about any fundamental transformations of the economy as Ghana was still heavily reliant on cocoa and other commodities. From the late 1980s to the early 1990s structural adjustment policies had resulted in cutbacks at state and private companies that added more than two hundred thousand people to the country's unemployed rolls; this segment of unemployment was blamed on the structural adjustment process (Konadu-Agyemang & Takyi 2001, 29). More importantly, it was clear that many Ghanaians had not benefited from ERP (Unicef/Oxfarm 1999). Indeed, Castells (1996) argued that structural adjustment programs like Ghana's institute abstract formulae grounded in free market conditions that have resulted in making most of Africa economically less viable in the informational/global economy.

Additionally, given that the Rawlings regime was not a democratically elected one, it needed a mechanism to legitimize itself. The vocal criticism and advocacy of prodemocracy groups for a return to civilian rule could no longer be ignored in light of the World Bank/IMF-supported agenda the regime had underway. The regime therefore began exploring a return to constitutional rule. Democratic elections held in December 1992 legitimized Rawlings as the military man morphed into a democratically elected civilian president. In 1996 Rawlings was re-elected for a second term as president. Constitutional rule allowed Rawlings and later presidents to continue the ERP/SAP by launching a fourth phase (1994–1996), a fifth phase (1995–1997) and a sixth phase (1998–2000).

In December 2000, John A. Kufuor of the New Patriotic Party (NPP), the main opposition party leader, won the largest share of the presidential vote. As President Kufuor took the oath of office on January 7, 2001, he was the first elected president in Ghana's history to succeed another elected president. He won re-election in December 2004. His second term marked another milestone—he was the first civilian president (without a military background) to serve his full term and be re-elected. In January 2009, Ghana's democracy managed another peaceful transfer of power as it elected John Atta Mills, Rawlings' handpicked successor to the presidency (Polgreen 2009). Finally, it seems that Ghana's political institutions are getting a chance to mature. One outgrowth of the maturing process is the increasing confidence investors have in Ghana's economy. Banking, telecommunication, mining, and infrastructure building have attracted capital and have created jobs. Ghana is touted as a model for restructuring that others can emulate (Konadu-Agyemang & Takyi 2001, 25).

The economic restructuring program has relied on extensive borrowing. The national debt which has been growing at a seven percent rate forced the country to opt for debt relief under the Heavily Indebted Poor Country (HIPC) program in 2002. The country was also included in a G-8 debt relief program decided upon at the Gleneagles Summit in July 2005. The Kufuor government set priorities under its $38 million Poverty Reduction and Growth Facility (PRGF) that included tighter monetary and fiscal policies, accelerated privatization, and improvement of social services. In 2006 the country received a Millennium Challenge Corporation (MCC) grant to assist in transforming its agricultural export sectors.[5] Still the extent of the country's external indebtedness can be seen in the CIA's 2007 estimate of debt to GDP percentage. For Ghana the public debt is 59.6 percent of GDP or $4.668 billion as of December 2007.

There is no question that under Rawlings Ghana finally began developing political institutions that would become the foundation for stability and by some measures even a measured prosperity. It is this relative prosperity that has made it a "darling" of the World Bank and the IMF. The Kufuor and Atta Mills governments continued the process of turning the Ghanaian economy around. This said, some observers point out that the government has continued to placate Western donors and international financial institutions in order to continue attracting international investment. In 2007, commercially viable deposits of crude oil were discovered off the coast of Ghana. Crude oil began going to the market in 2011. Oil exports will be a potentially critical source of revenue for the country if it is to achieve the goal of becoming a middle income nation in the next decade.

Critics have isolated multiple costs of structural adjustment. A critical one is the obligation to service such debt. Debt servicing curtails Ghana's ability to invest in socio-economic programs that will assure its long term viability. Ghana spends roughly "four times more on debt servicing than on health care" (Konadu-Agyegum & Takyi 2001, 28). The ERP, with its focus on cutting government expenditure, resulted in drastic cuts in social services such as education, health care and welfare. Another cost is the devaluation of the currency, which has had consequences. Massive unemployment and underemployment has created an informal labor sector of unskilled and unprotected work that offers low wages. And as Ocran (1998) points out, these labor-related dynamics are likely to exacerbate gender, class, geographic location and disability-based inequalities in employment. A recurrent challenge for successive Ghanaian governments therefore has been the country's high unemployment and underemployment rate. The many government employees who lost jobs during the structural adjustment process had to find alternative means of generating income. For many, migration became an attractive option. Ghanaians, particularly women, are now a large contingent of the contract workers in the care industries in the global North. Migration and other disruptions for survival therefore have been direct consequences of the ERP/SAP project (Hawkesworth 2006). It is such effects of EPR/SAP and other globalizing dynamics on the global South and its ramifications for communities, particularly women that have been a focus of feminist scholarship. Debt burdens such as Ghana's lead anti-globalization activists to question neoliberal ideologies and their effect on the global South in general.

An obvious area of intense debate is the impact of donor policy expectations on recipient nations. Activists continue to contest the general impact of ERP/SAP processes on nations in the South. The World Bank-supported SAPRIN (Structural Adjustment Participatory Review International Network) process highlights these tensions. A SAPRIN report on structural adjustment, "The Policy Roots of Economic Crisis and Poverty," studied adjustment processes in Bangladesh, Ecuador, Ghana, Uganda, Zimbabwe, Hungary, and others. The authors show that structural adjustment policies "have contributed to the further impoverishment and marginalization of local populations, while increasing economic inequality" (Bretton Woods Project, May 2002). This is a conclusion other scholars and anti-globalization activists have reached independently.

Population growth and cuts in government expenditure in social programs have contributed to the increase in the unemployed/underemployed population. As the population grows, so has the proportion of those without access to wage labor or other viable options for economic participation. World Bank data suggest that Ghana has an active labor population of 11.29 million. 60 percent of this labor population is engaged in agriculture and a sizeable percentage of these workers are women. While wage labor options have dwindled, both the population and the work force have continued to grow by between 2.5 and 3 percent (Panford 2001). Young women and men graduate from universities with very limited career opportunities. Though women are gaining access to wage labor in the official economy, this access is directly constrained by limited access to education and limited public or private sector employment opportunities.

## EDUCATION IN GHANA

Reciprocity between employment and education are critical to any sustainable development agenda. Yet until the ERP process in the 1990s the many years of instability had left Ghana's education system underfunded and teetering on collapse (Panford 2001). Nkrumah's post-independence project of decolonization was defined in terms of modernization.[6] What figures prominently in the discourses of modernization and development is literacy teaching and learning. Historically, as result of this link, projects funded by the World Bank, UNESCO, UNDP, USAID and International Monetary Fund (IMF) in Ghana, as in other areas of the global South, have been tied either directly or indirectly to education and literacy acquisition. That agenda underscored Nkrumah's ambitious construction projects that depleted the national coffers but which also created the country's educational and economic infrastructure and still sustain it. In fact Ghana's economic restructuring process necessitated a commitment to Basic Education and required a long term shift of tremendous resources to Basic Education. According to Panford (2001) the shift of resources to Basic Education was based on a "belief that primary/elementary schooling is inexpensive and the most cost effective investment for the country" (229).

Education in general and literacy learning in particular are now seen as a means for fighting off social exclusion and for access to the "benefits" of globalization.[7] By 2007 access to education for young people by gender had almost evened out. Activists, NGOs, and donors successfully persuaded government agencies, and local groups to utilize a mass public service campaign to heighten public awareness on the merits of educating girls. Chapter 3 examines gender and the specific location of girls and women in more detail.

The public education system, a remnant of colonial domination, continues to offer access to alphabetic literacies—reading, writing, and computing—as mechanisms for self development and for employment (Okedara 1999; Herbert & Robinson 2001). Of course this coupling of education and economic progress is not only applicable to nations such as Ghana nor is it prevalent only in these times; as Grubb (1997) has noted for "most of the nineteenth and twentieth centuries, education has been promoted as the solution to economic problems" (259). The coupling of education with employment and the adoption of free market policies, however, means that versions of human development that are appropriate to citizens' aspirations are only accessible to those with means to pay for quality education and all that goes with it. As part of the ERP, the Ghanaian government brought free market logic into its education reform process using a cost recovery program—what the government called "cost sharing." The government began expecting students to bear an increasing portion of the cost of education and education supplies even in Basic Education. As a result the poorest Ghanaians are unable to afford even basic schooling.

Education reform that fuels economic growth and positions communities to participate in what transnational nongovernmental agencies now label as "knowledge" work or work in the "knowledge economy" has shaped the focus of restructuring programs in the South. These reform initiatives are attempts to construct transnational laborscapes. The

**Table 2.1.   Primary Education Enrollment**

|  | M | F | Both Sexes |
|---|---|---|---|
| 2000 | 1,000,107 | 930,622 | 1,930,729 |
| 2007 | 1,278,377 | 1,187,683 | 2,466,060 |
| 2009 | 1,345,504 | 1,294,584 | 2,640,088 |

Source: UNESCO Institute for Statistics.

World Bank (2003) underscores the argument that in a globally competitive environment, nations in the global South are in effect in the same boat as those of the North as all citizens compete for the best jobs their skills can get them. Such arguments make radical education reform an attractive option if nations in the South want access to the benefits of globalization. And reform requires substantial financial infusion into education systems as well as the development of other mechanisms and models for career training. As Farrell and Fenwick (2007) have pointed out, reform under these circumstances also necessitates the "transformation of the social, cultural and pedagogical assumptions underpinning local education systems" (14). Indeed the World Bank underscores the need for reform thus:

> Developing countries and countries with transition economies risk being further marginalized in a competitive global knowledge economy because their education systems are not equipping learners with the skills they need. To respond to the problem, policymakers need to make fundamental changes. They need to replace the information-based teacher-directed rote learning provided with a formal education system governed by directives with a new type of learning that emphasizes creating, applying, analyzing, and synthesizing knowledge and engaging in collaborative learning across the lifespan (World Bank 2003, xvii–xviii).

Tikly (2001) isolated the complex and layered intricacies of reform in this environment by pointing out that the outcomes of a blanket reform tailored to the global economy are multifaceted and not at all predictable. Different areas of the education process may fit different sectors of an economy at different times requiring a constant tweaking of education/training to projected needs. Further as Tikly noted, when nations invest in providing high standard education to citizens, that education may also become the catalyst to migration and brain drain.

Indeed Ghana experienced a brain drain prior to and during the ERP/SAP process. Thus while providing basic education or low-end skill training can improve the wage earning capabilities of the poor, such training also becomes a segregating barrier across regions (Farrell and Fenwick

**Table 2.2. Secondary Education Enrollment**

|        | M        | F         | Both Sexes  |
|--------|----------|-----------|-------------|
| 2000   | 491,880  | *406,483  | 898,363     |
| 2007   | *780,886 | *677,757  | *1,187,683  |
| 2009   | *778, 648| *682,245  | *1,460,893  |

Source: UNESCO Institute for Statistics. * Denote estimates.

2007). Such barriers reduce whole regions to a permanent labor under-class in the global laborscape.

Basic Education in Ghana consists of six years of primary school and three years of Junior Secondary School (JSS). Beyond those nine years, some students go on to Senior Secondary School (SSS) for three years. Young people in Ghana have twelve years of pre-tertiary education. Options in tertiary education are three to four years of training at a polytechnic, teacher training college or other training institution or university. The education system considers primary education its foundation. The objectives of primary education are: to develop numeracy and literacy abilities, facilitate the development of the ability to count, use numbers, read, write and communicate effectively; to lay the foundation for inquiry and creativity; to develop sound moral attitudes and a healthy appreciation of Ghana's cultural heritage and identity; to develop the ability to adapt constructively to a changing environment; to lay the foundation for the development of manipulative and life skills that will prepare the individual pupils to function effectively to their own advantage as well as that of their community; and to inculcate good citizenship education as a basis for effective participation in national development. Under the reform program a centralized national curriculum requires primary schools to offer mathematics, science, social studies, cultural studies, Ghanaian languages, English, agriculture, life skills and physical education.

Junior Secondary Schools (JSS) provide pupils with a broad-based education including pre-disposition to technical and vocational subjects and basic life skills which will enable pupils to: discover their aptitudes and potentialities so as to inculcate in them the desire for self-improvement; to appreciate the use of the hand as well as the mind and make them creative and self-employable. English is the medium of instruction in all Junior Secondary Schools. Junior Secondary School builds on the primary curriculum but it offers students Integrated Science, English Language

**Table 2.3.   Lower and Upper Secondary Education Enrollment**

|  | M | F | Both Sexes |
|---|---|---|---|
| *2005* |  |  |  |
| Lower | 450,598 | 371,606 | 822,204 |
| Upper | 208,924 | 144,416 | 353,340 |
| *2009* |  |  |  |
| Lower | 677,717 | 593,918 | 1,271,635 |
| Upper | 303,876 | 236,573 | 540,449 |

Source: UNESCO Institute for Statistics. Data is total of enrollment in all programs.

instruction, Technical Drawing, Basic Technical Skills, Vocational Skills (here regions select subjects of study for which they have qualified instructors) and an optional curriculum in French.

Beyond JSS, students may continue Senior Secondary School (SSS) — a system that caters to students between the ages of sixteen to eighteen. The objectives of the Senior Secondary School system are: to reinforce and build on knowledge, skills and attitudes acquired at the Junior Secondary School level; to produce well developed and productive individuals equipped with the qualities of responsible leadership capable of fitting into a scientific and technological world and to contribute to the socio-economic development of their own areas and the country as a whole; and to increase the relevance of the content of the curriculum to the culture and socio-economic problems of the country. Senior Secondary School students study seven core subjects: English, mathematics, science, agricultural and environmental studies, life skills, Ghanaian language and physical education (which is not examined externally at the Senior Secondary School Certificate Examination). In addition, each student selects three subjects from a wide range of curricular options to be studied under five specialized programs.

Access to education is gendered however and a key factor in this gendering process is cost. Formal schooling starts at six and Basic Education requires parents to cover the cost of uniforms and other materials under a "cost recovery" program. This cost puts Basic Education beyond the reach of poor families and in such situations girls are less likely to have access. In 1989-90 for example, government statistics showed that more males continued to be enrolled in schools than females. One result of this state of affairs is that in the first six grades of the educational system, only 45 percent of the students enrolled were female. The percentage of females in the school system decreased at the secondary school level, to 27 percent. At the tertiary level that number continues to fall with universities recording numbers as to as low 19 percent. These disparities in the male/female ratios found in the schools had improved significantly so that by 2005 the gap between the sexes had either narrowed or evened off. However, gender disparity is still prevalent as the level of education rises.

A key goal of the reform process was to make the "curriculum functionally more relevant to Ghanaian society" (Panford 2001, 203) by emphasizing practical knowledge application and the acquisition of competence. For supporters of the reform process the new system created spaces to move students into technical, vocational, business and agricultural institutions so that young people who do not gain admission into Senior Secondary School (SSS) will be better equipped to enter the wage labor market with technical skill sets.[8] The user-payer system, the cuts in funding and the general lack of textbooks, equipment, trained teachers, etc., continue to plague the reform process. These issues are also increas-

**Table 2.4.  Secondary Education Enrollment by Gross and Net Ratios: 1991–2009**

|      | Gross | Enrollment | Ratio | Net | Enrollment | Ratio |
|------|-------|------------|-------|-----|------------|-------|
|      | M     | F          | M/F   | M   | F          | M/F   |
| 1991 | 42%   | 27%        | 34%   |     |            |       |
| 1999 | 41%   | 33%        | 37%   | 34% | 29%        | 32%   |
| 2002 | 41%   | 34%        | 38%   | 34% | 30%        | 32%   |
| 2005 | 47%   | 40%        | 43%   | 39% | 35%        | 37%   |
| 2009 | 62%   | 55%        | 58%   | 49% | 45%        | 47%   |

Source: UNESCO Institute for Statistics. GER: Percentage of pupils enrolled in a given level of education regardless of age in theoretical age group for that level of education. NER: Percentage of enrolled pupils in theoretical age for the same population.

ingly making education a privilege and thereby short circuiting a once viable route to social mobility. The consequences of these issues for women are explored in chapter 3.

One outcome of the reform process has been the proliferation of private institutions at all levels. Private institutions are resource rich and offer education that only the elite can afford. Despite the considerable national focus on education and a rather large school population, Ghana's literacy rate, although among the highest in West Africa, was relatively low by world standards at 57.9 percent in 2000 and 67 percent in 2009. The rate is based on the criteria of being 15 or over and having the ability to read and write. The 2000 numbers have clear gender based disparities with the rate among males at 66.4 percent while females have only 49.8 percent. However the disparity all but disappears in 2009 data as females continue to gain ground steadily. In 2009, the female literacy rate was up to 79 percent compared to the male rate of 81 percent. It is clear that the current education system is heavily tied to the country's development agenda and the aspirations of a government constrained by its ability to create new jobs and thus make some inroads with unemployment and population growth. The rise in poverty associated with economic restructuring and the cost of education may account for declining enrollment (Panford 2001, 229–231).

## LITERACIES, DEVELOPMENT, AND WORK

Scholars now acknowledge the complexity of the link between control of literate abilities and economic development. As Windham (1999) argues, the link between literacy and economic development is at the very least a

**Table 2.5.    Tertiary Education Enrollment**

|                  | M       | F      | M/F     |
|------------------|---------|--------|---------|
| 2005             | 77,776  | 41,783 | 119,559 |
| Science (2005)   | --      | --     | --      |
| 2009             | 127,603 | 75,773 | 203,376 |
| Science (2009)   | 16,308  | 6,464  | 22,775  |

Source: UNESCO Institute for Statistics. Data is not available for Science (2005).

complicated one. He notes, "Stated simply, literacy skills help determine the rate and form of economic development at the same time that the nature of economic development creates opportunities for and puts limits on the economic value of literacy skills for the individual and the society" (342). The complexity of the linkages between literacy and economic development are captured in the multiple forms those linkages take as well as the layered reciprocity of the relationships and interactions between the two. Discussions of the contributions of literacy to economic success that fail to appreciate these complexities, therefore, run the risk of at very least distorting policy debates on literacy and development (Windham, 1999). Donor countries and agencies, critics point out, nonetheless continue to uphold the potential economic benefits of literacy for employment, improved general productivity, increase in earnings, and changes in the patterns of consumption in the communities they serve. I am not suggesting that literacy learning or education generally are bad things—nor am I suggesting that they be withheld from individuals and communities that desire access to them. Rather I am making the case for avoiding simplistic equations of literacy to progress and economic development (see also Hull 1997). Street (1999) underscores this concern in his discussion of the pluralization of literacies when he points out that "In development circles, where agencies present literacy as the panacea to social ills and the key ingredient in modernization, the dominant assumption has been of a single autonomous literacy that is the same everywhere and simply needs transplanting to new environments" (7).

Similarly, Hull (1997) questions popular notions of literacy as a neutral, generic skill, "the intellectual equivalent of all-purpose flour" that "once mastered can and will be used in any context for any purpose" (17). Though Hull's focus is on North American workplaces, it behooves us to consider the implications of her insights for work settings in developing countries. She notes:

> I believe that, in order to understand literacy at work, one must situate one's study of literacy not only within the immediate work environment, but also within the larger cultural, social, and historical milieu. It's not sufficient, I would argue, to simply go into a workplace and

collect the documents people are required to read and build a curriculum around those. One needs rather to take into account how work is organized and how that organization affects who is required, allowed, expected to read and write and why. (Hull 1995, 7)

Links between literacy and employment in development settings are occurring at a time when debates about work in the global North are shifting. Street (1999) draws attention to this shift in discussing how this "New Work Order associated with globalisation of production and distribution" should be examined in order to understand its implications for the "language needed in work and educational contexts" (3). Common in the literature on the "new work culture" are references to the "knowledge economy" that is precipitating adaptations to literacy practices in workplaces. Hardt and Negri (2000) describe what they term the "postmodernization" of "immaterial labor in the information economy" by noting how it is rewriting the rules of production, communication and supervision of workers. In the outsourcing settings that have now become the work environment for many in non-dominant economies, production is not about manufacturing goods, rather it is about generating process-related services for clients in settings that, though bounded as physical sites, are nonetheless immaterial as production often takes place in ICT-enabled network environments (292–300). The unification of the world markets, the use of ICT-enabled networks, and the spread of the western industrial model of labor organization to peripheral regions create a sense of proximity that, according to Hardt and Negri (2000), is also simultaneously isolating. For example, while ICTs mean that workers in Ghana are close to their counterparts in the United States by their "virtual" proximity, contingent workers—and often that is what workers in outsourcing are—operate on the margins of American companies or for their second- and third-tier subcontractors.[9] Complicating issues further is the nature and direction of labor flows; almost always the direction has been from dominant economies to the so-called "less developed" ones. This all but assures that the discourses of literacy and work prevalent in the dominant economies will migrate into non-dominant ones. When that migration is unmitigated, is required and enforced in workplaces in unproblematic ways, and is cast in a rhetoric of progress whose logic originates from outside the receiving communities, it can only be described as a mode of colonization. As scholars examine Ghana's evolving new work-places and the work practices associated with them, we can begin to understand the interconnectedness of inequitable education, free market competition, and the effects of lax labor laws on ordinary citizens (Konadu-Agyegum 2001; Konadu-Agyegum & Takyi, 2001; Panford 2001).

For sub-Saharan Africa, a region Castells (1996) defines as part of the "Fourth World," ICT-enabled work environments exist in the larger context of the region's comparative exclusion from capital flows and new technologies (Baldoz, Koeber & Kraft 2001; Hardt & Negri 2000). The language-mediated practices in ICT-infused settings and the identities they open up for workers are situated in these contradictions and discontinuities. Ironically, the nature, functions and ideological underpinnings of workplace literacies have been and continue to be interrogated even in the dominant economies (Castleton 2002; Hull 1997; Hull & Grubb 1999). Researchers continue to assert that workplace practices are never neutral nor are they simplistically functional. Other researchers have offered critical investigations on how information communication technologies are shaping the ways people work, play and live (Feenberg 2002, Luke 2000, Selfe 1999). These projects have not, to date, examined the effects of these technologies on work in outsourcing settings in non-dominant economies. Such explorations are necessary if only because they have acute policy implications that may shape the lives of communities in whole parts of the global South.

As much as outsourcing creates employment and integrates communities into the global information network, it is still the case that the communities' "struggle for self-determination" is enacted "under technological conditions produced elsewhere" (Penley & Ross 1992, ix). Ghana's general unemployment rate was estimated at 20 percent during the late 1990s (CIA, UNDP) and during the early phases of the ERP process. Other researchers have offered estimates of from 7 percent to 10 percent for late 1990s and early 2000s (Mainsah & Ikezi 2004). Most recent (2009) World Bank data puts unemployment at 10.4 percent of the total labor force. Panford (2001) estimated that Ghana has to create two hundred thousand jobs annually in order to meet the needs of young adults entering the labor market. Clearly the government is struggling at job creation even as it strives to meet IMF and World Bank benchmarks. It is in this context that transnational companies and other foreign investors have established entities that employ many Ghanaians. A British Broadcasting Cooperation (BBC) Online report on Ghana in 2003 quotes one investor, Frank Schooster, who was then setting up an outsourcing center thus: "I believe that the talent and resources in Ghana are just about the equal of India and not quite up to the level of the Philippines." Schooster noted that "It [Ghana] has a ready available pool of highly skilled labor, not quite so proficient in hi-tech as in India, but certainly worthy and knowledgeable enough to handle basic customer support" (BBC 2003). This burgeoning outsourcing sector is a rich ethnographic space for learning how work practices are adopted and adapted in work environments with globalized dimensions.

My interest in this multi-sited ethnographic study has been to understand the nature of the literacy practices the women (who make up 92 percent of the work force at CTI and 72 percent at CDN) use in their workplaces. For my purposes, literacy denotes a "repertoire of practices

**Table 2.6.  Literacy Rates**

|  | Adult | | | Youth | | |
|------|------|------|------|------|------|------|
|  | M | F | Both | M | F | Both |
| 2000 | 66.4% | 49.8% | 57.9% | 75.9% | 65.5% | 70.7% |
| 2007 | *71.7% | *58.3% | *65.0% | *79.7% | *75.8% | *77.8% |
| 2009 | 72.8% | 60.4% | 66.6% | *81.2% | *78.9% | 80.05% |

Source: UNESCO Institute for Statistics. Adult: 15+ years; Youth: 15–24 years. * Denote estimates.

for communicating and for getting things done in particular social and cultural contexts" (Nixon 2003, 407). In order to get at this, I have had to develop a level of understanding of the culture of particular Business Process and Information Technology outsourcing environments. Further, because the practices that occur in these settings are embedded in specific cultural contexts, in this case the social contexts within which outsourcing transpires, I have also had to embed these understandings in larger Ghanaian education, literacy and employment patterns.

*Introduction to Field Sites: The Companies, Management Personnel, and Research Participants*

Client Technology Industries (CTI) is a branch of a transnational company with operations worldwide. In Ghana at the time of my field work CTI employed about 1600 people. Of the 1600, 92 percent or 1,472 were women. The company began operations in Ghana in 2000 with only 60 employees. CTI offered 24-hour coverage, seven days a week. The company's literature describes its workforce as highly educated, skilled and English speaking. CTI supported operations for industries such as communications, healthcare, insurance and transportation and provided business process outsourcing services in claims processing, transactional processing, data verification, data correction, and quality control. The Ghana site's operations were housed in more than 42,000 square feet of a multilevel office space that utilized two E1 data lines. At the time of fieldwork the site had twenty-one semi-autonomous departments, some with as few as five employees per shift and others with as many as sixty per shift. The workplace was paperless—all work was done online in a company-owned networked environment.

The official language of work was English but the employees, like many Ghanaians, spoke multiple Ghanaian languages: Twi, Fanti, Ga, Ewe, and Hausa were the most common. Further, because of Ghana's colonial experience under the British, the version of English taught and used in the country tend to approximate British English. The language version prevalent in the work the women did was Educated American English. CTI was unofficially a multilingual workspace.

Employees were acculturated into a parent company culture that promoted teamwork, focused on service, professionalism, and employee enthusiasm. CTI expected employees to uphold quality and to keep client satisfaction a priority. In company literature, management urged employees to pay attention to their work, to be creative, and to collaborate with their coworkers. This official culture was conflicted and contradictory and it was resisted, hybridized or appropriated by employees to serve their own ends. For example, memos were routinely signed with the collective "management" or "human resources" and thus at the very least rhetorically positioned non-management and non-human resources personnel as marginal members of the team. CTI management refused, for example, to stock restrooms with toilet paper because they claimed "people will abuse it." These conflicting values shaped CTI.

For fieldwork at CTI I concentrated on the following departments: Delta, Alpha, Gamma, Omega, and Sigma.[10]

## JACK HALLE (SITE MANAGER)

Conversations in Jack Halle's office the first day set the stage for my work and oriented me to the cultural landscape of CTI. CTI was administered by a country/site manager (a Caucasian American, Jack Halle and later Nate Mackman) who was assisted by a tier of executives, all Ghanaian— these were vice presidents for Business and Marketing (Kwame Hills), Process/Production (Yaw Sammy), and Human Resources (Mida Bostia). Jack Halle had worked for CTI beginning in 1999. Before taking the position in Ghana he had worked in the Philippines, Mexico and Taiwan. Halle left the Ghana site in August to take a position with a CTI competitor. At a meeting to set down ground rules for working at CTI, Jack Halle declared (in response to my request to join the women I was hoping to recruit for the study in the lunch room) that "we make sure they eat because for many of them food at work is all they get." He further commented that they had to make sure their employees eat "to keep up their strength" so they can work. The comment took me aback, though I consciously masked my dismay. I wondered why women working in a place where, according to World Bank literature, workers typically earn $300 per month, had to depend on the sole meal provided by their employer for sustenance. Considering that Jack Halle's two Ghanaian assistants, Bostia (HR) and Hills (Business & Marketing) were present, I discreetly looked over but they betrayed no discernable reaction. Halle, perhaps having registered how his comment might be taken, offered further explanation: his position, he said, was related to his concerns about productivity. It was important to keep high productivity levels at the site because their numbers have to be sent in to headquarters at the end of each month. And their numbers had to be up in order to compete. Halle also warned me of the "grumbling" by employees who ask about why they are not getting the equivalent wages that their American counterparts get. I was warned to stay clear of such topics.

Also, during that meeting Halle tried to make a case for why the Ghanaian employees were paid what they were paid—I had no idea about wages at this point. He argued that if he were to pay the Ghanaian employees the same wages as their U.S. counterparts, the company's profits would be wiped out. Without those profits, they would just as well keep their jobs in the United States.

Nate Mackman took over from Jack Halle as CTI country manager in August and served in that role until my exit from the field. Like Jack Halle before him, he had held a similar position in Mexico. When Nate Mackman took over the management of CTI Ghana, apparently no one at the home office or at the Ghana site informed him of the presence of an academic researcher at the site. I saw him frequently as I interacted with employees and greeted him often—he apparently assumed I was a CTI employee. He would only find out about why I was there during an exit interview. He was not happy to learn of my presence, but his superiors had granted permission based on the Institutional Review Board documents I had made available to them and the written consent of the employees and departments I was working in. In the end he opted to revoke access to production floors in late November. I shall return to these issues in chapters 6 and 7.

## OTHER ADMINISTRATIVE FIGURES AT CTI

Mida Bostia was Vice President for Human Resources and the highest ranking female employee at CTI. Her responsibilities were mainly recruiting, enforcing rules and sustaining the workforce. Her office provided care and support for employees. She had an MBA and worked closely with Jack Halle and later Nate Mackman and with the other Ghanaian vice presidents in business, production and IT. Mida Bostia had a team of assistants who worked for her. Her assistants were important in shaping the overall tone and culture of CTI.

Willy Kofi was a middle level staff member at CTI's Human Resources division. He reported to the Vice President for Human Resources and was responsible for HIPAA (Health Insurance Portability and Accountability Act) compliance, training, and orientation of new employees to the culture, discipline, rules and expectations of CTI. He was responsible for helping production managers and supervisors translate CTI handbook expectations for rank and file employees.

Tricia Mamala was a Human Resource officer and secretary to the Vice President for Human Resources, Mida Bostia. She functioned as a gatekeeper to Mida Bostia. She ran the company's screening programs, graded applicants' tests, wrote warning letters as well as termination letters and was largely seen by employees as the "enforcer."

On the production side, CTI had a three-tier structure below the vice president of Process/Production, (Yaw Sammy): These were: Process/Production Managers (PMs), of whom there were a few women but mostly men; Process/Production Leaders (PLs), who were evenly split between men and women; and data entry clerks who were called Data Processors (DPs), who were mainly women. The participants in the study were from the ranks of the Data Processors.

CTI operated on a twenty-four hour, seven days a week schedule using three shifts. The first shift began at 6:00 am and ended at 2:00 pm. The second shift came in at 2:00 pm and worked until 10:00 pm and the last shift worked from 10:00 pm until 6:00 am. During the first week in the field I made a decision about how many days I would spend at each site. Thus I visited CTI on Mondays, Wednesdays and Fridays and visited CDN Tuesdays, Thursdays and Saturdays.

*Data Processor participants at CTI*

Nola Addy (focal participant at CTI) was single and lived at home with her mother, the family matriarch, and her three siblings. Her father passed away in 1999. Nola had attended Senior Secondary School—the equivalent of the American high school, and then gone on to a government secretarial school that is recognized as being the best for office technology training in Ghana. She worked as a secretary at a number of local establishments before leaving to work at CTI as part of the first cadre of recruits when the company started operations in Ghana. She volunteered for the study when her colleagues at Alpha told her about my research after she returned from vacation. After discussing my project and providing her with a consent form to read at home, she returned the form two days later as I was observing her production floor. By this time I had been at the site for about two weeks. My first interview with her occurred shortly afterwards and we continued to talk extensively in and out of the workplace. After my fieldwork ended, Nola and I kept in touch and still correspond electronically occasionally. In addition to work at CTI, Nola was studying for a bachelor's degree in psychology at a university. She attended classes after work. She was also very active in her church—she was a member of the choir and had been the church secretary the previous year. These obligations required Nola to invest time but Nola simply lacked time.

To get to work by the company bus required an hour and half commute: It took longer without the company bus service. Since Nola's shift started at 6:00 am she had to be at the bus pick up point by 4:30 am. On Tuesdays Nola had an exceptionally long day; she worked from 6:00 am to 2:00 pm, had classes from 4:30 pm to 6:30 pm and then went on to choir practice. She was respected by her peers and was a leader amongst them.

Shakira was a close friend of Nola's. She was at the center of Nola's network of friends. She was practicing Muslim, was married and had family responsibilities. She too had gone to Senior Secondary School (SSS) and a secretarial school beyond that. Like Nola, she had had other jobs and had been at CTI at the start of operations in Ghana. Shakira's work terminal was next to Nola's.

Zita Teiko (focal participant at CTI) was single and lived at home with her mother. Her mother had her own business and Zita admired the independence this provided her mother. She had two siblings. All three of them were raised and supported by their mother. She had gone to SSS and to a private secretarial school. Though she was a trained secretary, she disliked working as a professional secretary because of workplace harassment issues. She therefore found working at CTI a better alternative. In addition to working at CTI, Zita had started a small trading business that she intended to grow. She often said she was working at CTI until she could strike out on her own.

Hagar (focal participant at CTI) was single and barely twenty one years old when she went through the CTI screening and hiring process during field work. She had traveled multiple times from Tarkoradi in the Western Region of Ghana to Accra, the capital to test, and then interview for a job. She did get a job at CTI and offered me a window into her socialization on the job.

Fatuma and Zamila (Nola's friends), Toni, Sarah (Zita's friends), Zonna, Lina, Gifty, Emma, Regina and Liza are all Data Processors at CTI who provided insights, shared their work and time, had conversations and provided their perspectives on the work done in other departments.

## CLIENT DATA NETWORK

Client Data Network (CDN) was a collection of comparatively smaller semi-autonomous entities operating under one roof. The official language of the workplace was English though all the employees spoke multiple Ghanaian languages.[11] The company was owned by a collective of expatriates and Ghanaian partners. The company was located in a commercial section of a city centre and offered 24/7 coverage with some employees working three shifts while others worked an 8:00 am to 5:00 pm schedule. The company had four distinct departments: a department that served the general public as a cybercafé, a department that did data entry and used AutoCAD to provide services to clients, the Client Computing Services Department (CCSD); a department that provided voice-related

**Table 2.7.   Client Technology Industries (Departments in Study)**

| Department | Services |
|---|---|
| Delta | Health and Dental |
| Sigma | Health, Dental, Vision, HMO, PPO, Prescription, COBRA, Medical, Hearing, Ambulance, and Chiropractor |
| Alpha | Dental |
| Omega | Correspondence related to Health, Dental, Vision, HMO, PPO COBRA, Pharmaceutical, and Chiropractor |
| Gamma | Health, Dental, and Vision |

transcribing services, Selective Data Solutions Department (SDSD); and lastly a department that did high-end work with software development, Quality Option Solutions Department (QOSD). QOSD had a female manager, Naku, and fifteen programmers only one of whom was female. QOSD offered solutions for clients in the areas of IT architecture, design, development and programming. In the course of fieldwork I had numerous conversations with Naku and the programmers who worked at QOSD. Departments at CDN had different productions schedules tailored to meet their needs. My discussion leaves out the café as it was not a focus of the project.

Client Data Network's day-to-day operations were managed by a Chief Executive Officer, Liela Nowa. Leila Nowa granted me blanket access to the site but left department managers some flexibility in deciding when I could not be in their departments. There were a few times when the sheer volume of work and the pressing nature of their deadlines led managers to request that I stay away. Liela Nowa was assisted by a group of second-tier executives: one for human resources, one for business, and another for production. Each department had a manager. On the "production" floors CDN had supervisors who worked closely with rank and file employees and reported to the department managers. Managers consulted with the executives as well as Nowa routinely. Nowa had a very visible presence around CDN and spoke to rank and file employees regularly. Often she walked through various areas several times a day and worked closely with the collective of owner partners.

## DEPARTMENT MANAGERS

Naku Quaye was the manager of Quality Options Solutions Department (QOSD). Her department was almost all men except for Maye Noonu, the only female programmer. Naku was a good source of information on women in IT in Ghana. She was very active in both formal and informal networks of technology professionals. She was a mentor to young women in the profession. In addition to Naku, Eddie Laryea managed the Selective Data Solutions Department (SDSD) and Saaka Bono managed the Client Computing Services Department (CCSD).

## EMPLOYEE PARTICIPANTS AT CDN

Zoe Bentell (focal participant at CDN) was in her twenties and had a degree in Psychology. Zoe had been working at the company since graduating from a university in Ghana in 2003. Zoe lived at home with her parents and had siblings who were still attending university. She saw work at CDN as a stepping stone to something else, though she was not sure what. Zoe felt lucky to have a job; as she said many university graduates had a difficult time landing jobs after National Service. Zoe had a few close friends at work but maintained a professional relationship with her co-workers. Zoe considered Moe and Mona her good friends.

Maye (focal participant) was the only female programmer in QOSD. I was particularly interested in how Maye negotiated a work environment that was male dominated. I was also interested in how having Naku for a manager affected her sense of the climate of the work environment.

Hawa (focal participant) was one of the few women who had utilized her own resources to secure technology-related training prior to coming to work at CDN. Since this was the prevalent dynamic at CTI, I wanted to understand what issues, if any, surrounded her experiences.

Other employees at CDN who shared their perspectives were Audrey, Abigail, Noe, Boe, Moe, and Mona. Though these women had different jobs at CDN the experiences they shared enabled me to get a richer understanding of the workplace.

Data collection was based on interviews (informal and semi structured—see Appendix B), artifacts, field notes, analytic memos, my observation commentaries, photographs, texts available from public online

**Table 2.8.   Client Data Network**

| Department | Services |
| --- | --- |
| Client Computing Services Department (CCSD) | AutoCAD-related services, customer support |
| Selective Data Solutions Department (SDSD) | Voice-related services—transcription, indexing |
| Quality Option Solutions Department (QOSD) | High-end software development and support |
| Cybercafé | Internet services |

**Table 2.9.   Focal Women and their Network of Friends**

| | |
|---|---|
| Nola Addy (CTI) | Shakira, Zamila, Fatuma |
| Zita Teiko (CTI) | Sarah, Toni, Kora |
| Hagar Assa (CTI) | Maya, Janet |
| Zoe Bentell (CDN) | Moe, Mona |
| Hawa Moyo (CDN) | Sara, Joe, May |
| Maye Salwa (CDN) | Sam, Nora (different departments) |

spaces of CTI and CDN, documents, records and memos. Recorded formal and semi formal interviews from both sites amounted to 1440 minutes. At CTI my extended field notes yielded 224 pages of text while extended field notes at CDN yielded 133 pages of text. In addition analytic memos yielded another thirty three pages of text. The categories that emerged from my cycles of coding, categorizing and re-categorizing data yielded the themes, concepts and trends that are used to frame my discussion. Participant voices are present throughout the text and those voices are used to illustrate the trends in the data. I return to these discussions in chapter 5.

A final point; in representing these workplaces, I do so mostly in my voice, in the context of the analyses of the various data sets as well as the experience of doing fieldwork at the two sites.

## NOTES

1. Central Intelligence Agency declassified documents now suggest at least prior knowledge of governments of the global North of the coup plot. www.ghanaweb.com/GhanaHomePage/history/24febcoup.php Or Johnson Library, National Security File, Memos to the President, Robert W. Komer, Vol. 21, 3/3/66-3/20/66. Confidential. A handwritten "L" on the source text indicates that the memorandum was seen by the President.   See   https://www.cia.gov/library/publications/the-world-factbook/geos/gh.html

2. There are extensive histories of Ghana such as (Agyeman-Duah, Ivor, Kelly, Christine (2008) Eds. An Economic History of Ghana: Reflections on a Half-Century of Challenges and Progress. London, UK: Turnaround Publisher Services and F. K. Buah. (1998). A Short History of Ghana. London: Macmillan). I have merely summarized key moments for my purposes here. However because economic issues frame the current conditions of Ghana, I will highlight a socio-economic history in more detail. www.ats.agr.gc.ca/sahara/4211_e.htm        lcweb2.loc.gov/cgi-bin/query/r?frd/cstdy:@field(DOCID+gh0079)

3. Devised by John Williamson, an IMF advisor in the 1970s, it seeks to reform the internal economic structures of indebted nations so they can pay their debts. In practice its some scholars have argued that it can only be labeled "a new form of colonialism" (Steger, 2003, p. 52).

4. Konadu-Agyemang & Takyi, 2001 pages 25–38 discusses some of the human cost of structural adjustments on the poor.

5. "Ghana Meeting the Challenge of Accelerated and Shared Growth: Country Ecomomic Memorandum," World Bank 2007 shows that in 2005 the country's per capita GNI was $450. Further since 1990s, Ghana's economy has begun to advance. The country has sustained real GDP growth of above 4 percent and per capita growth of approximately 2 percent. "These figures have elevated Ghana toward the medium growth performance among African countries over this period. Economic growth has averaged over 5 percent since 2001 and reached 6 percent in 2005–06. Some human development indicators improved, and aggregate employment increased, although much of it was in the informal sector. However, while Ghana did well in primary education in terms of enrollment, ensuring that children stay in school and make progress has been a challenge. Secondary and university education has not always provided the skills needed by the growing economy. And rural-urban migrations continue unabated, putting pressure on the already high urban unemployment." See also      info.worldbank.org/etools/docs/library/117347/PresentationproposalforGhana-Team26September2003.pdf.

6. The modernization and development discussion from Konadu-Agyegum (2001) As Hardt and Negri (2000) point out, the discourse of development operational in donor accounts envision all countries following a single model of development; that which the dominant economies in the global north followed. Presumably, if countries pursue this trajectory, they will one day attain the status of being developed. Even then as the authors argue, such prescriptions fail to acknowledge the economic and political arrangements that continue to keep such economies in subordinate positions.

7. I use literacy learning and education interchangeably as control over literate practices is critical to any formal/school-based education project. Barton, David. *Literacy: An Introduction to the Ecology of Written Language.* Malden, MA: Blackwell, 2009 and Brandt, Deborah. *Literacy in American Lives.* New York: Cambridge U.P, 2001 both explore this deployment of literacy learning in place of the larger education project.

8. These programs are i) Agriculture ii) Technical iii) Business iv) Vocational v) General (Arts & Science) Programs. At both basic and secondary levels of education, the inquiry method is the instructional method used. Pupils and students are led to use their creative skills on projects and find out things for themselves. Students are encouraged to read, observe, explore and experiment.

9. A number of companies now specialize in business process outsourcing and are now hubs for companies looking to shift back office process functions elsewhere. The popular press has been documenting these offshore operations and with that has developed anxieties about American jobs, etc. While India and the Philippines have become synonymous with offshore outsourcing, South Africa and Ghana and also attracting a fair share of this work on the African continent. Work at these companies is done in virtual, fluid and digital environments. Thus while these outsourcing sites are physically located in Ghana, the work is done on a virtual network and the solutions the Ghanaian employees offer enable a number of companies to tailor solutions to their American clients almost instantaneously and often with the help of other sites on this virtual web of networks. This back and forth between sites on a virtual web of hubs raises questions about the location at which a researcher studies such a work place.

10. For an exhaustive discussion of gaining and negotiating entry to CTI and CDN, see See Quarshie Smith, B. "Researching Hybrid Literacies: Methodological Explorations of 'Ethnography' and the Practices of the 'Cybertariat.'" In *Digital Writing Research: Technologies, Methodologies, and Ethical Issues,* edited by Danielle DeVoss and Heidi Mckee. Cresskill, NJ: Hampton Press.

11. See Jenkins, Jennifer, *World Englishes* New York: Routledge, 2009 for a discussion of the role of English and the specific inflections of Ghanaian English.

# THREE

## Gender Politics and Women in Ghana: A Short "Herstory"

> I think that in Ghana and the Third World generally, researchers do not have the luxury to cleanly demarcate the separations [between activism and research]. If the person is genuinely concerned about justice and change then s/he will, whether activist or researcher, merge the two. . . . Also because Third World intellectuals are still very much free to confront and struggle for all kinds of democratic and political changes, they/we are compelled to act. (Research Participant quoted in Manuh, 2007)

Ghana's current economic circumstances, as previous chapters have shown, are linked to larger global economic and political changes, and as chapter 2 demonstrates, are related to the relationship between the State, and the IMF/World Bank and other transnational nongovernmental organizations. In this chapter the goal is to examine the situation of women in the Ghanaian workforce. The chapter examines gendered work in Ghana by looking at common roles of working women and linking these roles to education, the impacts of the Structural Adjustment Program (SAP) and Economic Recovery Program (ERP) on women, access to economic opportunity, access to the official wage labor market and women's activism in relation to these issues. The last part of the chapter connects these currents to transnational feminisms and globalizing processes. It is against this backdrop that Part Two of the book takes up a broader review of feminist responses to the "woman question" in the globalization debate as feminists and activists assess the impact of these processes on the women who increasingly work in the emerging Information and Communication Technology (ICT)-infused workplaces in the global South.

## WOMEN AND EDUCATION

Women and girls make up 51 percent of Ghana's population, but lag behind men and boys in education, training and employment (Panford 2001). That there is a disparity in access to western style education between the genders in Ghana (as indeed there is in other areas of sub-Saharan Africa) is beyond dispute. Gender disparity can be traced to the introduction of a colonial education geared toward educating boys and men to serve in low levels of the colonial infrastructure, and to the simultaneous introduction of capitalist economic structures and the "monetization" of goods and services (see Egbo 2000). These dynamics shifted the focus from the family as the principal locus of production to wage labor outside the household. The shift put women at a significant disadvantage. At the end of the colonial encounter, the new Ghanaian state enacted a progressive education-for-all policy. The Education Act of 1961, which ensured virtually free education for all, including girls, was coupled with the expansion of the public sector. Public sector expansion improved the socio-economic mobility of women in the 1950s and 1960s. Nkrumah's government pushed its education agenda as part of a strategy of modernization for accelerated nation-building. Even then gender-based disparities persisted across all phases of the educational system in Ghana.

Contemporary women's activism began with efforts to equalize gender-based disparities. Manuh posits that activism on behalf of women's interests in Ghana can be traced to the post-independence moment when "the new nation sought to project women onto the political and social scene in the interest of the nation building project" (Manuh 2007, 129; Manuh 1991; McClintock 1995). Manuh terms this move "the first uses of affirmative action" that resulted in measurable improvement in the education, employment, and social well-being of women even though it was precipitated by the calculated political self-interest of the Nkrumah government. Because the ruling party co-opted women's issues into its structure and prevented the formation of independent women's groups; it effectively ensured that only state actors could take up systematic policy and advocacy on issues important to women from 1957 until the end of the 1990s (Manuh 2007). Thus while contemporary Ghanaian women's activists point out that Nkrumah's progressive policies actually gave women access to the public sphere far more than any administration after it, activists such as Mensah (2003) have pointed out that the regime also in effect ensured that the years of political instability beginning with the 1966 coup that overthrew it resulted in women being reluctant to be involved in politics, relying instead on state actors to work in their interest.

Years of political and economic instability and the ERP/SAP processes that sought to correct them have had significant consequences for women and girls. Surveying ERP/SAP's effect on women and girls, Panford (2001) concludes that prior to ERP/SAP processes women and girls were making "substantial social gains" because of the equal access policy particularly in the education arena (232). But the cost recovery program instituted as part of the ERP process affected school enrollment of girls. The introduction of user fees of about $200-$400 beginning in the 1999/2000 academic year at the tertiary level drastically limited access to university and other tertiary-level education for the poor and for young women in a country with a per capita income of $500. Indeed, as Nola and her co-workers often pointed out to me, when families weighed the cost of educating daughters and sons in the context of their limited resources, families often opted to support their sons. Panford (2001), citing Greenstreet (1979) supports this point, and describes the logic behind this stance:

> Generally, parents who have insufficient financial means give preference to boys over girls in respect to education, and particularly higher education. This reflects the idea prevalent in most societies that a boy, being a future breadwinner, has the first claim on education in order to better his chances of employment. (233)

Of course, the sheer number of the women who inhabit the ranks of outsourcing in Ghana demonstrates that securing economic viability to support family and community is an aspiration that women too share in contemporary Ghanaian society. Sadly, as in many sub-Saharan African countries, the number of women and girls who complete their education is considerably lower than that of boys and men even though educated women participate in all segments of society (Berger and White 1999; Dolphyne 1991; Panford 2001).

Indeed, as Panford has demonstrated, the adverse effects of ERP/SAP on the position of girls and women is acutely visible in the number of street children, many of school-age, and mostly women and girls "who roam the streets of Accra and other urban centers hawking items and using markets such as Makola (in Accra) as their permanent homes..." (Panford 2001, 233). It is not only that the cost of education is now high, but it is also that even with education, job prospects are poor. Many parents under these circumstances steer girls and young women into trading—a situation that leaves girls and young women outside of formal wage labor; keeps them from building long term economic independence through systematic structures such as retirement funds or contributions to state sanctioned social security; and diminishes their prospects for upward social mobility (Panford 2001).

## WOMEN: A POLITICAL AND ECONOMIC EVOLUTION

The 1975 International Women's Year and the declaration of the "decade for women" provided renewed impetus for reassessment of issues affecting women sponsored by the state as well as by Non-Governmental Organizations (NGOs). Ghana established a National Council on Women and Development (NCWD) giving it a mandate to work toward gender equality while monitoring the nation's progress in meeting obligations and implementing commitments to international agreements such as the Convention on the Elimination of all Forms of Discrimination against Women (CEDAW) adopted by the United Nations General Assembly in 1979, the Nairobi Forward-Looking Strategies of 1985, and the Beijing Platform for Action from the Fourth World Congress on Women in 1995.

From the early 1980s through to the current Fourth Republic, Ghana has, in many ways, successfully constructed an image of itself as a progressive state by ratifying international conventions and internationally approved legal instruments concerning women and making commitments to social justice and equality at home for women. The 1992 Ghanaian Constitution for the first time explicitly guaranteed women's rights. Laws have been passed to end problematic traditional practices such as widowhood rites and ritual servitude that targeted women and girls (Manuh, 2007). Women's rights in marriage and divorce have been codified under the law. Ghanaian law now has a set age for marriage and a legal framework for intestate succession. The country now has a Ministry of Women's and Children's Affairs (MOWAC) which acts as the executive branch umbrella for policy, monitoring and advocacy for women and children. The ministry's cabinet-level status is meant to demonstrate a state commitment to gender issues. Human Rights groups have mobilized on behalf of women around issues such as domestic violence, advocating for the passage of a Domestic Violence Bill, and lobbying groups such as the Ghana Medical Association for support. In 2003 these groups coalesced around a demand for the repeal of Section 42g, the marital rape exemption of the Ghana Criminal Code (Act 29). The exemption made it impossible for a wife to bring rape charges against a husband. A comprehensive domestic violence act was passed into law in 2007 (http://www.mowacghana.net/files/dva.pdf).

Gender politics in Ghana from the mid-1980s through 2003 merit close analysis. During the Rawlings regime, Nana Konadu Agyemang Rawlings, the then First Lady, established a women's group, the December 31st Women's Movement (DWM), which sought to address issues affecting women. Relying on her proximity to President Rawlings, DWM and Agyemang Rawlings made the needs of women an active focus of policy and planning within the government. While DWM underscored the critical place of women in politics and in the political party structures, it also occupied a contradictory space. At times DWM was branded as an arm of the Rawlings regime—a "wing of the December 31st revolution" (Manuh 2007). At other times it was an independent gender-focused NGO—a broad-based development-oriented movement committed to the emancipation of women at every level. In its own literature DWM professed a goal of mobilizing women to contribute to and benefit from the socioeconomic and political progress of the country. In the late 1990s the group claimed to have about 2 million members. The prominent role of the First Lady assured DWM access to state funds; and in the view of some activists even a monopoly of state resources for gender work (Manuh 2007).

DWM advocated for a re-socialization of women who, it argued, had been socialized into believing and accepting their subordinate positions in society. What is beyond debate is that Agyemang Rawlings used her position to facilitate the development of positive images of women. She advocated for processes and policies to help women take control of their lives and saw DWM as a mechanism for securing the welfare of women and children in the Ghanaian society. DWM conceptualized women's empowerment beyond economic development, contending that empowerment is also about sensitizing women to political issues in the public sphere as they relate to the state and their communities. It is also important to note that whatever we judge the contributions of DWM to gender activism to be, it is clear that DWM enabled and thus helped reproduce the political co-opting of women's issues under the purview of the state and therefore re-enacted what had been part of the Ghanaian scene since the First Republic. While state actors, in decisive policy initiatives, may hold the key to bending the arc of gender equity towards girls and women, gender-focused activists see a need for multiple voices in policy debates. DWM's connections to the Rawlings regime and later the first civilian government of the Fourth Republic provided access to donor resources (Manuh 2007) that amounted to an "undisputed control of the space for gender work for nearly two decades" (130). This monopoly has had some consequences.

When state actors monopolize gender work, that work tends to advance their particular agenda. Some scholars have questioned the viability of state co-option and or sponsorship of gender work, pointing out the limits such sponsorship places on advocacy, practices and policies on behalf of women. Yet as Panford and others have pointed out, without state-sanctioned intervention, private entities and citizens lack the means to reverse the harm done by systemic inequalities. State monopoly translates into first, the gendering of the state itself as it tends to promote policies that do not contest this status quo. Second, some scholars argue, the state tends to promote policies that reinforce the "super ordination of men over women" in both the public and the private spheres. Third, institutions of public life in Ghana (and in much of Africa for that matter) are male-dominated and have remained that way in spite of efforts by activists to change this profile (Manuh 1991, 1993, 2007; Tsikata 1989, 1997). As Charmaine Pereira (2002, 6) has shown, even gender-focused research in Africa often tends to be "malestream" so that male researchers who are sensitive to women's activism function in a gender-blind vacuum that fails to contest the "accepted norm." As a case in point, in the analyses of two studies on militarism and structural adjustment programs sponsored by *Le Conseil pour le Développement de la Recherche en Sciences Sociales en Afrique* (CODESRIA), edited by Mkandawire and Olukoshi (1995) and Hutchful and Bathily (1998), Pereira noted that while both militarism and SAP are deeply gendered processes that have adverse impacts on women, the absence of gender-sensitive analytical lenses meant that even progressive African male researchers made invisible the significance of these processes on women.

## WOMEN AND WORK

The situation of women in the economic sphere is conflicted and contradictory. Their paths to equitable engagement are either eased or constrained by education, policy, laws or "tradition." Control over literate practices and education, researchers and development agencies point out, can be a powerful catalyst to political and economic access and participation as well as a foundation to the personal development of women and girls. Activists point out that enhancing women's development is key to enhancing the quality of life for families and communities. Women's access to the types of wage labor associated with globalization, I would argue, is directly tied to their access to a specific English-language-mediated education and literacy. Women who do outsourced work, as I will demonstrate in later chapters, function in environments that require sophisticated language-mediated practices. While equitable access to public wage labor has been a significant objective of the women's movement worldwide, in Ghana, as in many so-called "less-developed" economies, women have always participated in economic activity be it agrarian, commercial, or "official" wage labor (see Berger & White 1999; Dolphyne 1991; Parpart & Staudt 1989). Often, women's labor generates a separate revenue stream that they control but may use to support family and community. In rural areas Ghanaian women work on farms or make crafts that they sell for independent income. Women engage in subsistence farming that either feeds their families or generates extra produce to be sold to supplement family resources. In urban areas women sell cooked foods, produce, textiles, local and imported foods and other household items to generate incomes for themselves and their families. These separate revenue streams afford Ghanaian women of all social classes economic independence and this point was made repeatedly by the women who worked at both CTI and CDN.

*Education and Structural Unemployment*

What progressive education policies during the transition to independent rule and beyond did was to enable Ghanaian women to make inroads in employment in the official economy. This point is underscored by Berry, who notes, for example, the inclusion of women in higher education:

> Early 1990s data showed that 19 percent of the instructional staff at the nation's three universities in 1990 was female. Of the teaching staff in diploma granting institutions, 20 percent was female; elsewhere, corresponding figures were 21 percent at the secondary school level, 23 percent at the middle level, and as high as 42 percent at the primary level. When women were employed in the same line of work as men, they were paid equal wages. (Berry 1995, 101–102)

Ghanaian labor laws up until the inception of the SAP/ERP process were considerably pro-women. Labor Decree 1967 (NLCD 157), for example, sought to protect pregnant and nursing women from losing their careers and jobs. The law assured women equal work for equal pay and granted women paid maternity leave (Berry 1995, 102). Under NLCD 157 women secured twelve weeks of *post-partum* leave with full pay; complicated pregnancies documented by physicians protected women by granting them leave from work for six weeks at half their salaries. Women employees were provided two half-hour breaks to breast feed their infants. Other pro-women law policies made it explicitly illegal to dismiss a female employee on account of a pregnancy. Greenstreet (1971, 18) aptly notes that in the workplace in the Ghana of the 1970s "complete legal equality in rights and privileges exists. . . . Where there are special laws relating to women exclusively, these are aimed rather at improving the position of women in relation to men rather than at discriminating against them."

These pro-women labor practices have been sharply constrained under the pressure of SAP/ERP. Downsizing, cost cutting, wholesale trade liberalization, and pressure from donor nations for the creation of a business-friendly environment that will attract transnational companies have led the government to be "less stringent over the enforcement of labor market regulations that protect workers" (Panford 2001, 227). Further, Panford notes that the World Bank explicitly urged the government "to reduce labor cost, especially wage gains through collective bargaining, to make Ghana attractive to overseas investors." These conditions, as I will demonstrate in later chapters, are precisely what frame the experiences and practices of the many women who work in outsourcing.

*Changes in Access*

A contemporary barrier to women's access to wage labor is related to the high level of unemployment further exacerbated by SAP/ERP processes. The economic collapse of the 1970s and the SAP/ERP plans adversely affected the quality and access to education in general. Education reforms initiated in 1986 tended to foreground vocational education. For women and girls this vocational focus would affect the post independence gains that had translated into jobs in secretarial, teaching and administrative positions in both private and state-owned factories. Indeed a World Bank study (EIU Country Report, Ghana 1998) admitted that both school enrollment and the levels of literacy acquisition were falling for women and girls. UNICEF data for 2003–2007 shows a literacy rate of 65.5 percent for females between 15–24 (www.unicef.org/infobycountry/ghana_statistics.html, accessed March 3, 2010).[1] The SAP/ERP goal of downsizing and reducing labor cost, particularly in the public sector, limited the education and career prospects of women and girls. Mhone (1995, 51) demonstrated the unequal effects of SAP-induced layoffs on women. In considering these converging forces, Panford concluded that "There may be a correlation between retrenchment and declining women participation in the wage economy" (2001, 235). Though men have lost jobs, Mhone stated that the "proportion of women . . . fortunate . . . to be employed . . . has diminished" (51). Women have fared badly under structural adjustment programs. Indeed it was the criticism by advocates for women that led the government to establish an $85 Million Program of Action to Mitigate the Social Costs of Adjustment (PAMSCAD). Ghana's general unemployment rate was estimated at 20 percent during the late 1990s (CIA, UNDP). Current estimates range from 7 percent to 15 percent. The unemployment rate among young people between ages 15–24 is, according to Youth at United Nations, about 15.9 percent. The rate is only slightly lower for those in the 25–35 age groups. These age groups constitute about 21 percent of the total population of roughly 22 million. Aid agencies and women's groups note that employers given the opportunity to select from a labor pool of men and women offer work to men over women (Baden, Green, Otoo-Oyortey & Peasgood 1994; Dolphyne 1991). Further, girls and women are more likely to be steered towards gendered employment categories by key structures and institutions in society—families, churches and schools (Dolphyne 1991). One result of this state of affairs is that as more and more women seek access to wage labor, they find that what is available is gendered work; it is work that men find less desirable. These factors may partially explain the high number of educated women in the ranks of those who work in the outsourcing industry. In effect, access to work and the technologies of work is mediated by an economic and social environment of structural unemployment and women's vulnerability in that environment. In the absence of viable local employment, many women seek access to "lucra-tive transnational" care work (Hawkesworth 2006, 2) as contract workers whose foreign wages and remittance become part of what the nation uses to service IMF and World Bank loans. In some respects therefore, the colonial gendered education project whose main goal was to socialize girls into acceptable societal roles has really not changed much in postco-lonial times (Berger & White 1999). And it is these gendered education experiences, enculturation, norms and values that have created a labor pool suitable to Western companies in need of relatively cheap skilled and semi-skilled workers. This relocation of work from the industrialized global North has created unique opportunities for women to enter the wage labor market though a considerable number of the work opportu-nities are low end and routine.

## WOMEN AND WORK IN NEW TIMES

The advent of "official" wage labor related to the economic activities underwritten by globalization and the types of work globalizing process-es have created have led to an influx of women into workplaces, particu-larly those that provide services, the only sector that seems to have grown under SAP/ERP (Panford 2001). What outsourcing is precipitating for women is at once a change in the nature of work as well as terms and conditions under which that work is done. The shifting dynamics wrought by globalization are rewriting the conditions under which citi-zens, particularly women, participate in "official" wage labor. Female workers have tended to dominate the workplaces that global North transnationals and their contractors operate offshore and this has gone beyond apparel and electronics manufacturing, areas that have historical-ly tapped female labor. As the late eighties and early nineties unfolded, microchip and other technology hardware production began appearing offshore. These "new" offshore workplaces employ a high percentage of women (Huws 2003; Ross; Terry & Calvert 1997) who are often labeled flexible employees, casual workers, temporary or part timers and who work under conditions that Mitter (1997) notes "conjure up invariably the image of a worker who is a woman, and whose status as a wage earner does not necessarily carry with it automatic prospect of career progres-sion" (163). Female labor and the products of that labor have provided key components for the development of information communication net-works which have become the infrastructure of globalization. For periph-eral communities the access these technologies create is synonymous with progress and development and exclusion from it has thus become a defining characteristic of communities that are non players in the global economy.

## CONCLUSION: TRANSNATIONAL FEMINIST ACTIVISM AND CROSS-BORDER ARTICULATIONS

Clearly Ghanaian women and men who support a progressive women's agenda, and the strategies for confronting gender inequities do not function in isolation—groups and NGOs have linked their projects to transnational ones. Women's continued advocacy for access to wage labor, labor protections, and roles in politics and policy-making has not happened in a vacuum. Rather these strategies and practices are linked to transnational gender activism. Transnational feminisms/gender work is, as Moghadam (2005) has demonstrated, intricately woven into globalizing processes. Globalizing conditions and processes induce activists on the African continent to hitch their projects to those of others. Global groups such as Women's Empowerment Research Project Consortium (WERPC), provide forums for women from Ghana and other parts of the world to collaborate on creating pathways to empowerment for women.[2] For Ghanaian women then, employment, literacy and activism are all tangled in global flows. I turn to a discussion of the transnational nature of equitable gender relations, knowledge work, and development in chapter 4.

## NOTES

1. See Table 2.5
2. See www.un.org/Africa/osaa/ngodirectory/dest/Women.htm#Ghana for a directory of active gender focused NGOs.

# FOUR

# Gender, Knowledge, and "New" Work

The contours and consequences of globalization have been the focus of passionate scholarly conversations for nearly two decades now. There are the old disagreements about when those processes began, where they might end, and what dimensions and dynamics constitute their critical components. There are new disagreements about the effects of 9/11 on globalizing processes. And there are debates about the impact of the global economic downturn on these processes. These debates and analyses have tended not to engage the implications of gender explicitly. Rather, they have focused on macro analyses of globalizing processes. Feminists have critiqued the absence of "the woman question" in several authoritative accounts on globalization, pointing out that this absence implies that these processes are somehow neutral or that their consequences are the same for women as they are for men. And feminists have also sought to foreground the impact of these processes on women. Moghadam identifies the emergence of at least two lines of feminist inquiry in this area: the first entails analysis of the "operation of capital via state, global economy and international financial institutions" using gender and class. She labels this line of work a Marxist-feminist or feminist political economy approach. A second line of inquiry involves analysis of "symbolic representations of economic globalization, gendered binaries in the construction of knowledge about globalization, contradictory and decentered organizations, and heterogeneous subjectivities" (2005, 26–27). This line Moghadam describes as postmodernist or postcolonialist in its orientation. As gender-sensitive lines of research and theory-building have evolved, the feminization of migration, poverty, and labor have emerged as significant issues. These lines of research have also highlighted feminist transnational networks and activism. Feminist

scholars argue that bringing a gender perspective into studies of globalization both enables and requires looking at micro-phenomena like wom-
en's activism, work, knowledge, access to literacy, access to technologies,
family and community disruptions, etc., that affect women's lives in significant and immediate ways (Hawkesworth 2006; Moghadam 2005).
Macro- and micro-gender-focused analyses in effect illuminate the extent
to which globalizing processes are gendered, resulting in differential impacts for women and men. In other words, such analyses allow us to
examine "globalization from above" as well as "globalization from below" and thus open up vernacular and indigenized globalization dynamics for critical analysis.

In this chapter I argue that discerning the links between globalizing
processes and feminization processes demands situated research in specific "global/local" spaces; that is, we need to study particular local and
sub-local communities that are overtly shaped by global dynamics. This
is precisely what a deployment of multi-sited ethnographic research in
outsourcing workplaces can provide—a situated examination of the impact of globalizing processes on particular women in particular workspaces. Here I will situate the intersections of globalizing processes, gender, knowledge, and "new" work in Ghana. The general consensus of the
authoritative scholarship on globalization is that Africa is by and large
affected by globalizing processes rather than being a player of any significance. A gender-focused exploration of the intersections of globalization,
knowledge, literate practices and "new" work in outsourcing in Ghana
sheds light on how the supposedly inconsequential actors in the "global
now," particularly women, may be rewriting the terms of their "exclusion." I will invoke feminist scholarship that explores the intersections of
development studies and globalization in order to theorize and locate the
specific practices of outsourcing generally and in the process locate the
industry in Ghana. My interest here is not to offer exhaustive examina-
tions of either the globalization or the development studies literature.[1]
Rather I seek to use these critical discourses to situate outsourcing and
the literate practices they appear to promote among workers in the global
South.


## GENDER IN THE GLOBALIZATION DEBATE

Macro-analyses of globalization are exemplified by the work of theorists
spanning a wide disciplinary and ideological spectrum. These analyses
have areas of agreement and disagreement but their one uniting characteristic is their failure to address the gender dimension of the phenomenon in any noteworthy manner (Hawkesworth 2006). For example, Waters (2001) offers a definition that foregrounds the issues of time and
space as well as economic, political, cultural and social integration. Glo-

balization encapsulates a set of multidimensional social processes that cannot be confined to any one thematic framework. Steger (2003) articulates four features of globalization that, by and large, converge with Waters: (1) there is the creation of new and multiplication of existing social networks that increasingly prevail over traditional political, economic, cultural and geographic boundaries; (2) there is the expansion and stretching of social relations, activities and interdependencies; (3) there is the intensification and acceleration of social exchanges and activities with the local and global interacting symbiotically and (4) there is creation, expansion, and intensification of social interconnectedness and interdependencies beyond the material, objective level and into the subjective plane of human consciousness. The conception of globalization as ongoing non-static processes with multiple dimensions forces us to pay attention to shifting perceptions of time and space and requires an attention to theorizing the configuration of the social space of the workplace. Such discussions of globalization while significant, privilege the internationalization of capital, economic centralization of power in the hands of international institutions such as the World Bank and the International Monetary Fund, the erosion of the sovereignty of nation states, exponential increases in labor migration, the compression of time and space through the creation of computer-mediated interactions, or simultaneous pressures toward homogeneity and differentiation of cultures (Hawkeworth 2006, 3).

By contrast feminist scholars have argued that the absence of gender-focused analysis wrongly suggests that "gendered power relations are not at play in the complex process of globalization" and that "globalization is not and has never been a women's issue" (Hawkesworth 2006, 3). Hawkesworth points out, "the complex and contradictory economic, political and ideological transformations wrought by capitalism play a central role in this narrative [of globalization], providing a framework in which women in various regions of the world struggle to sustain themselves, their families, and communities" (5).

Indeed, transnational networks of women's groups have taken up looking at gender issues and issues affecting women and mobilizing on their own behalf and on behalf of their communities. Women have developed collective vehicles for political action of their own and have used the United Nations as a stage for advocating for human rights, and against oppression.

Perhaps no theorist has done more to situate communication technologies and the information age within ongoing globalizing processes than Manuel Castells in his three volume treatise on the Information Society. In his trilogy Castells argues that global space has progressively been divided into the "space of flows" (or the realm of the Net) and the "space of places" (or the realm of the Self). He notes that "our societies are increasingly structured around a bipolar opposition between the Net and the Self" (1996, 3). He characterizes the Net as the material time-sharing behaviors and actions that are no longer place-bound, such as electronically-mediated communication, capital movements and other financial transactions and the movements of the world's elite managerial classes (1996, 412). The new global economy intertwines the informational and the global. The economy is informational because it depends on the ability to generate, process, and apply knowledge-based information efficiently. It is global because its core processes—production, consumption, circulation, finance, raw materials markets, etc.—are organized on a global scale either directly or through a network of links. Using technologies that have transformed how information is processed, offshore outsourcing locations enact practices that obliterate the constraints of space and time.

As one of the few globalization theorists to address the "woman question," Castells (1997) offers an extensive discussion on the "the end of patriarchalism." Castells' prognosis for women's economic and social advancement under globalizing processes is optimistic. He points to the fact that women's participation in wage labor has increased over the last twenty years and attributes these changes to transformations in the economy and labor markets coupled with advances in reproductive technologies and global feminist activism. Castells also points out that what women have going for them in these emerging labor spaces are their interpersonal skills, their flexible work patterns, and their lower levels of pay—all characteristics that fit the demands of postindustrial economies. It will come as no surprise that feminist scholars have objected to the way Castells' analysis casts women in the role of exploitable labor in the "global now." Saukko (2003), for example, critiques Castells' analysis of the transformation of women's economic position, the impact of feminist activism and the trends that undermine the traditional patriarchal nuclear family on the global stage. She argues that the methodological resources and the positions Castells adopts limit the politics he is able to advocate for. As Saukko points out, these limitations mean that Castells is able to see the entrance of women into wage labor (positively) but unable to confront the exploitative conditions under which many women work. Saukko's point, one which other feminist scholars share, is that while Castells' structural analysis documents the profound transformations in women's economic power, it does not foreground the exploitative features inherent in their location *vis a vis* the new economy. Pointing to the low wages and difficult working conditions in the flexible sweatshops that are now the workplaces of many women around the world, Saukko argues that positivist macro-analyses cannot adequately illuminate the dynamics that exploit women and men who work under these conditions. For Saukko, these conditions can only be foregrounded by a gender-focused analysis and to do that one needs different sets of methodological lenses.

Feminist epistemology deploys gender as a heuristic to guide research, utilizing it as an analytic category to shed light on questions, hypotheses, and concepts (Hawkesworth, 1997).

To deploy gender as an analytic tool, we have to move beyond the usual uses of the term for cultural constructions of masculinity and femininity. Joan Scott articulates the theoretical basis of gender as a concept involving two interrelated but analytically distinct parts: "Gender is a constitutive element of social relationships based on perceived differences between the sexes, and gender is a primary way of signifying relationships of power" (1986, 1067). In teasing out how gender is a constitutive element in social relationships, Scott highlighted the fact that gender functions in various capacities. For example, gender functions in the symbols that cultures make available to people, it functions in social institutions, in the formation of our subjective identities, and in organizations (1067–1068). For Scott gender is a useful analytic category by virtue of the fact that "it provides a way to decode meaning" (1070). Decoding the meanings of gender makes possible the uncovering of how "gender hierarchies are constructed, maintained, subverted, and changed through the complex interaction of norms, symbols, interpersonal relations, social practices, and religious, economic, and political institutions" (Hawkesworth 2006, 10). Gender power permeates international relations, financial and economic processes, state organizations, development policies, the structures of institutions, symbol systems and interpersonal relationships (Hawkesworth 2006). It is the deployment of gender for analytic purposes that has allowed feminists to examine and shed light on the power relations between women and men, and the mechanisms that structure privilege or disadvantage on the basis of race, sexuality, ethnicity, nationality etcetera. This feminist analytic perspective reveals dynamics about the experiences of women that macro-analyses overlook because they do not differentiate women and men as social agents and therefore do not consider the complex dimensions of subjectivity that feminist theory elaborates.

For feminist scholars another aspect of the deployment of gender for analysis is that it underscores the dynamics of uneven power relations on the global stage. Gender power works by excluding, lessening the value of what women do, belittling or even prohibiting women from participating in certain facets of society. Gender power frames the social opportunities available to particular women and men by creating systems that embrace and reward qualities associated with masculinity and maleness while devaluing qualities linked to women and femininity. These power structures then become culturally sanctioned systems upon which social space, labor, and other choices and opportunities are made accessible to men and women (10). Like other feminist theorists, Hawkesworth argues that it is in this way that gender is seen by women's activists and scholars as "integrally related to inequalities which become embedded in institutions and structures that operate independently of individual volition and intention" (10–11). It is under these circumstances that men's interests and power related dynamics get promoted as the norm in the process and leave women's needs and interests hidden. Deploying gender as an analytic tool in an examination of globalization makes it possible to uncover the gendered dimensions of the process. As Hawkesworth notes, "Investigating its complex economic, political, technological, and ideological dynamics, feminist scholars construe globalization as a thoroughly gendered phenomenon" (11). Feminist analyses have linked globalizing processes to the feminization of poverty, migration, and labor. Other analyses have theorized the gender structures of the process by showing the changing sexual divisions, by making visible the ways in which priorities in economic policies are masculine-oriented and thus privilege a male bias. Feminist have also deployed their theoretical project to link these gendered dimensions of globalization to development.

There is one aspect of the ongoing debates about globalization about which both feminist scholars and those who have not focused on gender by and large agree—the global economy is not planetary because the whole planet is not on the global circuit and does not participate in the logic of the economy even though the whole planet feels its impact and is shaped by it. In other words, there is segmentation; however this segmentation is not static and countries, regions, local societies, and economic structures may enter and be dropped as a result of the ever shifting (re)alignment of processes of accumulation and consumption (Castells 1998, 102). I want to pay particular attention to Castells' discussion of Africa under the global economy. "It is precisely the feature of this new economy," he writes, "that it affects the whole planet either by inclusion or exclusion in the processes of production, circulation, and consumption that have become at the same time globalized and informationalized" (133). These conditions lead Castells to note:

> Overall, the systematic logic of the new global economy does not have much of a role for the majority of the African population in the newest international division of labor. Most primary commodities are useless or low priced, markets are too narrow, investment too risky, labor not skilled enough, communication and telecommunication infrastructure clearly inadequate, politics too unpredictable, and government bureaucracies inefficiently corrupt. (135)

In other words, Castells' systemic analysis arrives at one conclusion— Africa's structural irrelevance in the new global economy. Other globalization scholars concur, though they may not characterize issues in such dire terms. Beck (2000), Hawkesworth (2006), Moghadam (2005), Steger (2003), and Waters (2001) all acknowledge that globalization is uneven and that whole regions in the global South do not have equal access to global networks and their infrastructure. While the 1970s marked an accelerated expansion of global exchanges in the global North, they also marked the simultaneous marginalization of most areas in the South. That marginalization is also related to the emergence of neoliberalism and development programs offered by the North. Though my main concern is with the economic and cultural dimensions one cannot really separate the economic from the political dimension. For example, telecommunication and media are unhampered by national borders or geography; as a result the proprietary networks of transnational companies within which business services are offered at offshore sites know no borders. But transnational companies also need weakened national governments that are willing to follow IMF and World Bank directives to open their markets in order to set up shop. Thus there is a chain of global economic interdependency and interconnectedness that is facilitated by political decisions, and contemporary Ghana is squarely linked to this chain.

## DEVELOPMENT, GENDER AND MACRO/MICRO-ANALYSES OF GLOBALIZATION

Development and modernization are, as I have asserted in chapter 2, central to the aspirations of nations and peoples in Ghana and other parts of the global South. As Appadurai remarks, for many societies in the global South, "modernity is an elsewhere, just as globalization is a temporal wave that must be encountered in *their* present" (Appadurai 1996, 9, emphasis in original). Yet for many citizens in the global South modernity is becoming an experience of here and now as the lines between elites, between producers and consumers, between workers at different levels of production, and between different locales have shrunk (Appadurai 1996). Beginning with modernity, one has a kind of globalization based on the establishment of the nation state, colonialism and the poaching of natural resources from the periphery to the centers of power in the West. In the current moment of post-colonialism, post-modernity, post-industrialization and post-nationality, there is a kind of globalization of production and distribution of material resources and of commodities on a scale unlike any we have seen before. The current moment has created situations where postcolonial communities such as Ghana are being drawn into the capitalist framework in a different way.

Development and its practices are directly related to contemporary globalizing processes. Nation-states in the current stage of globalization have by and large ceded their development agenda to transnational organizations such as the IMF and World Bank. Joanne Wright's (1997) essay noted that development is a twentieth century touchstone that is "a theory, a process, a project, and a prescription that was conceived by the West for the Third World" (FN2). Prior to the 1980s, development and modernization programs were largely uncontested and their inherent assumption was that the end result of the process will be "development" that resembles that of the developed global North. President Truman famously offered his 1947 development strategy of "fair dealing" to address the poverty and misery of "underdevelopment" in the Third World. In the Truman development doctrine underdevelopment was believed to pose a risk to world security. Saunders, however, points out that the so-called "fair dealing" doctrine was related to a strategy of keeping emerging nation states from the "seductions of communism." While this development strategy was supposedly earmarked to support democratic economic relations between the United States and the Third World — something rather revolutionary for the time, considering that the colonial apparatus had sought to "civilize" the peoples of the South through controlling and 'developing' raw materials, administrative infrastructure, education, and instilling western values — Truman's programs could not be "fair dealing" given that protectionist trade practices and the debt trap created an imbalance between North and South (Saunders 2002, 2).

*Feminisms, Politics, Labels, and Discourses on Gender*

The impact of development on communities and the fact that the power structures within the non-governmental organizations prescribing and overseeing development projects lacked gender-sensitive perspectives have led activists to challenge these NGOs on two fronts: 1) activists have worked within the structures of NGOs often forming groups with distinct feminist agendas; 2) other activists have worked outside of these NGOs. The focus of these groups has been to challenge projects and prescriptions on the bases of their impact on women and communities and in the process argue for versions of the feminist project. I discuss these developments below.

An underlying logic of the development prescription is obviously that the West has attained a superior stage of existence that others need to emulate in order to have access to the good life. As I have noted in chapter 2, in the 1970s and 1980s the economic structures in place in the global North, the debt of the South, the shock of oil prices and the collapse of commodity prices all added to the collapse of many Third World economies; a situation that produced untold suffering, especially for women, as we have already seen in the case of Ghana. These conditions are also linked to the cementing of American global political and economic hegemony (Wright 1997, FN1). The collapse of Third World economies and the advent of feminist activism during the 1970s and 1980s led to the interrogation of patriarchy and male domination in peripheral societies and in the development community. Feminist activism led to the interrogation of modernization and other development practices. An outcome of the feminist critique of the development project is that development studies now has orientations that are decidedly conscious of gender though their specific ideological foci continue to evolve. Yet it is also the case that even postmodern critiques of the development project left intact the "specifically gendered layers" of the process (Wright 1997, FN2).

Prior to the current stage of globalization nation-states controlled their development agenda and often positioned projects within a liberal humanist ideology that by and large left patriarchy unchallenged. Under modernity, the nation-state had some autonomy in directly setting the contours of its own social and industrial development. For a brief postcolonial moment the emerging decolonized states of Africa saw a flowering of enlightenment humanist ideals as they developed their own autonomous, locally/nationally directed gender-neutral projects that preserved patriarchy but offered access to services such as education that some women could use to advance themselves. As I have argued in previous chapters, structural differences in economic and political power between North and South made this moment rather brief. A neoliberal development agenda shaped by the global North has become the reality for many communities in the South. The differential consequence of this development agenda for women has prompted feminist scholars to examine it. The process has uncovered and made visible the contested terrain of feminisms, particularly western feminisms and activism *vis a vis* women's issues in the global South, the role "third world women" have or should have in examining and advocating for their own communities, and lastly the differences between the feminist elites and other women within both North and South (Saunders 2002).

Welfarism, as a development orientation, was grounded in western liberal ideology that specifically sought to address the needs of women. Moser (1989) identified three kinds of welfare programs. These addressed physical survival (providing food aid in times of disaster for women and children); combating malnutrition (food and nutrition education for pregnant women and children of ages five and under); and mother-child health programs including family planning (Saunders 2002, 4). This approach to development came under attack from the group within the development community that called itself Women in Development (WID). WID attacked Welfarism for its paternalistic reproduction of existing gender roles and its re-inscription of patriarchal power of the state and family. Some feminists saw Welfarism as sexist, reproducing sex roles, and socializing Third World women into these roles by defining "women's nature as biologically wired to nurture rather than to be rational, aggressive and competitive" (Saunders, 5). Ironically, as Saunders points out, while feminist professionals fought for self-recognition, they nonetheless "continued to perpetuate the images of impoverished Third World women as helpless victims of patriarchy" because this "authorized their right to organize a planned liberation of this client population" implying that this client population lacked the power to liberate themselves (5). The heterogeneity and tensions within various feminisms in the North, and the relationships between these approaches and their consequences when theorists and activists engage gender activists of the South raise politically charged questions about who speaks for whom and to what ends. What is clear, as Saunders and others have demonstrated, is that feminists and other women's activists do not hold a homogenized position on women, gender and development, much as the field does not hold a singular view on the impact of globalization on women.

Feminist positions on development studies have evolved along the trajectory of feminist scholarship and theory development. Women in Development (WID) takes a western liberal orientation to development and focuses on women's labor and its invisibility yet centrality in Third World development. WID also promotes legal rights and has advocated for gender equality. WID positions assume that a gradual process of incremental change will eventually result in gender equality. Feminists such as Esther Boserup (1970) examined the status of women in the Third World using compelling analyses to call into question the assumptions that male dominated aid agencies made about the location of Third World women. In Ghana, a NCWD review conducted between 1999 and 2000 concluded that development projects conducted by the DWM were stuck in the WID paradigm even though the group had couched its discourses in the language of progressive gender politics (Manuh 2007). WID positions on issues such as the exclusion of women in development programs have been challenged by another prespective within the development community—Women and Development (WAD) (Saunders, 7).

Women and Development (WAD), owing its emergence directly to United Nations conferences, has been mobilizing women around the world, often bringing legitimacy to broad feminist agendas on the global stage. WAD has contested WID hegemony and the "gradualist" assumptions of WID. WAD sees global capitalism as inequitable to both men and women in the Third World. This WAD position has in turn been challenged by proponents of a Gender and Development (GAD) orientation. Gender and Development adherents argue that WAD does not pay enough attention to gender relations, and class-based differences. WAD, it is argued, privileges class over gender. GAD on the other hand takes on a socialistic orientation by highlighting the social responsibilities of the State while examining gender ideology. Wright (1997) pointed out that Women in Development approaches are guilty of focusing on the integration of women in development without much attention to the larger development paradigm. When these approaches look at the larger context of their integration agenda, development is cast as a benevolent project (Wright 1997)—a position that is at the very least problematic.

Gender activism around development within agencies has tended to represent the voices of those in the North. In order to inject a specific

Southern perspective into development discourse, a network of research-ers interested in Africa founded the Association of African Women for Research and Development (AAWORD). AAWORD takes a distinctly feminist orientation and rejects the way in which sex-based inequity is seen as the foremost problem for women. AAWORD members argue that class and national hierarchies create barriers and thus it behooves acti-vists to recognize the multiplicities of needs and interests among women. AAWORD's founding has been hailed as a crucial moment in the decolo-nization of research on African women. Though AAWORD still operates, its influence has receeded.

Another Southern voice in the development sphere is Development Alternatives with Women for a New Era (DAWN). The DAWN network has interrogated the western oriented focus on sex-based equality and notions of sisterhood defined by First and Third World elites (Saunders, 7). DAWN has suggested that integrating women into development is dependent on breaking down local biases against women's partaking in the process. DAWN positions women's desires to be free of class, race, gender and national inequalities as basic rights. For DAWN, empowering women means creating spaces for critical reflection that is grounded in the multiplicity and heterogeneity of feminist viewpoints (Saunders, 12).

As much as feminists and gender activists have worked to push gen-der-sensitive approaches to development within transnational agencies such as the World Bank, it has become clear that agencies can co-opt the agenda to serve their own goals. Empowerment of women, for instance, has become a World Bank goal, though many activists find the bank's deployment rather problematic (Moghadam 2005; Saunders 2000).

Gender-focused analyses of the development agenda in the current stage of globalization shows among other things that first, the nation-state is no longer the sole arbiter of development choices as IMF, World Bank and global capital increasingly shape that agenda. Second, in this stage, capital determines the distribution of resources and tends to ex-ploit the path of least resistance. This ironically has tended to focus some development initiatives on women and their labor. It has shifted gender-neutral development to gender-sensitive development; in a back-handed way this creates access to the knowledge that women need in order to work in sectors like outsourcing. I shall return to this issue below. Third, this current stage has weakened the nation-state—some feminists argue that the nation-state has in fact been "feminized," though ministries and agencies that reinforce or assist global capital in its "coercive and surveil-lance capabilities" are paradoxically masculinized while those that focus on domestic health, education and social welfare are feminized (Marc-hand and Runyan 2000, 24). A key ideology that undergirds this process of feminization of the nation-state is neoliberalism.

## GENDER AND NEOLIBERALISM

The financial institutions that control development projects in the global South are guided by a neoliberal agenda. Neoliberal ideology borrows some facets of Adam Smith's *The Wealth of Nations* and privileges the "invisible hand of the market" as the sole arbiter of economic growth. Neoliberals advocate for the free reign of the market as a moderator of individual behavior and argue that individual interests ultimately take on social benefits. Free markets, neoliberals argue, force producers to find cheaper ways to produce their goods and services. The free market also compels them to offer prices cheaper than those of their competitors. Consumers reward producers who offer the best goods and services at the lowest prices and push less competitive ones out of the market. Thus, the neoliberal argument goes, consumers benefit while also helping competitive producers amass private wealth. In this process, producers and innovators are forced to develop new means for producing ever cheaper goods and services. For neoliberals the role of the state is to support an unrestricted open market. Nation-states provide the legal protections for private property and contracts. They also secure law and order and provide defense services. Neoliberals argue for free market ideology even in the areas of civil welfare: they argue for states to privatize publicly held industries, removing market regulations on trade, reducing public expenditure on education, health, welfare, labor, prisons and others. These neoliberal positions are at the core of investment and loan service agreements and practices of transnational agencies such as the IMF and the World Bank. For these agencies, free markets and globalizing processes are all for the collective good. Critics of globalization and the wholesale exportation of neoliberal policies into the global South point to the economic and social dislocation caused by practices such as structural adjustment and economic recovery plans and their impact on Third World peoples, particularly women (Hawkesworth 2006; Moghadam 2005). Feminist scholars such as J.K. Gibson-Graham see globalization as a masculine project. L. H. M. Ling refers to it as "hypermasculinity." Charlotte Hooper and R. W. Connell argue that inherent in the gender politics of neoliberalism is a "transnational business masculinity" (cited by Moghadam 2005, 28). Along the same lines, Marchand and Runyan note:

> In the neoliberal discourse on globalization, the state is typically "feminized" in relation to the more robust market by being represented as a drag on the global economy that must be subordinated and minimized (14).

Ghana's economic and political upheavals during the 70s and 80s are already well documented in previous chapters. Its emergence as an IMF and World Bank "darling" has also been discussed extensively. Here I want to link Ghana's economic "transformation" to the neoliberal ideology on which it is based. The Economic Reform Program (ERP) the IMF and World Bank imposed upon Ghana as a condition for a bailout in the late 80s is heavily entrenched in neoliberal ideology. Structural adjustment unleashed drastic economic and social dislocation with mass layoffs of workers (many of them women) as the state shed investments or privatized them. The public sector, the biggest employer in the country up to that point, shed workers in unprecedented numbers from banks and other state industries as these were restructured or sold to private investors. Sectors such as banking and telecommunications employed a disproportionate number of women and thus added numerous women into the ranks of the unemployed. At the same time, under IMF and World Bank "guidance" the state removed barriers to trade and investment, thus opening the door for many transnational corporations to set up shop in Ghana. World Bank brochures now hail Ghana for having entered "the knowledge economy" as it becomes a hub for transnational corporations providing outsourcing services. The ideology of neoliberalism where the market eliminates or supplants political actors and where we end with the rule by the market inevitably reduces the multidimensionality of globalization to a single one—economics. Of course leaving issues such as ecology, culture, civil society, and politics under the sway of economics is at the very least suspect. Thus it is not surprising that, like modernization and development before it, globalization generates considerable suspicion, particularly in the global South and among activists.

The supposed systemic irrelevance of Africa (except for pockets like South Africa), its uneven access to globalizing networks, and its situation as a region that is affected by globalization rather than affecting the process continues to be the conclusion of analyses of the process (Steger 2003; Waters 2000). Thus, Castells' gloomy outlook notwithstanding, one still has to account for the precise nature of the impact of neoliberal practices on countries such as Ghana. Clearly, there are winners and losers in globalization and Africa is sadly on the losing side of the equation. Yet the issue of who wins and who loses in contemporary globalization is ultimately related to social justice. It is for this reason that Beck (2000) argues that issues of social justice need to be handled differently both theoretically and politically under globalization. It is an issue of social justice, specifically, the gender disadvantage that women in the Third World have been saddled with as a result of globalizing processes—that has prompted a feminist intervention in the globalization debate.

## GENDER, TECHNOLOGY AND GLOBALIZING PROCESSES

Technology and technological innovation are the infrastructure of global-ization. Technology provides the architecture for globalization while also creating the conduit for linking various dimensions of the process. Draw-ing on Harvey Brooks and Daniel Bell, Castells defines technology as "the use of scientific knowledge to specify ways of doing things in a reprodu-cible manner" (1996, 29–30). Castells sees information technologies as "the converging set of technologies in microelectronics, computing, (ma-chines and software), telecommunications/broadcasting, and optoelec-tronics" (1996, 30). Popular conceptions of globalization point to technol-ogy as its single most important characteristic. Ordinary folks render globalization as fuelled by "new" technologies such as the internet, cellu-lar phones, fax machines, satellites, high definition televisions, digital cameras, etc. Certainly these innovations have played a role in the pro-cess. Networking capabilities have developed at an accelerated pace and with that development has emerged ever cheaper ways for moving data and processing information. According to Castells, the cost of informa-tion processing had fallen from around $75 per million operations in 1960 to less than one-hundredth of a cent by 1990 (Castells 1996, 45). For this reason shipping data offshore has become considerably easier and cheap-er, and offshore processing further reduces cost. Global networks offer flexibility. Indeed, technological change in the last three decades pro-vides rather compelling evidence of the major transformations that are occurring as a result of globalization.

Economic globalization refers to the intensification and stretching of economic interrelations around the globe. Here however, some regions are more fully integrated into these economically globalized networks than others—again Africa is really peripheral in many respects. Massive flows of capital and technology have generated huge markets for goods and services, and markets now have global reach through the linkages among regional blocs and national economies. As a result of these dy-namics huge transnational corporations have emerged, as have powerful international economic institutions and regional trading systems. For scholars such as Beck (2000), Steger (2003) and others these regional blocs and transnational networks are becoming the building blocks of a twen-ty-first century economic structure.

Feminist scholars, while acknowledging how modern technologies are embedded within patriarchal social relations, have nonetheless noted women's ambivalent assimilation of technology (see, for example, de Beauvoir 1953; Firestone 1970; Haraway 1995). Exploring this complex relationship, Terry and Calvert (1997) argue for the understanding of the inherent moral and political issues of relationships and exchanges among machines, their designers and their users. Terry and Calvert call for understanding technologies in relation to the particular historical, economic, and cultural context of design and use. The machine/human interface, they point out, is situated in social relations, and these affect the configuring, effecting, mediating and embodying functions of technologies. The political issues for feminists in relation to globalization generally and to the emerging technology-infused globalized workspace are who controls the technologies of work, how is that control organized socially and institutionally and for what ends? A further point is that the social relations into which the machine/human interface are embedded also offer slippages and spaces for resisting, and/or re-appropriating technologies for purposes and ends other than those intended. Female-dominated outsourcing is a particular historical context of technology use that is layered by the terms with which we structure and understand masculinity and femininity. While work in these contexts is done via technologies that exploit patriarchal gender hierarchies and traditional notions of gender, as I will show in later chapters, the technologies may also be appropriated in opposition to gender oppression.

## GENDER, KNOWLEDGE, AND "NEW" WORK

In chapter 2, I discussed education in Ghana's development agenda and the country's goal of becoming the IT hub in sub-Saharan Africa. As with other nations vying to compete in this global economy, IT-enhanced work and the knowledge that makes that work possible has become a critical component of Ghana's drive for global relevance. In chapter 3, I offered a historical analysis of gender politics in Ghana since independence. In this section I will use these discussions to look at how what constitutes work-related knowledge is constructed and represented in relation to the new work that workers are doing in outsourcing in Ghana.

Work-related knowledge is now a key characteristic in economic development and this reality makes the development of appropriately trained workers critical to the new economy. The new focus on knowledge also underscores changes in notions of what counts as knowledge, who gets to define it, what in fact constitutes "knowledge work," and what counts as working knowledge. A 1996 OECD (Organization for Economic Co-operation and Development) policy document entitled "The Knowledge-Based Economy" pointed out that "knowledge is now the driver of productivity and economic growth" (4). That sentiment is shared by the World Bank. In its policy brief on lifelong learning the writers noted that "A knowledge-based economy relies primarily on the use of ideas rather than physical abilities and on application of technology rather than the transformation of raw materials or exploitation of cheap labor" (1). Powell and Snellman (2004) defined the knowledge economy as:

production and services based on knowledge-intensive activities that contribute to an accelerated pace of technological and scientific advance as well as rapid obsolescence. The key component of a knowledge economy includes a greater reliance on intellectual capabilities than on physical inputs or natural resources. (Powell and Snellman, 201)

As Farrell and Fenwick (2007, 5) have pointed out, while the Robert B. Reich (1991) argument that the global economy depends on elite symbolic-analytic knowledge—that is, the aptitude to "generate, design, manipulate, and translate ideas" and the versatility to move such knowledge across audiences and language—there appears to be other components of knowledge construction in the emerging workspaces of the new economy. For instance, the processes of symbolic analytic knowledge making also entail management, mediation, mobilization of knowledge and the development and maintenance of networks for partnership and collaboration. Knowledge making and the connecting of that knowledge to others encompasses divergent levels of abstraction and translation. Workers at different levels of the hierarchy translate and/or adapt and re-present what symbolic analysts create into different localized work processes and knowledges. What constitutes "common knowledge" in a particular work site is how the adapted, improvised knowledge is acted upon, and this knowledge, as Farrell and Fenwick (2007) noted, may be so much taken for granted as how things are done that it may not even be codified in any systematic manner at all. Workers who function with localized knowledge in sectors that the global economy has created are indeed "knowledgeable" in the spaces in which they work. Furthermore, as Christopher Newfield (2008) argues, earlier assessments of knowledge in the new economy offer us far less complex and nuanced understandings than current characterizations permit. Newfield, drawing on "Knowledge Management" (KM) and "Innovative Management" literature analyzes the practices the KM field uses to isolate subgroups of knowledge workers. Newfield notes:

> "Knowledge management" acknowledged the importance of culture and, at the same time, subordinated it to financial goals. KM wanted to improve the freedom of the human interaction that enhances knowledge work while translating individual labor into value for the firm. KM had two main ways of seeking this synthesis. It aimed to stratify knowledge workers into clearly identifiable subgroups, which would then receive disparate treatment. Second, it aimed to transform "human capital," owned and controlled by employees, into what the field called "structural capital," controlled by the company. (Newfield, 130)

KM delineation stratifies knowledge work into four distinct categories and offers insights into the implications of this stratification for American public higher education. Here I focus on Newfield's discussion of the four categories of knowledge work. The first is knowledge work that is information-based and done by highly skilled workers who are difficult to replace but are low value-added. What the new economy's logic demands for this class of workers is to deskill them as much as possible and outsource the skilled work they do. As Newfield notes, workers in this category are necessary to the firm but are not valued by customers. These workers he notes, "have learned a complicated set of ropes but pull no strings" and they include "skilled factory workers and experienced secretaries" and bookkeepers (131). They are also workers who have the cultural knowledge that is not easily codified or transferred. Therefore, in order to maximize profits, the firm needs to minimize its dependence on these workers as much as possible. The goal is to strip away all non-essential tasks from the job description (through outsourcing or automation), so that fewer of these workers are needed. The second category is knowledge work that is done by workers who are easily replaceable and are low value-added. The new economy's logic is to buy machines to replace these workers. A third group of knowledge workers are easy to replace but high value added. These workers are highly-skilled but happen to be in a class whose skilled compatriots are many in the global labor market. Their jobs may be outsourced to markets that offer the same highly-skilled labor but for less. The last category is the star class of knowledge workers: they are highly trained, difficult to replace and are high value added. They are the workers who deserve full capital support and they get into this class "by being competent, brilliant, and unique" (132). Newfield's analysis therefore avoids the danger of oversimplifying the relationships among knowledge, training and work in the new economy. It also provides a far more sophisticated heuristic for analyzing the class of workers who are doing outsourced work off-shore, as I show in later chapters of this book.

Capital markets are a dimension of globalization that is truly globalized, as they are managed around the clock in a globally-integrated financial market powered by technologies. Labor, according to Castells (1998) is the least globalized. Labor is least globalized because only a small fraction of scientists and professionals, that is symbolic analysts, are able to work where they choose. Hawkesworth (2006) however suggests that this may be changing as labor migration is becoming far more prevalent among all classes of workers—for example, she points to the 60 million or so women who migrate to work in the care industry as contract workers in the global North and parts of the South such as the oil-rich states of the Persian Gulf. Though labor is not as fully globalized as capital and technology, it is nonetheless a global resource in three ways—(1) companies may choose to locate anywhere worldwide to find the labor supply they need—in terms of skill, cost or social control, (2) firms anywhere may solicit labor from everywhere if they are willing to pay, and to provide agreeable working conditions, and (3) labor will enter any market on its own initiative as a result of a number of concerns—war, poverty, hunger, etc. The processes by which people work, that is the knowledge and expertise people control, are at the center of the social structure of communities.

Given the historical context of women's access to education and wage work, I will argue that gender is the underlying structure that mediates access to knowledge and expertise deemed appropriate for participation in the global economy. Further, women's access to knowledge is shaped by gendered constructions and representations of the kinds of knowledge that are most valued in the new economy. As Castells (1998) argues, the extent to which technology and the informational paradigm transform labor, production and managerial functions determines how globalization affects societies and communities. And, I will add that the extent to which these functions operate to limit access of women determines the position of women and communities in the new economy. Labor dynamics under globalization are intimately connected to technological developments. It is technology that opens up the possibility for transnational corporations to export jobs to places where they can find cheap labor and/or to places where they have low workplace safety and environmental protection obligations. Computers and other networks generate worldwide proximity and enable the breakdown and dispersing of goods and services. Production is done through the division of labor at different parts of the world. Transnational corporations are then in a position to play off countries and regions against each other in order to get the most favorable fiscal arrangements or friendly investment environments (Beck, 2000). These conditions limit the scope of self-determination for countries in the global South like Ghana, countries that must attract capital in order to survive. In some instances, this can lead to greater autonomy for women, and sometimes it leads to exploitation. While mainstream analyses of globalization identify these labor-related consequences, they often do not articulate the gendered characteristics of these consequences. Part of the feminist project has been to theorize the link between globalization and labor practices in gender-sensitive ways.

A key labor shift that has emerged with globalization is the centrality of work in the service sector of many economies. Since the late 1970s, women have entered the wage labor market in unprecedented numbers, working in both the formal and informal economies. The idea of the "feminization of labor" or the "feminization of employment" captures the dual sense of the increase in the number of women in the labor force as well as the worsening conditions under which men and women in these arrangements work. Hawkesworth (2006), citing Wichterich (2000), points out that in export processing zones (EPZ) around the globe, in employment such as textiles, pharmaceuticals, electronic and leather goods production, one finds 70 to 90 percent of workers are women. With global corporations carving out export zones within borders of nation-states but outside the judicial oversight of the states, workers labor under appalling conditions as labor laws, environmental and safety regulations, labor unions and even defined working hours are set aside. As outsourcing and off-shoring becomes ever more attractive to transnational corporations looking for ever cheaper and cheaper labor, "200 million women" end up in these labor dynamics as employees of contractors or subcontractors (Hawkesworth 2006, 12). As I will demonstrate, women in these labor arrangements may work for long hours for low wages, they may have no choice but to meet production deadlines that require them to work overtime, and they may be required to work flexible hours, part time, as temporary workers or under a corporate regime of just-in-time production. In Ghana as in Latin America workers may leave their families by moving to cities to work, a condition that not only puts enormous pressure on families but also exacerbates the consequences of urban migration.

Globalized labor arrangements pose severe health risks for women: repetitive stress syndrome, carpal tunnel syndrome, miscarriages, premature babies, babies born with low weight and many more. Feminists argue that labor gets feminized under these conditions not only by virtue of the fact that women populate these worksites but because these practices now affect the work that both men and women do. Telecomputing, and other mechanisms for "informationalization" and "flexibilization" of work have also led to more home-based work, at least in the global North. Saskia Sassen (2002) argued that these arrangements make homes the sites for active economic activity. These practices offer flexibility, but, more importantly, they reduce labor costs for employers. Space and infrastructure expenses, Sassen points out, now become costs that the worker bears. Thus it is not only labor that is feminized under globalization but also the conditions of work. Under these conditions the barrier between work and family life is erased, often to the detriment of family life.

To further underscore feminizing processes, one can point to the gendered structure of service work in the global economy. Some areas of the service economy are male-dominated, are highly valued by globalized labor arrangements and practices and are accordingly rewarded. Service workers in finance and information technologies by and large receive attractive wages. Women who provide services in areas such as care, cleaning, the lowest tier of the health care industry, retail sales, customer services, and data entry are comparatively poorly paid. According to Wichterich, (2000) a majority of women who do service work only receive subsistence-level wages and this makes women vulnerable to poverty. It is these structures that feminize poverty and contribute to the staggering percentage (by some accounts 70 percent) of the women in the ranks of the global poor (Hawkesworth 2006). Indeed outsourcing sites where a large cadre of women renders low-end services fits squarely into this sector though their work is complicated by the use of technologies and the navigation of virtual spaces in which they work.

*Literacy, Outsourcing, and the Field Sites*

Advanced telecommunications capabilities make the location of BPO and ITO work in Ghana possible. Outsourcing constructs conflicting narratives about globalization, technologies, development, gender, and work. For some women in Ghana, ICT-enabled process outsourcing has provided an entry into the global information technology network as western companies cut labor costs by shipping service jobs there. For these women global connectivity is transforming their working lives even as it defines and shapes what they do. The unemployment rate, the size of Ghana's national debt, and other complex geopolitical dynamics mean that the state's ability to create viable employment opportunities is greatly curtailed. These pressures and the competition among non-dominant economies for outsourcing opportunities have led to the creation of attractive incentive packages and general attitudes of compliance of host communities to the desires of companies. For Ghana, as I have shown, these dynamics are further compounded by a public education infrastructure that has remained fairly stagnant, its practices focused almost entirely on alphabetic literacies, even as the state pushes for the creation of work opportunities related to IT and BP outsourcing that require abilities beyond the alphabetic. As the state proves incapable of underwriting a public education congruent with its aspirations of benefiting from globalization, even as it strives to position itself as an IT hub for sub-Saharan Africa, neoliberal inspired private market entrepreneurs are shoring up the gaps and thereby underwriting the terms under which citizens participate in globalized work. As the experiences of women at CTI and CDN demonstrate, it is mainly from these private sites that localized knowledge is acquired by prospective outsourcing employees.

The exportation of jobs that western companies see as less desirable or cost too much for labor in dominant economies invoke two simultaneous yet contradictory impulses. Considering where such jobs go, it can be argued — and indeed agencies like the Organization for Economic Cooperation and Development (OECD), IMF and World Bank take this position — that such jobs integrate "developing nations" into the global economy and therefore further the pace of their "development." However it is also clear that such communities have human resources that companies tap into cheaply. As one outsourcing entrepreneur put it "Ghana's low cost of living, stable democratic government and literate, English-speaking population make it well-suited as an outsourcing location" (Slayter 2004). Thus, while those who do such work in post-industrial first-world settings may be paid low wages (Hull 1997), the comparably literate workers in offshore settings are paid comparatively even lower wages. In another account of such an outsourcing enterprise in Ghana, *The New York Times* reported on women who work in offices that visitors "jokingly call [the] 'electronic sweatshop'" and use high technology to process tickets issued by New York City police and other agencies for various ordinance violations (Worth 2002, A17). The manager notes that the company is in Ghana because it, "is safe, and the government is democratic and has been stable for twenty years. And, of course, because labor in Ghana is far cheaper than the United States" (Worth 2002, A17). While competition for the low wages of Ghanaian workers obviously costs American jobs and drives down wages for American workers, the Ghanaian women, at least by published accounts, are nonetheless generating income levels impressive by local Ghanaian standards.[2] Globalization advocates will point to such examples as evidence of the markets spreading their benefits into even "excluded" regions of the planet. They may argue that even in these workplaces, people have choices. But anti-globalization activists might look at these dynamics and charge that they are evidence of the impact of the "juggernaut of untrammeled capitalism" that is "ruled by profit seeking corporations" (Lechner and Boli 2004, 1).

The Ghanaian women workers in the *New York Times* story raise yet another critical point about outsourcing work in the global economy: they discuss what can only be identified as a shaping of desire and aspirations. Virtual work not only makes "virtual immigrants"[3] but it also becomes a conduit for imagining the possibilities of self-making. The women use the subject of their work and their analysis of it to imagine a first-world city that is, in their view, sparkling clean. To them part of the translation of work-related knowledge is also cultural. That cultural knowledge is processed through local and imaginary know-how. It leads to assumptions such as those of Susuana Okine, a 26-year-old woman, who comments that "I know that New York is beautiful: the streets, the flowers, and the people too. I can also testify that it must smell better than Accra," based entirely on ties to the city through the maps she consults daily at work. That outsourcing work inspires self-confidence and new desires is evident in remarks like these from Christine Mensah, 35, a manager, who said, "It's easy to look at New York and see where you are going, it's not like Ghana. With a map you can go anywhere," and Nora Kraku, 28, who told the *Times* reporter, "I am very used to the rules and regulations of New York now, so I think I can live there" (Worth 2002, A17).

The dominance of women in the new workplaces of outsourcing and the conditions, under which they work, as I have sought to argue, should be of interest to scholars for a host of reasons. For example, CTI employed 1600 workers at the time of my field work. Women were 92 percent of that workforce. Why are so many of these workplaces populated primarily by women? One answer is that many outsourcing jobs utilize what appear to be low-end skills, are repetitive, and require abilities that are generally associated with secretarial work—a profession most modern cultures assign to women. CTI required successful applicants to type between sixty to sixty-five words per minute minimum but often sought those who could type at even faster rates. Thus while the women's work was enabled by high-end technology, what they did with that technology was, apparently, low value-added work. The interface appears to be just a conduit for repetitive unimaginative work. Further, the presence of so many women in these workspaces also meant that the men who ended up in these jobs devalued what they did.

During the long process of industrialization, modern western societies developed complex social infrastructures to compensate for the social costs to families and communities stretched thin or broken by the relentless escalating demands of capitalist modes of production. As increasing numbers of women are drawn into the outsource economy, it is becoming clear that Ghanaian society lacks the social infrastructure to fulfill the family and community functions women traditionally performed. Women are therefore encumbered by both public employment as well as their domestic "employment" in families and communities. These dynamics point to the general failure of what Manuh describes as the "dominant development agendas African states have pursued under the direction of the international financial institutions that have failed to give women and poorer people generally equal rights in the neo-colony" (Manuh 2007, 144).

It is these cultural, economic and geopolitical contexts that frame how host communities such as Ghana's evaluate outsourcing arrangements for the cheap labor they provide and the dependence on foreign direct investment such arrangements may foster. These conditions also underscore the paradox of women's access to work-related knowledge and wage labor, even as they highlight the unintentional consequences of the feminization of labor and the disproportionate burden women bear as a result. Indisputably, then, deploying a gender-focused perspective to examine the convergence of technological innovation, the global restructuring of capital, and the knowledge and literacies that enable participation in the networks and forums in outsourcing workplaces can broaden our understanding of the specific inflections on workplace literacy practices for those who work in these settings. A gender-sensitive analysis also foregrounds the conflicting and often contradictory relationships among rhetorics of work, skills, literacy, development and the bottom line of companies. A situated multi-sited ethnographic study opens up possibilities for examining the precise relationships among globalizing processes and feminization at least in the specific setting of CTI and CDN.

## NOTES

1.  For fairly exhaustive discussions on globalization for development studies see Erik S. Reiner (ed), *Globalization, Economic Development and Inequality: An Alternative Perspective* (Cheltenham, UK: Edward Elgar Publishing, 2004), and Ian Goldin and Kenneth A. Reinert, *Globalization for Development: Trade, Finance, Aid, Migration, and Policy* (Washington, DC: World Bank Publications, 2007).

2.  World Bank posters and newspaper accounts suggest women in outsourcing in Ghana make anywhere between $72 and $300 per month. As chapter 6 and 7 will demonstrate the published income levels only tell a partial story.

3.  See "the virtual immigrant" project www.annumatthew.com/Portfolios/virtual%20immigrant/ta_Virtual%20Immigrants.htm

# FIVE

# Multi-Sited Ethnography
# and Hybrid Spaces

As I have already noted, the global restructuring of capital and the Information Technology (IT) and Business Process (BP) outsourcing arrangements this has engendered now mean that thousands of people in the global South engage in work practices that are directly tied to global connectivity and the digital networks that connectivity makes possible. These workers do not only inhabit their disembodied virtual work spaces—there are physical, material places that they call "work." In order for us to begin to understand the literacies related to these material/immaterial workplaces there is a need to refashion traditional research practices, like ethnography, to study both the physical and the virtual spaces that such workplaces constitute. That re-fashioning process necessitates an approach that accounts for the multi-sited research locales as well as understanding the continuities and discontinuities in practices within and across them. In this chapter, I draw on qualitative research sources to theorize the methodological decisions and practices employed in the course of the project. The chapter also adds more depth to descriptions of Client Technology Industries (CTI) and Client Data Network (CDN).

Ethnographic practices have traditionally been utilized to examine physical, bounded spaces, and CTI and CDN are in fact, physical material places that can be examined using ethnographic practices. The physical locations provide embodied spaces from which virtual work is launched. But there are also ways in which they are not easy to categorize spatially. At CTI in particular, employees worked in a paperless online environment that was part of a transnational corporation's global network. When an employee logs onto the CTI global network, in what sense is that employee still working in Ghana? When one studies such a work community with ethnographic practices, what adaptations should be made to traditional research practices? These and other questions frame my discussion in this chapter. I will start with a description of my practices, addressing issues such as the politics of entry, empirical materials collection, and Institutional Review Board (IRB) processes and their implications for doing research in these hybrid spaces.

My goal in adopting ethnographic practices to study CTI and CDN was to understand, in some significant detail, how the people in these two workspaces think about their work, how they develop their particular viewpoints and what literate practices make their work possible. I wanted to understand worker and supervisor behaviors, workplace organization, inter-worker relations, and the nature of the work done in these companies. In short, I wanted to understand the culture of these workplaces. Here I am using Spradley's notion of "culture" as "the acquired knowledge people use to interpret experience and generate behavior" (Spradley 1980, 6). In *The Culture of Experience*, John McDermott notes that "At its best, an ethnography should account for the behavior of people by describing what it is they know that enables them to behave appropriately given the dictates of common sense in their community" (McDermott 1976, 159). The ethnographer's goal is to share in the meanings that participants take for granted and to portray these to outsiders in ways that preserve the voices and realities of communities under study. In studying CTI and CDN, I focus on the literate practices that frame the work life of the women who work in these communities. As a consequence, what is generated is very much in keeping with what Athanases and Heath term "slices of organizational life within complex societies" (1995, 265). I focus on uncovering and understanding the cultural contexts, cultural patterns and practices within which literacies are acquired and used in the emerging workspaces of outsourcing in CTI and CDN.

Given the multi-sited design of this project one challenge was how to theorize ethnographic practices in such a way that the two locales could be studied with some level of comprehensibility. The approach I adopted is grounded in Saukko's (2003) rereading of Marcus (1998a) and Appadurai (1997). Saukko provides a hybrid, dialogic theoretical orientation. Using Marcus's idea of "multi-sited ethnography" and Appadurai's idea of "scapes," various practices in canonical ethnography can be brought together in dialog and thus provide a heuristic for "how to study social issues and events from two different dimensions" (Saukko 2003, 177). Appadurai uses the notion of "scapes" to denote spheres of life. He refers to the various layers of social reality such as the sphere of economic as "financescape," media as "mediascape" and people as "ethnoscape." This heuristic allows for the study of the various instantiations of the practices of business process outsourcing at two different locations (sites) in order to examine what these practices look like within and across locations. The idea of "scapes" opens up the space for examining the particular Business

Process Outsourcing (BPO) practices from the perspective of media, or people, or finance, for example. While "site" and "scape" are closely related, the concept of scape enables a dynamic understanding of space. Appadurai contends that "scapes" are not static layers of reality—they are "flows" (of money, people, and images) that join people and places. Methodologically then, what my project does is study how two different outsourcing "sites" are connected with and disconnected from one another by diverse flows that articulate diverse "scapes" (177). As I will demonstrate in the next chapter, the deployment of this hybrid heuristic also creates the space for a montage, or mosaic of the two workplaces. Such an approach allows one to do justice to differences among contemporary social and political environments while looking at unities across differences.

According to Green, Dixon and Zaharlick (2003), the very logic of ethnographic inquiry means that hypotheses and lines of inquiry emerge *in situ*. This is not to say that the researcher does not make certain decisions even before entering the field. Indeed the researcher's general interests often translate into the theoretical and conceptual frame upon which concrete descriptions are fashioned. These can in turn help identify settings in which data may be collected. It was my general interest in the implications of globalization for the so-called developing world, gender and access to work in "developing" societies, questions about access to digital technologies, post-colonial theories, and methodological questions about canonical ethnography that provided conceptual foundations upon which to develop a project exploring the literacies of women in outsourcing. However, the idea that hypotheses and lines of inquiry should develop *in situ* has implications for how one's protocol is framed for the IRB process. Certainly these practices of ethnographic work clash with the expectations of the Institutional Review Board process that obliges researchers to know their research questions, understand the dynamics of the cultures they are going study and so on. As I sought approval for the protocol for Ghana my colleagues questioned the extent to which I would stick with what they were approving, given how vague my materials were. In order to protect institutions, participants and others, the IRB process necessarily has to demand transparency. But how does one provide that transparency when what happens in the field cannot be anticipated? As Jorgenson (1989, 28–29) shows, in such cases the parameters of how research ethics and responsibilities are articulated frame how these guide one's practices. As a researcher I knew what my interests were but my interests did not necessarily match what I discovered in the field. Contending that as an inductive researcher I propose to go into the field assuming I know little but rely on questions that might emerge through fieldwork to guide my exploration would have been unacceptable to colleagues. As my protocol (see Appendix A–D) shows, my interview guides, and empirical material collection guides are therefore all flexibly crafted to provide me with the latitude needed.

As I have argued elsewhere, using ethnographic practices to research outsourcing settings raises a number of questions about how one studies these workspaces.[1] For example, given the fact that all work is done online in a network environment, where is the workplace located? Are traditional ethnographic strategies adequate in studying these work-spaces even if one does not gain access to the whole web of virtual net-works? Under the conditions in which access is gained, what constitutes a participant observer stance? Is that stance applicable only to what the researcher does at the physical location? Should one's stance be that of an observant participant? Could one conduct ethnographic research in such workplaces without being in any of the physical spaces and if so which site is such work studying? Given how controversial outsourcing itself has become, what ethical issues confront a researcher whose work might end up being a record of where American jobs have gone? How does a researcher protect company confidentiality in situations where identify-ing the country where the research takes place may be enough to lead to company identification? In other words when a company requests confi-dentiality, does that preclude the identification of the country where the research is conducted?

## SEEKING ACCESS

Getting permission to conduct research at CTI and CDN required iden-tifying "gatekeepers" who control access to potential participants. Part of the general background work a researcher does is getting to know who the gatekeepers are in a setting so entry can be negotiated. At both CTI and CDN this meant knowing the hierarchical structure of the compa-nies. Intermediaries had provided names, roles, phone numbers and email addresses. At CTI, having the name of the site manager—Jack Halle—enabled me to call his secretary to ask to talk to him. That prelimi-nary phone call resulted in an appointment and a meeting in his office. At this initial meeting I explained what my interests were and why I had chosen that company. I described my research interests broadly. The site manager, though agreeable to my request, explained that he did not have the authority to grant permission. Any request was to be cleared with his corporate bosses in the United States. Knowing that his corporate bosses in the United States weren't going to grant me entry unless the site man-ager was open to my research there, I asked him what it would take for me to gain entry if he were the sole decision maker. I was alert for signals about potential issues that might influence how the corporate office re-sponded to my request. Jack Halle talked about the nature of the work CTI did at the Ghana site—processing health insurance and other healthcare-related information and the federal privacy laws they had to follow. He was concerned about the potential impact my presence would have on worker productivity. It also became apparent that Jack Halle was concerned that employees would use my research as a vehicle to agitate about working conditions or union organizing. These concerns had to be addressed in order to gain his support on my behalf. I used the IRB process as my legitimizing tool. I explained the process to him and high-lighted the fact that he could call or email my university about my proto-col. Here, my academic affiliation gave him some cover and provided me with legitimacy. By the time I left, it was clear I had won Jack Halle over. He provided me with names, email addresses and phone numbers for his bosses.

At the CTI site the next stage of the process of gaining entry involved three-way conversations among the home office personnel, Jack Halle and me. This took a few weeks to work out. Addressing concerns about who would take responsibility for allowing an academic researcher access to the work site meant having conversations with a number of people at the company's corporate home office on the phone and by email. Eventually, permission was granted for me to work at the Ghana site. The home office agreed to a blanket access request with the qualification that the site manager would sort out the logistics and conditions with me directly. This meant that I still had to negotiate the specific conditions of access with the local site manager. In emails we agreed to a face to face meeting in his office during my first week back in Ghana. Jack Halle—the only American at the site, was joined by his two Ghanaian assistants for the meeting. Mr. Kwame Hills was the Vice President for Business/Marketing and Ms. Mida Bostia was the Vice President for Human Resources and the only female executive at the time.

Jack Halle shared his conditions for my having access to the production floors and to employees in the presence of his two assistants who did the day-to-day management of employees. It was clear that he was granting access but also providing himself with some built-in surveillance capabilities. The message was very clear: "they will be watching you!" The conditions under which I could study the site were that my presence had to be as undisruptive as possible. I was to have Health Insurance Portability and Accountability Act (HIPAA) training as per federal government guidelines because of the health care content the site processed. I was to protect company and client confidentiality. I could not be at the site after midnight. I could not have unfettered access to the company network—to learn what is there I could only rely on observing and talking to employees as they did their work. Formal interviews could not be conducted on company time. I could not discuss union organizing—I asked if I could listen if that came up—the answer was yes. I could photograph employees but not screen shots—photographs may not identify company or its clients. Initially, for example, Jack Halle wanted to

make certain that client-related data was off limits. This would have restricted my access to the literacy practices at the site enormously. I therefore had to think of alternative ways of protecting what he wanted protected while having access to what I needed. I asked rather directly about
what his concerns were and then suggested ways to address these concerns. For example, he was concerned that company and client names
might be made public. He was also really concerned about the effect my
presence would have on employee productivity. The Institutional Review
Board (IRB) approval documents and my assurance that I am committed
to and ethically bound to protect confidentiality put him at ease. Finally, I
shared the fact that his corporate bosses had requested that I write something about my work for the company newsletter—this changed the ten-
or of our conversation somewhat. It became a case of "if they can trust
her, I guess she is alright."

Another condition was that the human resources director would work
with me to draft a memo to employees introducing me and my research
and asking for volunteers. With the Human Resources manager in tow I
visited each of the departments at CTI and was introduced to employees.
Ms. Bostia took me to the production floor twice (once to be introduced to
the morning shift and the second time for the afternoon shift staff). She
sent out an email to the night shift supervisors so I could be introduced to
those employees. At each department, Ms. Bostia gave me the opportunity to tell employees what I was doing and how long I planned on being
there. Shortly thereafter volunteers started coming forward. This process
yielded the participant pool. Given the sheer size of CTI's operations—
something I had not anticipated—I spent my first few weeks visiting the
departments in order to decide on how I was going to collect my empirical materials. These visits immediately raised some critical logistical
questions. How would I establish parameters for what I was calling the
field when Client Technological Industries (CTI), for example, had twenty-one semi-autonomous departments—some with as many as 250 employees and others as few as six employees? Surely, I couldn't possibly
observe, participate, and collect empirical materials in all these physical
spaces? While I could not do credible work in all of the departments, I
had nonetheless to find some systematic process for choosing which to
study. After "the weeks of my grand tour" of the establishment, I developed a set of criteria to guide which departments to focus on. These were:

- Gender dynamics among rank and file employees and between employees and supervisors and managers
- Nature and variability in the literacy practices of the departments
- The dynamics of the interpersonal relationships among the women
  in particular departments

This process also facilitated the identification of three focal women and
their immediate networks of friends whose practices became key ele-

ments of my explorations. All of these decisions were made in the process of working at CTI: they emerged *in situ* but the nature of my protocol design granted the flexibility to respond to existing conditions in the field.

Given the circumstances by which I gained access to participants at both CTI and CDN, what exactly constituted informed consent? Is an employee really willingly consenting to participate in a research study when her boss introduces a researcher and requests that she cooperate? Does the employee get to decide to continue cooperating even after the boss decides the research process is gaining access to practices he'd rather the researcher didn't know about? What are the ethical responsibilities for the researcher if employees are told not to cooperate but decide to cooperate, nonetheless, as happened at CTI? Fien (2003) discusses the whole informed consent dilemma—Consent for what and from whom? If relying on participants as windows into a community is problematic, it is even more so where certain aspects of a community's existence are off limits. Here the CTI officials were being as accommodating as they could while also trying to protect what they considered company confidentiality. This meant that I would rely on participants to offer explanations of their actions and intentions while also recognizing that what was offered were their accounts, stories, and explanations of what transpired and why.

At CDN (a comparatively smaller outfit) gaining access was fairly straightforward. During my exploratory visit in the summer of 2003, I identified this workplace as a potential research site. When I returned in early summer 2004 I emailed the Managing Director—Ms. Leila Nowa—and asked to meet with her. At a meeting in her office I described my interests and why I had chosen her site. While she saw the merits of my proposal, her concern was about what the women had to gain from participating in the research process. While I could not promise her anything, I pointed to the possible policy implications of such an investigation; that is, that it could help policy makers by providing them with information from those in the trenches of IT outsourcing work. This seemed acceptable to her. She gave me a conditional approval to work at the site if I would provide her with copies of the IRB approval and consent forms. When I arrived back in the United States, I emailed the materials Ms. Nowa sought. A week after that email exchange, she approved my request to conduct research at the site. During my first visit to the site when I began field work, the Managing Director invited three members of her management team to meet with us. At this meeting we discussed what I wanted to do and how they could help. An email broadcast introduced me to all employees and described my research project. It also invited interested employees to meet with me. This is how the participant pool at CDN was generated.

As I noted in the preface, biography was a critical factor in this project. Being Ghanaian-American, I had cultural background knowledge and a general familiarity with the country and its people. During the summer of 2003, I visited Ghana and explored the extent of the outsourcing economy. This provided the groundwork for identifying outsourcing companies for the study. Though I had a general sense of how to approach companies in order to gain access, I knew nonetheless, that having spent most of my life living elsewhere, I was going to have to do some learning in order to figure out how the particular outsourcing companies I wanted to study worked. At both CTI and CDN my initial overriding concern was to negotiate conditions of access that would not foreclose on possibilities I did not know about as I went into the field. With my rather limited knowledge about the sites at that time, I wanted to seek as vague an entry as I could negotiate while also leaving open the possibility of renegotiating access to people, places and spaces as the research evolved. Given the nature of the settings and my interests, I had to gain access to both the physical production floor and the virtual environment in which production was carried out. While access to the physical space was initially considered a thorny issue, it was understandably even more so with access to the virtual environment. This is because the virtual networks were proprietary spaces for these companies and companies needed to protect them for both legal privacy issues and for securing their operations. I had to be both creative and flexible, often thinking on my feet as my work evolved. For example, when Jack Halle apparently resigned in August and was replaced by another site manager, Nate Mackman, I decided to keep working since, I reasoned, the corporate bosses of Nate Mackman knew they had granted an academic researcher access to the site and its production floor. This decision permitted me to continue my work at CTI until the point when I was beginning the process of leaving the field. It was only at this point, in late November 2004, that I asked to interview Nate Mackman. It was also when he first found out that I had been at the site for months—and he was not happy.

## EMPIRICAL MATERIAL COLLECTION

A fundamental principle in ethnographic practice relates to the role and stance of the researcher in the community once the researcher has gained access. The overriding goal is to make the researcher's presence as undisruptive as possible in its effect on the daily routines of community—one condition of access to production floors at both CTI and CDN stipulated categorically that my presence could not impair the daily operations of the women. Within such parameters the role the researcher is able to negotiate frames the extent of participant observation. For me this meant following the spirit of the conditions I had agreed upon while also maximizing my engagement in those activities I could participate in. In the cases where participation was off limits, observing activities, people and situations in the communities became exceptionally important to developing an understanding of workplace culture. These processes and practices allowed me to experience an assortment of the actions of the community as fully as possible. Empirical data collected were based on interviews (informal and semi-structured—see Appendix B), artifacts, field notes, observation commentary, photographs, public online spaces, documents, records, and memos from each site. That said, there were instances where I consciously shifted my stance to an "observant participant" as an inherent acknowledgement that understanding and describing the lives of others is a process that is "mediated by our own autobiographies" (Florio-Ruane & McVee 2002, 84). In my view, the status of observant participant stance is one of the critical methodological issues for ethnographic research in hybrid and proprietary environments that deserves further exploration.

At each site I took scripted notes on the production floor, and extended these into detailed field notes with analytic memos on my observations at the end of each day. Analytic memos often highlighted practices I had not understood. I also listened to audio recordings I had made on the production floor. It was imperative that I listen to production floor recordings at the end of each visit as the floor was often noisy yet they were also the times when women talked me through their practices in spaces I could not enter on my own. This listening process was critical to questions I asked on subsequent visits. Usually when women were working in networked areas that were off limits to me, I had them talk me through what they were doing. They would describe their practices and the reasons for them. I would repeat these to ensure that I had understood what they were doing. At each site I usually arrived around 9:00–9:30 am and stayed until 4:00–4:30 pm. This meant that I got to interact with two shifts of employees. Occasionally, but particularly during my first few weeks of fieldwork, I returned to the sites in the evening to observe the night shift. With these different sites and their different work foci, field notes and other empirical materials started piling up fairly quickly.[2] I return to this discussion later on in the chapter.

At CTI the empirical material collection process started with a round of informal interviews of those who accepted Jack Halle's request to cooperate with my research. These were on-site in a room on the second floor of the building where employees usually took short breaks and unauthorized naps. Part of the space was used for storing old computers but it had tables and chairs and it was very quiet. It was also far from where management offices were. Because I could not interview on company time, volunteers had to come into work early or leave late after work. Even so I had twenty-eight initial participant volunteers at CTI. I explained in general terms what I was doing, gave them the letter I had written to get consent and then read them the consent form. If after reading the material they still wanted to participate, I asked them to sign the consent forms. Later I made copies of these and gave each participant a copy of what they had signed. Given what I saw during my first few days at CTI, I decided my focus had to be confidential so as not to put employees in any difficult positions. This cadre of participants also generated the three women and their network of friends who eventually became the focal women for the project. As I began to understand CTI, I made a very conscious decision to conceal the identities of the focal women. I usually invited them for extended interviews only by calling their cell phones outside of work and conducted these interviews off site—usually at restaurants or hotel lobbies and coffee shops. Also, I consciously interacted with employees who were not within the network of participants as another way of masking the identity of the focal women. As I will demonstrate in the next chapter, these moves were necessary so as not to jeopardize the women's employment.

Once each extended interview was completed, I listened to it again at the end of the day, annotated it, made notes of its content but did not transcribe it. Later I hired a Ghanaian doctoral student (Mike) to transcribe them. He, I surmised, would understand the Ghanaian language/s and accented English of the women as they talked about their experiences. After I got the transcripts, I listened to the tapes and the transcripts again to make sure they were accurate. There were instances where Mike, the transcriber, had told me he couldn't make some things out. Returning to them enabled me to figure out what was being said and to transcribe the texts in those places where Mike had indicated he could not make out what was being said.

## DESIGNING RESEARCH PRACTICES

Though I worked with an emergent design orientation, with a multi-site design, I began field work with a general sense of what I wanted to explore. My overarching interest was to understand how ICTs were shaping the literacy practices of the many women who now work in IT and BP outsourcing. Given that the IRB process required that I delineate some general areas that will guide exploration, these general questions served the institution's bureaucratic needs while providing a general guide to frame practices in the field. The following questions guided my exploratory directions in the field:

- In what ways and for what purposes do women in process outsourcing use digital and information communications technologies in their literacy practices in the workplace?

- In what ways and for what purposes do women enact gender and culturally specific literacy practices in their online and offline workspaces?
- How are constructions of gender implicated in the women's technology-mediated literacy practices within their online work communities?
- How do the local and the global intersect? That is to say, what are the global economic conditions that make this arrangement proliferate for outsourcing companies?
- What are the current and potential future political implications of such arrangements? How are these economic and political issues perceived by Ghanaian workers?

Even before I began I knew full well that new lines of inquiry might emerge and original ideas might be refined, altered or even set aside as data was being collected and analyzed. Thus, for example, though I had originally planned to focus a lot of my attention on the virtual environment in which the women worked, the companies' unease with letting me in to all areas of their networks meant that I had to refocus my attention on the areas for which I had access and then figure out how to get at other areas. In my general planning of the project, I had not anticipated the impact the conceptualization of the research space was going have on empirical material collection. This realization emerged as I began fieldwork.

## THE FIELD AND FIELDWORK IN ETHNOGRAPHIC RESEARCH

Fieldwork is the canonical practice of ethnography and it is crucial to the ethnographer's capacity to capture the behaviors and practices of the community under study. Fieldwork entails a reflexive and interactive-responsive orientation. What Geertz describes as the "thick description" of the culture under study (1973, 10–14) is based upon how participants describe their community. The descriptions offered by participants are themselves based on how as members of a community, they make meaning, and explain or interpret their communal social actions—that is, such descriptions are based on how participants enact their culture.

The empirical materials collection process is always informed by the conceptual and theoretical principles that orient the researcher and guide her practices. Empirical materials are what aid the process of interpreting and explaining the complex relationships at CTI and CDN. For fieldwork to be successful, I needed the support and cooperation of members of the community, particularly those who held intimate knowledge about the meaning of actions, events, objects and behaviors, values, beliefs and attitudes that were embodied in the community (see Zaharlick and

Green, 1991). These included the women who worked on the production floor, their supervisors, area managers, vice presidents and the site manger. Thus, part of my task was to be alert to learning the cultural knowledge of the communities even as that knowledge was being (re)negotiated.

Empirical materials were collected through sustained contact with participants in the places where they spend their time—the production floor, the lunch room, the break room, college and community activities in which the focal women and their immediate network of friends participated. In order to understand the literacy practices of the workplaces, I also had to develop a historical understanding of the setting. As pieces of information were gathered at the work sites they were analyzed by identifying patterns and relationships as they emerged. This process of inductive and cyclical analysis was taking place throughout the study. Early analysis helped refine/refocus ongoing work, often opening up lines of inquiry for the project. Participants were asked about what they were experiencing, how they interpreted their experiences and how they structured the social world in which they worked. In so doing the research process became an ongoing dialog with participants. Patterns and impressions that emerged were tested by comparing one source of data against another to eliminate competing explanations. Thus, for example, my notes were often checked against informants' explanations and vice versa.

Fieldwork in proprietary spaces raises dicey questions for a researcher. For this project, fieldwork took place from 2004 to 2005. Immersion at CTI lasted for four and half months. My immersion at CDN was a month longer—five and half months. CDN also agreed to return visits to the site whenever I was in Ghana. At CTI, Jack Halle the site manager who agreed to my researching the site left abruptly but I made a decision to keep working during this transition period as I reasoned that the corporate office was aware of my working at the site. I thus observed the new manager, Nate Mackman, as he came in, learned about the site, took control of operations; set in place his own management structure and watched the rank and file employees react to these changes. Significantly, Nate Mackman could not tell me apart from his rank and file employees—I am black and all his employees were also black. Or perhaps, his inability to differentiate between us was an indication of how well I blended into the community of female employees! Nate Mackman's obliviousness to my presence was all the more remarkable because as a new manager he had adopted a practice of visiting the production floor several times a week in an attempt (he claimed) to establish rapport with employees. He would stop and talk to women who were sitting with me, but I didn't speak with him. Thus I continued to observe, participate and generally continue my work for about seven weeks into his tenure. Interestingly, none of his Ghanaian assistants thought to tell him about my presence either. During the last week of November 2004, as I began the process of leaving CTI I finally asked Nate Mackman's secretary for a convenient time for an extended exit interview. Lisa, the secretary, set up an interview with Nate Mackman and informed him the day before the interview. Strategically, I had opted to keep certain questions about practices at CTI that different empirical materials had raised or had left unanswered or needed the site manager's perspective until this interview because I suspected asking them might provide evidence of how much I had learned. I also suspected that these questions might make management especially resistant to my presence. As I had surmised, Nate Mackman was really unhappy that I had been there in the first place, and that no one had told him. At the beginning of my interview he asked how long I had been at the site—I told him. He wanted to know how I got in—I told him. He wanted the name of the person who had granted entry out of the corporate home office—I told him. He then told me that he only had twenty minutes to spare, but he ended up talking with me for about an hour. At the conclusion of our conversation he wrote an email to his home office in my presence asking that his corporate bosses withdraw my access to the site. I requested that he copy me on the email—he refused. He did however offer to call me when he had a response. He called the following week to say I could no longer get on the production floor but that I could communicate with the women outside of work if I wanted to. Nate Mackman's tone was almost jubilant as he told me "they supported me—no outsiders can come in anymore and that the moratorium applies to you too—therefore you cannot go into CTI and definitely you cannot go on the floor. I have informed all my guys about that." Though he claimed that I could continue to work with the women on their own time, Nola and her peers however told me that Nate Mackman had instructed Ms. Bostia's office to tell all employees not to continue volunteering for the project. Of course as I had developed relationships with the women at this point, they called, they invited me to church, to weddings, etc. They engaged me in conversations that invariably included CTI.

What the foregoing discussion does is raise questions about informed consent, the vulnerability of research participants in these kinds of situations and the responsibility of researchers and the IRB process to protect them. These are things that the field has grappled and has come to some consensus on, by and large. But it also raises questions about the vulnerability of the research itself and of the researcher. I will return to these issues in the final chapter.

## ETHNOGRAPHIC PRACTICES IN HYBRID ENVIRONMENTS

The nature of ethnographic inquiry in literacy studies and the ways in which that inquiry has imagined and conceptualized the spatial has, according to Leander (2003), been "powerfully shaped by" situated accounts such as Heath's (1983) "place constructions of Roadville and Trackton." These accounts of "relatively boundless places" often analyze "texts, literacy events, classrooms, schools and communities" (396). To this list I will add workplaces. While traditional ethnographic principles provided ample research tools for studying these place-bound communities and practices, these approaches may not be as useful when we shift our focus to the hybrid environments created as a result of Information Technology and Business Process outsourcing. These environments are almost always powered by digital technologies that require users to combine "old" and "new" (Hagood 2003) literacy practices. Here traditional ethnographic methods such as interviewing, observations, video recordings, and artifact analysis may not account for the totality of the experiences of members of the physical and virtual communities we seek to study since we need "ways with words" that do not isolate virtual activity from its material settings. In order to get the full meaning of literacy practices in outsourcing, for example, we cannot bracket virtual work from the physical social situations that shape its meaning without losing sight of issues related to context and identity (Leander 2003). Saukko makes a similar point when she draws our attention to the methodological and epistemological assumptions of the "new" ethnographies. Using the work of Clifford and Marcus (1986), Appadurai (1997), Burawoy (2001) and others, she highlights the critiques of classical ethnography and foregrounds the ways in which "new" ethnographies blur "the distinction between, for instance culture, and economy," while leaving "shattered the idea of easily definable research objects, such as a subculture or a village." In making that point, she notes how new ethnographic practices lead researchers to see villages not as "isolatable locales but more like nodes in networks traversed and shaped by flows of transnational media, money, people, things and images" (Saukko 2003, 7). I would argue that this concept of "nodes" captures the essence of globalized work in the emerging workspaces of outsourcing and that our challenge is to develop approaches to studying them that will do justice to all their layered complexities.

Saukko is not the only scholar critiquing how "field" is conceptualized. Others have pointed out that traditional conceptions of the "field" have to be rethought significantly when research shifts into online environments (Bruce 1997; Clifford 1997). Indeed as Nixon (2003, 410) points out, the argument that research on the new media and online literacies needs to incorporate "thick description of interpretive acts, thick analysis and thick theorizing" may not be acknowledging the inadequacy of traditional methodologies for the task. Ethnographic work that targets internet culture significantly alters the nature of fieldwork as traditionally understood since in these circumstances it is possible for the researcher to complete fieldwork without ever meeting participants. The field in this case becomes an ever shifting milieu. As Leander argues, we need ethnographies of online literacies that examine the "field of relations" among multiple locations of practice (2003, 395). In my case, I have had to do field work in Ghana at two outsourcing sites—this work is congruent with traditional field work. But the immersion in these material workplaces is not the only "field" in which the work I observed is taking place and herein lies the challenge.

## ETHNOGRAPHY AND VIRTUAL WORK: OTHER CONCEPTIONS OF "FIELD"

Socially situated practices of hybrid workspaces pose some challenges because work in them is accomplished in dedicated corporate "owned" spaces that owners guard jealously. These spaces are the proprietary resources of their owners. CTI, for example, had a dedicated internet based network enabled by ICTs and satellites that allowed its employees in Ghana to work on Business Process (BP) solutions and transmit these back to the United States or other company BP locations on the company's virtual network of hubs. Thus in the placeless and immaterial internet environment employees as "users-readers-and-viewers" interact with the virtual from an "embodied space, a material place" (the work floor) (Luke 2003, 402). From this space they read and process transactions, sometimes in real time. There is a materiality to these interactions that traditional ethnographic practices can help a researcher investigate— there are real bodies working in real time (Luke 2003). However, there is also fluidity to this work that is difficult to track. Further, given the hybrid nature of outsourcing workspaces, it is hard to figure out how systematically to participate and/or observe practices associated with ICT use when corporate owners make certain areas off limits to a researcher. Given what I agreed to, I had negotiated to observe as employees worked in areas of their network which were off limits for me as a participant—in these instances, I became an observant participant and relied on focal participants to show me these places on the network that I couldn't physically get to on my own. While this made learning how these areas of the network worked rather difficult, I could count on double checking and rechecking my impressions and understandings with different participants for clarification. While I had access through the focal participants, I still had to figure out ways around the following questions: How do I collect data in a network I do not have total access to and therefore cannot master myself? How do I learn how workers navigate the work network given the constraints I have in access? How do I know I have actually learned how such a network works? There were a number of occasions where my conversations with focal participants, area managers and other personnel centered on my mapping out what and how I understood the work the women in the study did in the areas that were off limits to me. The goal was to share my learning, to check on the accuracy of my learning and to seek clarification from those who own the realities of working in these online spaces.

## METHODOLOGICAL CHALLENGES

Another problem one confronts when working in a hybrid setting such as I did is the methodological and conceptual problem of understanding practices from the community's perspective. As Bogdan and Biklen (2003) note, the viewpoint the ethnographer seeks is itself a research construct as there is a degree to which the attempt to understand someone's viewpoint inevitably distorts that experience or viewpoint. This is even more of an issue in an outsourcing setting where both management and employees are very much aware of the geo-political implications of their work and may have competing interests at stake. As the researcher, I addressed this issue by recognizing that the meaning people give to their experience and the processes they use in interpreting their experience are critical components of what that experience is. Thus in order for me to understand practices and behaviors, I had to understand the ways and processes by which people create them. In an outsourcing environment, though community members do not go about their work thinking self-consciously about their perspective on the literacies used in their community, I had to understand their practices and behaviors in the larger context of the work environment and the larger Ghanaian context in which that work environment was embedded.

The extent to which a researcher identifies with a community does affect the research process. Moss (1992) discusses the complex dynamics of defining membership and isolates some of the questions faced by ethnographers who study their own communities. In my case my being Ghanaian and my familiarity with the culture, some of the languages, history and customs provided a good starting point. I was not, however, a member of the workplace communities I had elected to study. Thus, though I was not in any serious danger of assuming that my mere identification with the group meant that I had access to the information I sought, I still had to learn how to seek information about the literacy practices of these workplaces and I had to know what kinds of questions would yield the information I sought. I also had to figure out how to participate/observe in the community without assuming I knew it. As

Moss (1992) deftly demonstrates, both community and researcher expectations have to be addressed. Having some relationship to the community under study required that I be self-conscious about how that relationship might affect my judgment about what I deem important and thereby affect how I make decisions about what is of value. There is also another side of this dynamic—the idea that working in a community that one knows means that one can identify patterns of behavior and their meaning to the community far more quickly than outsiders. Even though the communities of interest in my case were workplaces with which I had no prior relationship, my understanding of the larger culture within which these workplaces were embedded meant that I had to be cognizant of the danger of drawing on previous knowledge to make decisions about the meaning and significance of behaviors and patterns in the data collected. To guard against this danger, I relied on other empirical material sources and on the focal participants with whom I often checked, and rechecked my impressions and understandings.

## ETHICAL TENSIONS IN RESEARCH IN HYBRID SETTINGS

Another issue with using ethnographic practices in hybrid outsourcing settings relates to the ethical dilemmas a researcher has to confront. Some scholars have noted the new kinds of ethical responsibilities researchers assume when they research new media and communication technologies (Leander 2003; Luke 2003). As I drafted this manuscript, for example, I agonized that identifying the country where the research took place would be enough to identify the companies involved. Yet in not identifying the country, there is the risk of distorting the significance of the meanings that accrue from practices in these workspaces. I had either to rethink how to situate my research sites or identify the total number of such companies and therefore confidently avoid the likelihood that country identification would be an *ipso facto* company identification. I chose the latter—I found census data on the number of outsourcing operations and on that basis made the decision to identify the country.

Ethics is again an issue when it comes to protecting the various layers of confidentiality. In order to gain entry onto the "floor" where work is done, I committed to protecting the confidentiality of the companies whose work these sites did. Given my pledge to protect the identity of the sites, I felt obligated to do all I could to the deliver on that pledge. No matter what one's views on the topic might be, one is obligated to participants' portrayal of the practices of their community and how they situate these in the specific cultural context of their workplace. Though a number of scholars have isolated the nature of participant observation/observant participation online as a source of crucial methodological questions, hybrid research designs ease the tensions somewhat. For one thing there is still the place-bound physical space that both researcher and workers occupy on a day to day basis even while the workers do their work in the virtual spaces provided by global connectivity. As a researcher, I could participate and observe at the physical site, and I could participate and observe in some areas of the virtual work space that were accessible to me and through participant informants. Because the participants were engaged in work-related practices, and because they had to document their work online in order to be paid, they left traces in the form of logins, clock-ins, identification numbers and other network records. As a participant observer/observant participant, however, there were the ethical dilemmas about how to collect data that related to how employees often circumvented company directives by appropriating network capability for other uses. These illicit uses, such as gaming, movie watching, and cheating on time on task were enacted so as to leave few traces but were also bound up with the self-(re)presentations of employees.

As a participant observer/observant participant, I was often privy to these appropriations but was never sure of how to document them without compromising data sources. Depending on how entry is negotiated, a researcher is ethically bound to collect data without compromising the sources of the data. In this case, by the time I understood the nature of illicit technology use, I had developed relationships with a number of the women so that they were no longer hiding these practices from me though they continued to hide them from their floor supervisors. In order to underline my role to all parties, I took advantage of opportunities where women, supervisors and managers were together to reiterate the fact that my interests were only related the literacy practices at the workplace. In addition I made a very conscious decision not to discuss my observations of the production floor with supervisors and managers except when I needed their perspective on issues. Even here I was always careful about how my questions were couched. Often I used hypothetical questions such as "Assuming an employee wanted to inflate his/her productivity, how would you know they have done that?" Most of these conversations took place on the production floor. One of the ethical responsibilities that comes with my role as a researcher is to learn about what the women did—as I learned they did both that which is sanctioned by their employers as well as that which is not. As a result, I had to wrestle with both the ethical and the practical questions of how one collects such data in ethically responsible ways and how one collects quality audio data in a sometimes noisy workplace that at least in theory prohibits some of the evidence one seeks to collect. In the end I decided to document the illicit uses of network access in my field notes and then ask focal participants about these uses off site. This gave the women the opportunity to discuss their uses of these technologies from their standpoint.

## RESEARCHING WOMEN'S LIVES ON-LINE AND OFF-LINE

Because ethnographic approaches traditionally focus on studying bounded social spaces, they are ideally suited for studying the off-line lives of women in these work places. Their online lives, however, seem to disrupt this sense of bounded space. The coalescing of these two into what I call hybrid spaces requires rethinking the relationship between ethnographic practices and space while simultaneously accounting for the virtual. In investigating the online lives of women at work (given the conditions of access that I had), I had to address the problem posed by my limited network access. Given this limited network access, testing knowledge through direct experience and interaction online in all spaces was just not conceivable. I therefore reframed the issue somewhat by theorizing my role as being one of seeking similar experiences as those of the women—however these experiences are mediated (Hine 2000).

In order to get a better sense of the relationships between the online and offline lives of the women at these sites therefore, I extended traditional observation beyond the workplace. I met focal participants outside of work. I interviewed focal participants off the work sites on numerous occasions and developed friendships as a result. When the women began calling me with information about practices and issues that occurred on the days I was not at their particular physical site or in the case of CTI after I was no longer welcomed at the site, I knew I had been granted some level of acceptance. Even then, my approach here also highlights the difficulties of fashioning research orientations that allow one to study on and off line experiences in settings like these in a seamless manner.

Online research requires the researcher to have knowledge of and be immersed in the online culture she seeks to investigate. Yet in process outsourcing there is the dual level of privacy- and confidentiality-related issues. The outsourcing outfits would rather their identity is kept confidential and they definitely want client confidentiality upheld. Companies involved in outsourcing services do not want to be "outed." For the women who work in these environments however, there is the hope that a researcher's work would lead to disclosures that might mean better jobs, higher wages, better working conditions and others. For the researcher the issue of immersion is singularly fraught with tensions. The researcher as a participant observer/observant participant has to learn the network and the work that is done on it. She has to learn the processes used to complete transactions and in the process build some credibility with those who do that work. However, given the desire of companies to keep certain aspects of their operations off limits, there is only so much that a researcher can have access to. Thus, unlike research in some private/dedicated spaces like gaming areas on the internet, virtual workspaces cannot be accessed undercover. The researcher cannot lurk anonymously; she enters that space on record. In fact the whole IRB process means that researchers have to be "out" at least in a general sense about what it is they seek to study. As Jorgenson (1989) points out, covert strategies raise critical ethical questions. For some researchers deception is unethical under any circumstances as it misleads insiders. Since such insiders do not really know the nature of one's interests, the researcher does not in fact have consent. In this sense then the IRB process protects all involved.

The problems of grappling with the fluidity of internet-based research is evident in hybrid settings as well. Luke (2003), for instance, has called for analytic tools for tracking the fluid and highly mobile travel across links, knowledge domains, web pages, email routes, etc., to capture the ideas and practices of flows across the internet of global connectivity. While her focus is on the online lives of youth, these issues are also prevalent in the world of cyber work. In fact in the sites I studied tracking these flows are a crucial practice in the community and it required the development of a certain faith in the technologies used in the workplace. Online surveillance of employees was routine, but the utilization of that surveillance by the different parties differed. For management there was a sense that the virtual work space needed to be policed. Yet for the women the surveillance mechanisms could be appropriated for tracking their work volume and therefore their wages. However, the dynamic/ fluid nature of work in such a virtual network cannot be ignored. For example, there was a case where the women at CTI contended that their work volume for a whole day had "disappeared" and as a result their corporate bosses had not paid them for that work. There were back and forths about these "disappearing" workloads while I was working in this community. Often the women would share their version of events with me, no doubt with the expectation that I would be sympathetic. Management would also share its version on whether and how work does indeed disappear. In spite of these competing realities, as a researcher the very idea that work "disappears" on such a network was of theoretical interest to me. Clearly interviews, electronic transcript analysis, and network loggings alone were not going to be enough to capture the "practices of mobility and flows" (Luke 2003, 402) in such a work space. On the other hand, the fact that I did not have the permission to roam free on the network meant that I could not independently investigate the system. In this case I was forced to rely on the understandings of participants.

Theoretical and methodological challenges arise with the conceptualization of the location at which research occurs even in hybrid spaces. Online networks such as those used at CTI and CDN are really placeless though they are accessed from bounded physical sites in Ghana. Thus the question of the location at which research happens is an interesting one. For example, when the women in the study enter the company's internet based network, where exactly are they working and where is a researcher collecting data? Epistemologies developed with less fluid environments in mind may not provide adequate tools to research these spaces (Leander 2003; Mackey 2003; Nixon 2003). Recognizing the theoretical and methodological issues facing the field in relation to literacies and ICTs, Margaret Mackey (2003, 405) points out that "Now more than ever we need thick description of interpretive acts, thick analysis, and thick theorizing" in order to research the full range of issues associated with online literacies. Methodologically, for me at least, this research process raises the question of what ethnography looks like in the hybrid environments that have become the mainstay of ICT outsourcing work. It is for these reasons that Saukko's idea of creating a hybrid heuristic using multi-sited ethnographies and Appadurai's idea of "scapes" and "flows" open up new possibilities. They allow for a re-articulation of space and how that may be studied. As (Clifford, 1997) demonstrates, one can no longer study sites and "scapes" in isolation in this contemporary global environment where worlds are intimately connected to one another and infused with transnational flows of policies, politics, money, images and others. CTI and CDN, I will argue, are micro "worlds" that straddle a number of flows though studying their specific practices may uncover different agendas.

After my "grand tour" I observed and or participated in five departments—mini sites within CTI. Each of the five had its own unique way of doing work. Departments also had their dynamics and subcultures; it had a lot to do with the employees in the department as well as the specifics of its work. The origins of the work, where they returned and the cultures shaping work and workers exemplify the flows and scapes of CTI. The five departments, for my purposes, are Sigma, Delta, Alpha, Omega, and Gamma. Sigma processed health insurance, dental, vision, Health Maintenance Organizations (HMO), Preferred Provider Plans (PPO), Point of Service Plans (POS), Pharmaceutical and Prescription Plans, Consolidated Omnibus Budget Reconciliation Act (COBRA), medical, hearing, ambulance and Chiropractor claims for a company operating in the global North. Sigma employees worked with over fifty different claims types. The department had a female team leader, a female production supervisor and a female Production manager. Delta processed mainly health and dental insurance claims for its client. It had a female team leader, a male production supervisor and a male production manager. Alpha processed only dental insurance claims. Its team leader was female, its production supervisor was female and its Production manager was female. Omega dealt with claims and their related correspondences for health insurance, dental, vision, HMO, PPO, COBRA, Pharmaceutical, and Chiropractor. Omega's work was heavily text based. The team leader at Omega was male, the production supervisor was male but the production manager was female. Gamma was a relatively small operation that processed health insurance, dental, and vision claims.

Gamma had an all female supervisory structure. Each department "rents" space and equipment so that the more its space is used the less its overhead costs. There were a few departments, such as Gamma, that had two shifts only and did not work on weekends. The women here made less money because their department's overhead was higher than departments with three shifts and weekend work.

*Coding and Analysis*

Initial informal coding began in the field as data was read and re-read in the context of the research questions. This process guided further data collection and facilitated the process of double checking the accuracy and rigorousness of emerging first cycle trends. Data from each site was coded separately. Within each site, I coded data from each department as a separate set. As initial patterns in categories emerged within sites and across departments, they were cross checked against different sets of incoming data. Initial categories and codes were reorganized and re-categorized for another cycle of coding. The re-categorization process during the initial stages of the process was recursive. It is the categories that emerged at the end of these processes that were used for the analysis reported here. Themes, concepts and trends from these categories are used to frame my discussion and to theorize the various issues as they relate to the research questions. Participant voices are present throughout the text and those voices are used to illustrate the trends in the data.[3] My discussions here by no means addresses every issue in the data, rather it accounts for slices of the data.

One significant issue that has been dangling over this chapter's discussions so far is Nola's question. I end my discussion here therefore with a return to Nola's question—"Are you going to write about us?" I am of course writing about the many women and the not so many men who work in outsourcing at CTI and CDN. Like all academic researchers, writing about what I experienced in the field as I learned from and with participants is the final product of the research process. Yet I am also very self conscious of Nola's question and all thorny issues it raises. I have sought to theorize my work in ways that are responsive to the realities of the two sites. Given the theoretical orientations I have adopted, and the ways in which those orientations have been theorized, I hope to present slices of reality that capture the complexities of these communities. It is my hope that in the interest of Nola and her co-workers I have succeeded in doing a measure of justice to their complex communities.

## NOTES

1. See Quarshie Smith, B. "Researching Hybrid Literacies: Methodological Explorations of "Ethnography" and the Practices of the "Cybertariat."" In *Digital Writing Research: Technologies, Methodologies, and Ethical Issues,* edited by Danielle DeVoss and Heidi Mckee. Cresskill, NJ: Hampton Press.

2. Artifacts were dated, labeled and then filed with any contextual notes I had written to ground them. Reading and re-reading data kept me grounded in the data. These practices were part of my initial cycle of generating coding categories from the data itself. As patterns started emerging in certain data sets, they were cross-checked with others. Emerging patterns and issues were also cross-checked with participants at the two sites. When appropriate, I also then looked for opportunities to seek managerial perspectives on them. A separate work in process looks specifically at data analysis and the challenges they present.

3. I am exploring methodological issues specifically related to the challenges of data analysis in a separate work in process.

# SIX

# Outsourcing as "Glocalization:" Material Practices and Fluid Workspaces

The need of a constantly expanding market for its product chases the bourgeoisie over the whole surface of the globe. It must nestle everywhere, settle everywhere, establish connections everywhere. —*The Communist Manifesto* (1967:83)

Ethnography does not have to be limited to the, either disempowering or empowering, 'reception' of globalization (in the 'local') but can also study the way in which globalization is 'produced' by specific agencies, institutions and actors, which can be observed. —Saukko (2003, 179)

Information communication technology enabled networks were constitutive of the location of labor at both Client Technology Industries (CTI) and Client Data Network (CDN). The two sites were similar in the outsourcing services they provided, and the means by which they provided them but were different in their size and in their scope of operations. As I have argued in previous chapters, their very existence is a consequence of the current stage of globalization and its ancillary processes. CTI and CDN connected their respective workplace communities to different spheres of existence far removed from the quotidian physical experience of the workers. Within and across these work sites, "flows" of people, services, money, images, literate and labor practices connected workers and places but these connections were articulated differently as they got attached to and transformed by different actors and different "ways of knowing" and doing work. This chapter draws on data analyses to describe how outsourcing played out at the multiple sites, how various "scapes" and "flows" layered them and how these were "read" by the different actors. I focus on how participants experienced what I broadly define as the "laborscape" — the spatial geography of CTI and CDN, their labor practices, their networks, their official cultures and how employees "lived" these cultures, their uses of space and time and how that compression affected the pace of work. Cumulatively, these processes produced rhizomatic networks of lived experience as different actors created multiple and sometimes even contradictory realities from these experiences. These workplaces and the scapes and flows that traversed them were therefore learning sites where employees mastered the situated literacies of practices and thus what it meant to be literate.


THE "LABORSCAPE": CONTINUITIES AND DISCONTINUITIES

CTI as a subsidiary of a transnational offered business process solutions for healthcare and health insurance providers in the global North — mainly the United States. It offered services in claims processing, transactional processing, data verification, data correction, quality control, and communications. CTI Ghana was connected to the parent company's worldwide sites by an in-house proprietary network of information communication technologies. The Ghana site was located at the heart of a business district in a modern multistory office complex. Work at the twenty-one departments (nineteen by the end of fieldwork) was done at rows of Formica-covered long tables with terminals at which the women and the few men who were data processors sat and worked. Production employees' work space was defined by the length and depth of their terminals and since the terminals were used 24/7, they effectively shared that space with two other employees on the other shifts. As part of a benefits package, CTI provided all employees with a meal per shift, health insurance for up to two dependants, and transportation to and from work. Under Ghanaian law employees qualified for paid three month maternity leave as well as a three week annual vacation. Employees were paid biweekly through direct deposit and CTI required them to have accounts with the company's local banker. The company at the time of fieldwork according to its public records paid a piece rate of $1.00 per batch. However, for example, for a two week period Nola's pay stub shows that she processed 150 batches but the piece rate was in fact 47.99 cents (based on the then exchange rate of ¢9240 to $1.00. See Appendix G). After successfully completing three years of service employees were given a bonus of $100.00.

CTI meals were served in a break room that also doubled as a writing assessment area for job applicants. The meal service was outsourced and the food was brought to the site pre- packed in plastic containers. Employees provided their own silver ware, napkins, drinks, etc. Employees ate at long Formica covered tables similar to those they worked at. The floors also had the same terrazzo finish as the production floors. The schedule for lunch rotated monthly and was meant to make the process democratic.

**Figure 6.1.   CTI Multi-Purpose Room**

Unlike CTI, CDN was independently owned by a group of partners (Ghanaians and expatriates). The company was located in a commercial section of a city centre and offered 24/7 operations with some categories of employees working in each of the three shifts. At CDN departments operated with different productions schedules that met their specific needs. The company had four distinct departments: the Café, a cybercafé that served the general public; the Client Computing Services Department (CCSD) a department that did data entry and used AutoCAD to provide services to clients; the Selective Data Solutions Department (SDSD), which provided voice-related services—transcription, indexing, etc.; and the Quality Option Solutions Department (QOSD), which did high end work with software development. Each CDN employee had health insurance benefits, a three week vacation annually, three month maternity leave, a meal at work and five hours a week of internet access at the cybercafé. This online access was only to be used when no paying customers needed services. Employees used the benefits, often coming in on days when they weren't required to work. Unlike CTI employees, CDN employees had to make their way to work; this was an area of tension as participants felt the cost ate into their wages. CDN paid what independent analysts have termed "fair salaries"—for example, some programmers were paid between $350 and $600 per month—and these were directly deposited into employee accounts.

CDN had an area where employees took breaks and had their meals. Meals were outsourced to an outside vendor. For the employees who worked the 8:00 am to 5:00 pm schedule, lunch was provided around noon and the set up and presentation was different from that of CTI. I often joined the employees at lunch. Even CDN's lunch room and meal record keeping was computerized as the caterer used a Desktop computer to keep track of patrons. Lunch break was an hour long, and lunch was served with plates, silverware and tablecloths in a pleasant, relaxing atmosphere. Drinks like non-alcoholic malt, soda and bottled water were available for purchase. The food was dished out on site in the presence of employees. There was always a choice of food on the menu and there was always soap and towels in an open wash room adjacent to the break room where they could wash their hands.

Space and access to that space emerged as a significant marker of how hierarchy functioned at the two sites. The different spatial geographies of the two sites corresponded to different representations of hierarchical power. At the beginning of fieldwork, the CTI site manager's office was on the fourth floor—the highest elevation of its rented space at the time. Halle's office occupied the North West wing of the fourth floor. All his employees were either on the floors below or on the Far East wing of the fourth floor. Separating Halle's wing and the fourth floor production areas was a security desk managed by two guards. The production floors were factory-like, even though the office complex itself had an ultra modern exterior. With bare terrazzo floors, the departments where I spent my time were often hot and stuffy—fans worked at full throttle though they blew mostly hot air. Even though the office complex had air conditioning and other tenants in the complex (many of them global North organizations) tended to have functioning systems, for some reason the production areas almost never had a working system. The site manager's suite's air conditioning worked just fine however. Since CTI rented the space, its site management told employees that besides complaining to their landlord there wasn't much else they could do about it. The north wing of the third floor, the floor below Halle, housed the administrative areas. This was where all the Ghanaian employees in Human Resources, Business and Marketing, and secretaries were. The rest of the third floor housed production departments. Access to the entire third floor was controlled through security screening. Food for the Ghanaian administrative staff was brought to their offices. The second floor was made up of the employee eating area, a snack bar where soda, candy, bottled water and other snack foods were sold to employees by an outside vendor, and an open multi-use area. There was a multi-use south wing on the second floor that CTI used as a holding area for those seeking employment on days when it conducted screening. It was also an area employees used to take illicit naps, to socialize and to talk on their cell phones. This was the area I used for onsite interviews.

The location of Halle's office on the fourth floor, the fact that all the local employees occupied offices and production floors below him or as far from him as possible on the same floor, the fact that access to this area was through gatekeepers—security guards and a secretary—and the fact that often doors to this area and to Halle's office were closed were perfect metaphors for how power, hierarchy and access functioned in this workplace. This symbolic structure of power and access was disrupted when Halle was replaced by Nate Mackman. Nate Mackman relocated his office from Halle's to the third floor area where his assistant, Sammy, was. If space defined the location of employees then Nate Mackman's move to the third floor appeared designed to facilitate closer oversight of the production workers. Or it could also be read as an attempt to re-write the power and hierarchical structure of the work place.

The symbolic and physical uses of space at CDN offer another point of view on how spatial geography connected the two outsourcing sites as well as how space shaped relationships among those who worked at CDN. At CDN the production floors were configured around what the various departments did. Employees worked in cubicles with their own defined spaces. The air conditioning worked and most of the floor space was carpeted. Furniture and décor were coordinated with company colors, logos and other furnishings on the premises. A section of the first floor of CDN housed the cybercafé, print shop, reception desk and an area where patrons of the café watched television with satellite channels that broadcast UK, USA, and South African programs. The other floor of the building housed CDN's Business Process Outsourcing (BPO) and Information Technology Outsourcing (ITO) operations. These departments provided services such as software development, technical support and voice services for mostly global North companies. Other services provided at CDN were transcription, indexing, quality control and technical support. The café offered fee-based web access to the general public, but my discussion will exclude the cybercafé's patrons. Clocks at CDN were set for worldwide time—Accra, Lagos, London, New York, Hong Kong and Johannesburg. Except for the cybercafé and the QOSD department, the production floors of CDN were all on the same level as its management team. CDN had security presence particularly in the areas beyond the street level cybercafé. Each visit to the site required a check in with security who then escorted me on to the production floors where access was again restricted by security. The doors to the executive suite at CDN were open as were those of the other management personnel but there were security personnel and a secretary who were gatekeepers and screened visitors.

## THE NETWORK AND THE TRANSFORMATION OF WORK

Powerful networks function as work spaces for many outsourcing workers. At CTI the proprietary network was the medium for all work. Tasks
arrived at data processors' desktops via a virtual pipeline: A client in the
United States sent data to the U.S. CTI hub at the end of the business day.
At the hub documents were digitized and sent in numbered batches to
Ghana using CTI's 2 dedicated E1data lines. Individual CTI Ghana departments downloaded the data onto banks of servers. Downloaded
work was controlled and released to employees by supervisors. Employees only had access to network areas that they needed to get their specific
jobs done. In addition to processing the data, CTI Ghana also conducted
its own internal quality control. This process depended on the protocol of
the individual departments and these depended on needs of clients. In
the case of Delta, for example, at the end of the process the data was
uploaded for CTI employees in Jamaica who then conducted another
round of quality control before sending the finished product back to the
United States to be returned to the client. This whole process took a
maximum of forty-eight hours—what the industry calls turnaround time.
The company had its own backup generators to support operations during power outages. If there was a power outage, others on the network of
hubs had to be told. In 2003 CTI had only three such critical glitches and
they lasted no more than a few hours each time. Productivity was measured by batches of client data services processed and turnaround time.
Each department had banks of servers and local departments were
named for the global North clients whose work the departments did.
Thus if "Sigma Corporation" offered CTI its processing contract, Sigma
became a department at the Ghana site. The twenty-one departments
(nineteen by the end of field work) corresponded to twenty-one (nineteen) global North providers who were outsourcing data processing to
CTI.

   Access to the network at CTI was carefully managed. Firewalls
blocked the public World Wide Web from employees. The network also
restricted employees to online areas that they needed to do their work
and there was a system for tracking who used what and when. This
limited accessibility was a mechanism for controlling exposure to information and therefore assured compliance to the Health Insurance Portability and Accountability Act of 1996 (HIPPA from now on). Employees
were required to maintain password protected access to their desktops
and to lock their computers every time they stepped away from them.
They were required to login at the beginning of their shift and log out
when they took breaks as time on task was tracked electronically. These
logins and logouts therefore left traces of employee time on task.

Digital Communications networks and the virtual spaces they create can be thought of as blurring the lines of the material, the experiential and the symbolic contexts of their users. The material is captured by the physicality of the work site. Women at CTI did not only inhabit their disembodied virtual workspaces—there were also physical, material places that they called "work." Though their entire work was done in fluid and digitized environments, that work was enabled by a material foundation of infrastructure, hardware and software, and that work had real, material effects on peoples' lives. The women's work practices were also experiential in that they did capture how women encountered the virtual and interacted in it in order to work. I invoke the concept of "symbolic context" in order to foreground how the symbolic related to representations of the women's technologically mediated work experiences. These symbolic representations enabled the mediation of both the material and the experiential.

The network organized space and time in the work place and that configuration shaped how work was done. Besides the fact that globalizing processes made the location of CTI in Ghana possible, its operations further encapsulated a key dimension of postmodern globalization—the compression of space and time. This compression was critical to the logic and practice of business process outsourcing. Information technology-enabled networks were the organizational model for production and circulation at CTI. With sites around the world, these networks link bounded spaces in different time zones, thus providing clients twenty-four-hour coverage in real time around the globe: the network made distance irrelevant. At CTI, the ICT-enabled network "dis-embedded" what workers did from the locality at which they did it (Avgerou 2002). Workers at various physical CTI locations around the world entered the company's webbed network to offer process solutions thus annihilating space and distance among them. Theoretically, CTI occupied an interesting location. On the one hand its employees worked at a material, real place in Ghana. On the other hand, that work was done in a placeless, virtual network that was connected to other virtual/material places around the globe. A workplace like CTI raises questions such as where exactly is work done? Answering that question may require a re-theorization of workspace. Theorists such as Saukko (2003), Soja (1996) and Castells (1996) have offered various conceptualizations of space. Saukko, drawing on Soja's concept of "Third Space," argues for examining space from the dimensions of the material, the discursive and the lived—what for my purposes is more appropriately called the "worked" space. For Saukko theories of space should be seen as "performative" in that "instead of describing states of affairs they construct certain kinds of spaces and identities and politics that go with them" (167). Thus, CTI's material space was not bounded as an isolated locale; rather, considering the virtual interconnectedness that defined its existence and the many actors who functioned in it, CTI was a space that was at the crossroads of trans-national flows (see Saukko 2003, 178). More to the point, the material space that CTI employees inhabited was a "scape" in Appadurai's (1997) sense, as the idea of "scape" better captures the complex ways in which CTI workspaces looked to different parties from different angles. Seeing that workplace as a "scape" also highlights the ways in which various practices within it connected to different spheres of life. Employees, who often arrived at CTI as a result of migration from the village to the city within Ghana constituted a "landscape of persons" in a shifting world of work—a mini "ethnoscape" of sorts. Economic flows from market actors abroad propelled and regulated the decisions CTI's management team made. The virtual workspace and the technologies that power it con-nected various CTI actors speedily across boundaries that would have been previously impossible to navigate. These dynamics were all pro-foundly conditioned by globalizing processes.

The other side of the space/time dynamic is that the network also functions as a conduit for bringing the pressures of the global economy into CTI's "local" workspace (Avgerou 2002; Ó Riain 2001). The network shaped the rhythms of the workplace. At CTI this time-space compres-sion was manifested in the turnaround time for projects which ranged anywhere from a few hours to forty-eight hours. Since fairly short turn-around time was what clients expected and since delivering on promises to clients was the core logic of outsourcing, workers often had no choice but to meet these deadlines. Time differences among locations on the company's network either intensified the pressure or provided a respite of several hours. Pressure was also exerted through the network's enor-mous communication capabilities that made monitoring and policing workers rather straightforward for management. In this cyber workplace, workers were always tacitly under surveillance. However this surveil-lance did not stop employees from finding ways to break the rules—at least per the management's position. I will return to this issue below.

The time compression achieved through digital telecommunication enabled CTI to tailor solutions to the needs of its many American clients sometimes instantaneously and often with the help of other sites on each company's virtual web of networks. Production was decentralized on the transnational/borderless network and the immaterial products that were created by this new work were transported around the world instantane-ously. To some extent, the value added during this process can be seen as the mining of human capital rather than the production of value. That is to say, the data entry and similar activities performed by CTI workers was not better or faster than American workers, for example, could have done. But the American companies were able to reap the benefits of Gha-na's relatively good British-style educational system and under-devel-oped economy to employ qualified workers at cut-rate costs. In effect, the value of the work is equal to the value of such work done in the United

States; in this case, however the service is being indirectly subsidized by the Ghanaian people.

Business Process Outsourcing work at CDN had various foci but all work was done in a web environment using web-based technologies. For my purposes here, I will use two departments at CDN for illustrative purposes—SDSD and CCSD. Employees at SDSD and CCSD worked in a web environment using company proprietary software that allowed them to transfer voice communication and other data and images back and forth from their location in Ghana to clients in the global North. The network was the conduit for flows of nonlocal work into these spaces. All computers, head sets, and foot pads were supplied by the company and these were collected at the end of each shift. The bulk of SDSD work related to conference calls and most of the conference calls that the department transcribed ran for about four hours. Each employee was assigned about ten minutes of voice texts to work with. One group of employees did the initial transcription and another group conducted verification of that initial product. From the verifiers the job went to the unit supervisors who audited one more time. From the unit supervisor the job went to the manager for another audit. From the manager the quality control person did a final check before the job was turned over to the client. If the job had a four hour turnaround time—and most of SDSD jobs had four hour turnaround times—all these checks and balances had to be made before that four-hour time was reached. Though the women often talked about pressure they also often described their work as fascinating and interesting.

## "GLOCALIZING"/HYBRIDIZING LABOR PRACTICES: SHAPING WORK CULTURES

The combination of globalizing pressures and information technology changes fundamentally affected how work was done at both CTI and CDN. Practices were conceptualized and presented by management to their Ghanaian supervisory team members who then translated and operationalized them for rank and file employees. Practice, as I use it here, follows Baynham and Prinsloo's idea of it as "routinized" behavior with "several elements" interconnected with each other. Practice "is mediated action with a history" (2009, 6). At both CTI and CDN core practices such as security provisions and responsibilities for enforcement of laws, quality assurance, workplace ethos, safety, workers rights and responsibilities, definition of work hours/days were all part of how the sites functioned as in-between places—places where things were always fluid and under negotiation. They were places where global flows bumped against local ones. The resulting behaviors were observable, mediated with textually collectable artifacts, and therefore documentable. While the conditions were present at CDN, their negotiation was often more subtle than at CTI. Both employees and management at CTI were mutually mistrustful; often positioning practices to me as either problematic or as best practice in the business of outsourcing. Employees at CDN did not seem to see their employer-mandated practices as problematic enough to deploy my presence for negotiating purposes.

Quality control practices were critical to overall effectiveness at both sites. At least that was what management and the supervisory teams believed and that was what they wanted data processors and other rank and file employees to believe. But there were variations in the standards used by the different departments even within CTI. Here I will use Delta for illustrative purposes. For the Delta department the quality assurance standard at the beginning of fieldwork was 99 percent. That was adjusted to 98 percent by the production supervisor in an oral announcement to employees in August. This adjustment translated into four errors per biweekly pay period. Employees who didn't meet this target got warning letters and after the third infringement the consequence was termination. The production supervisor told the employees that people who had been given letters based on the 99 percent standard but who had met the standard of 98 percent would have their letters withdrawn. For the management team grading and posting worker grades was an incentive to spur productivity. For employees, it was pressure that brought on stress. For management the goal was a perfect/error free grade of "A" and in fact the company's piece rate of $1.00 per "batch" was based on this. Participants and other employees hardly ever met this perfect "A" target—hence the employee claim that the company does not in fact pay a $1.00 piece rate (see Appendix G). Interestingly, though the production supervisor at Delta shared the rationale for the change in the quality assurance standard with me, he did not tell his employees. They had set their grade at 99 percent per a client's request but the supervisor had made the change in consultation with his counterpart in Jamaica. As I will show below, the practice of not sharing critical contextual information with the women and the few men in production was routine at CTI.

Management set the length of the workday but there were variations among departments at each site. From the start of my fieldwork until my exit from the field, CTI required certain departments and their employees, (Sigma, Delta, Omega were examples) to work seven days a week, sometimes including overtime on regular work days. These employees were also required to work on both American and Ghanaian holidays. According to management this practice was necessary when the work volume was heavy. To management this was part of the "can do" ethos that undergirded CTI's corporate culture. Not surprisingly, employees had a different reading of this. To the employees this was understood as being required to work under conditions that amounted to coercion and intimidation. For employees, there was always the specter of getting terminated if one consistently refused overtime assignments. As one participant, Shakira, put it:

> They (supervisors) wait till the last minute to tell us we have overtime. Overtime is really not worth the money unless you do four hours because by the time you pay for transport all the overtime money will be gone.

Because of the irregular schedules overtime created, employees found their own way home and got reimbursed 5.00 Ghana cedis. This amount, according to the women, did not cover cost of taking taxis (what the women called "dropping"—a door to door service) home. Shakira, like other participants wanted me to understand what she perceived as unfair treatment by a management team whose practices she described as "the American way." Shakira noted:

> If I do my regular shift and I finish that without a mistake and then at a quarter to two my team leader tells me we have overtime and I stay and do it for four more hours ehh, are you with me? And I make an error; they will still charge me for the error. By God I am human—can they work for twelve hours and not make mistakes?

Shakira clearly wanted me to acknowledge that I couldn't pull that off either. And Shakira wasn't the only employee making such a case. For the management the women lacked a commitment to the company. To the women the company was only interested in its profit margins and lacked loyalty to its employees.

A contrastive point here is that even when CDN employees met with me off-site they shared positive stories about their work at the company. Zoe and Moe, for example, felt CDN treated employees fairly. Asked if there was anything they would change about their work both talked about wanting more money and or transportation to and from work.[1] The wage issue was often discussed in the lunch room but the discussion was not infused with frustration or resentment. Indeed sometimes these discussions took place in the presence of supervisors and managers. The atmosphere at CDN was generally casual but professional with interactions between management and employees and among employees, professional yet informal. For instance, at the beginning of the shift there was always a lot of back and forth between supervisors and employees as employees came in to get ready to begin work. Some of the socializing was about work but often it wasn't. In this workplace employees were permitted to consult, agree, disagree and communicate openly with their superiors.

CTI and CDN functioned within an outsourcing environment that was constantly navigating or absorbing global pressures and flows. Yet CDN appears to address these transnational flows somewhat differently than CTI. Mini-sites within CDN were empowered to function in ways that were responsive to the flows of work. Variability in the practice of setting the length of the work day was one way CDN addressed global pressures and it is illustrated by the Client Computing Services Department (CCSD). It was headed by Saaka, and the department provided business process, business re-engineering, and information technology solutions. One business process solution the department offered was data entry, provided by the eight women in the department. It was a relatively small department with twenty-eight employees. CCSD's client base was mainly US companies and other transnationals. Saaka characterized what CCSD did as high-end Business Process Outsourcing (BPO) and Business Process Re-tooling (BPR) work. This was because a major part of their work involved manipulating images, graphics, and technical data sets, putting them on the web and maintaining these sites for clients. CCSD worked with AutoCAD, other constructions of mechanical items, and repair manuals. Because of the specialized nature of what some CCSD employees did, they had schedules that reflected the nature of their work volume. When projects and deadlines demanded they worked fairly long hours—fifteen-hour days were sometimes necessary to meet deadlines. On the other hand employees stayed away on slow days when only a skeleton staff maintained the office. Further, CCSD rotated employee schedules so different employees covered the workplace on slow days.

Employees, contrary to what management assumed, had fairly sophisticated understanding of their place in the outsourcing industry. Lunch time conversation was a window into how employees located themselves at both CTI and CDN. At the start of fieldwork I initiated conversations but by late October employees, particularly at CDN, were engaging me in spirited conversations, sometimes even challenging each other on their views on outsourcing while inviting me to share my opinion. Our conversations in late November were particularly interesting as I had told them I was getting ready to leave. In November, a small group of employees started a conversation about outsourcing yet again. From previous conversations it was clear that the women followed media reports on outsourcing. Further, they were well aware of the backlash in the United States against outsourcing but had their own arguments about why it continues. A consensus position the CDN employees held was that if investors weren't looking for good profit margins, companies wouldn't feel compelled to look elsewhere so as to cut costs. Mona, a transcriber in SDSD, for example, acknowledged the competition that is developing among outsourcing hubs—this she said will increase pressure on employees like her and her colleagues to do more for less. Mona said, "There is the mentality that if you ask for too much your customers will go elsewhere—to India or Guatemala—they are ready and waiting." In other words, the women were very cognizant of the dual pressures on global North companies for profits and the pressures on the global South to create competitive packages to attract companies. For Mona and her colleagues there was one scenario that was not going to happen: she believed that bringing outsourced jobs back to the United States just wasn't going to happen. In her opinion, "too much has left and the price has gotten too cheap" for companies to decide to pay for the same service on U.S. soil. As she made this point, her peers nodded their agreement. In an observation commentary for early November I wrote this note about CDN:

> It seems to me that employees at this site are not treated as though they are company property. They certainly don't seem to feel patronized by their bosses. They seem to work, act and think about their work for themselves and actually buy into the customer service model that the customer calls the shots. Their morale is healthy—they do think their workplace can be improved; a point their managers tended to agree with. But this also raises some interesting questions: What makes for the differences in these two places (CTI and CDN)? Is it class/education or is there something else? Is it the focus of their work?

*Identification and Work*

In conversations at lunchtime at CTI the women offered particular understandings of the outsourcing industry, their identification with and its politics. There were discussions about pay, the treatment of employees, and the long work hours. But it was also obvious that members of the CTI community—whether rank and file employees, middle managers, supervisors or executives—inhabited their distinct places and understood what the company did and how it did things from their particular locations. The change in leadership at CTI at the site did affect some practices. Yet it was clear that the ways of doing that management provided employees were arguably deeply influenced by its origins as a subsidiary of a U.S.-based transnational. There were aspects of practice that were clearly "American" and corporate. But employees brought their own values and beliefs into CTI. What for lack of a better term I am labeling "American" corporate culture was manifested in how management constructed and then represented to employees an ethos of being part of a transnational corporation. Management cultivated this ethos explicitly and encouraged employees to develop feelings of loyalty and pride in the company. Management and company newsletters and other literature projected a need for employees to buy into a "can do" ethos that was constructed as a "core value" of CTI. Employees were advised to "go above and beyond" to satisfy client needs in order to stay competitive. On the production floor there were posters with the company's employees smiling and giving testimonials about being part of a global team. Posters were often positioned so they looked down on to the floor; a perfect but unintended metaphor for the surveillance capabilities of the networked environment in which work was done. Interestingly, the posters originated from elsewhere—there were no local employees in these posters. Lunchtime conversation provided the women the space to share their opinions on CTI official value narratives and to air their grievances.

CTI's proffered "American" corporate culture contended with the "local" values of its employees and the local context in which it did business. Both employees and the company were therefore navigating processes of identification in the context of the flows of work that the site did. In fact Nola and her peers often contended that CTI needed to adapt to Ghanaian culture. Even though CTI made a point of wanting to be a "good citizen" the tensions of negotiating these orientations framed how different parties understood how things were done at the site. For example, Ghanaians, according to the women, by and large place value on the group and operated with a conception of family that encompasses the extended family. This conception of family was the location from which the women negotiated their identification with CTI. For CTI on the other hand, "family" was defined as the nuclear family of western modernity. As a result, questions about who should be covered by an employee's health insurance, whose funeral an employee could legitimately take time off to attend, and even what counted as marriage were all contested and constantly under negotiation. The management team devoted considerable time and effort to asserting and explaining the company's positions on "family" benefits. For instance Kofi, an assistant to Mida Bostia (the HR executive) told new recruits to CTI during orientation that they could only count on getting time off for a funeral if the deceased were a mother, father, or direct sibling. As he put it, "don't come and ask to go to your mother's brother's wife's funeral." CTI's employee health insurance covered up to two dependants. Employees therefore had to choose who in the family would be covered if they had more than two dependants. But sometimes the company changed positions as with the case of defining what should count as a legal marriage.

From my field notes on November 22, 2004, I note:

> The Employee Welfare Association got an important concession out of management. In the past the company would only accept Western style wedding/marriage certificates as the standard for determining dependant eligibility on its health insurance plans. The women note that even though the company is working in Ghana and Ghanaian customary marriages are recognized by law it was the company's way or no coverage. The Employee Welfare Association has gotten management to accept and recognize traditional customary Ghanaian marriages as legally acceptable for determining dependant eligibility. Shakira and Nola seem to think this is a major accomplishment.

The conflicted processes of negotiating values and ideas in this workplace were epitomized by a sad event that occurred in early October. It was an instance where the "local" and the management understanding of practices collided. Somber Ghanaian funeral music announced the fact that one of the few male data processors had died on his way to work that morning in a motorcycle accident. The music was coming out of the Human Resource office. Everyone from the security guards on up looked distressed. The man—a twenty-nine year old—was well liked by his colleagues. I asked the Human Resource personnel if the employees will be given any time to process any of what they were going through—the answer from the HR secretary was "this is CTI, you just keep working through your tears." She volunteered that this was the third time they had lost an employee and this prompted me to ask about what the company does to help those employees left behind. The HR employee's response was that at CTI people die but "the work goes on." Employees still have to meet productivity targets. Indeed the women who worked in Alpha, the same department as the deceased man, wondered whether they would be granted permission to attend his funeral. That day I noted in an observation commentary that:

> Clearly, working for CTI means employees have to learn a new culture not only for the workplace but also for how they make sense of issues in their lives. Considering how Ghanaians deal with death and dying and their elaborate funeral rituals and ceremonies for the dead, CTI's adoption of what—for lack of a better term—I will call the western approach to death and work must have been disorienting at the very least. These employees have to relearn/readjust their values and their sense of what should be important in their lives at least *vis a vis* the workplace.

Paradoxically, neither what the company saw as its corporate culture and identity nor what the employees called their local culture were stable, coherent entities. In the case of management, the very conditions and location of its existence and the negotiations it had to make had, I would argue, already created a hybrid mutation of whatever its American version was, if in fact, there was ever such a version. For the employees, the nature of what they did, how they negotiated it and the contexts in which these were negotiated negated any claim to some static essentialized local culture that was uncorrupted by transnational flows. If CTI's management team constructed corporate practices that it proffered as desirable, its employees brought their own identities and subjectivities to negotiating and making sense of what was asked of them. Different parties read such appropriations and negotiations from their own locations and the frame of identification.

Another example is illustrated by employee practices that management labeled as "cheating." To management some employees "cheated" as a result of their attitudes to work; attitudes shaped by employees being accustomed to salaried employment under which they got paid whether or not they were productive. At CTI on the other hand, employees learned quickly that productivity was what materialized into wages. Indeed Kofi, who worked in Human Resources, conceded that adjusting to piece-rate and performance-based pay was difficult for employees. It required what Kofi called "discipline." At CTI time on task was tracked and that translated into wages. As alien as that was to the Ghanaian employees, according to Kofi, it was how CTI did business and the employees had to learn that quickly.

The management team pushed for high quality assurance and productivity to meet client expectations. From their management ranks "above" they understood this push in the context of the broader outsourcing economy, global competition for cost cutting while maintaining quality, and profit taking. For the management team there was a real danger that in not meeting productivity targets, in not having "good" profit margins, in not controlling the cost of doing business; the site would not be economically viable and work would have to go someplace else with cheaper labor and overhead costs. Indeed two departments saw this reality during my time at the site. But from their position "below" as data processors, rank and file employees at CTI were, at least according to management, often oblivious of the larger context in which the company operated. According to the management, employees did not relate to or identify with the company. While different data sources support this management position, the data also demonstrate that issues were far more complex and nuanced. Indeed interviews and lunch time conversations reveal that the women actually have a different reading of the workplace. Their perception was that the company was taking advantage of them because of Ghana's high unemployment rate and limited job opportunities. And they could also see the many people who came in for employment screening—a constant reminder that other people were eager to take their jobs. So even though the women resented the stress, the pressure they endured, and the many grievances they eagerly catalogued, they continued to work at CTI. Nola and many of her peers often told me they were grateful to have viable employment because for many of them there were no alternatives.

The different contextual variables that framed management and employee locations at CTI also therefore shaped the conception of the practice of "cheating" by the various actors. Cheating, from a management perspective, was described by Kofi thus:

> Some people think they are smarter than the machines. They don't realize that the machines and programs were written by people. They think they have found a short cut to processing claims in ways that allow them to get through a high number of batches and therefore make more money. One way they do this is by hitting the numeric key 9.

According to Kofi this key takes one through a document faster therefore resulting in high volumes of processed data and high wages as a result. Kofi noted that though CTI had a number of IT persons who track employees online, they were busy people and could not track all employees at all times. As a result some people cheated and got lucky. However if a spot check (usually one is run on an employee because of errors: or because as people cut corners simple entries are missed and this raises red flags; or as a function of the network's built-in program that can audit all of an employee's work in order to note time on task, etc.) reveals that the employee has cheated, it was automatic termination. That was the case with the people whose identification cards were in a stack on Kofi's desk during a routine visit. Kofi's practice is also however further evidence of the level of surveillance in this workplace.

The practice that management labeled cheating was an example of the conflicted practices and ideas under perpetual struggle in these workplaces. Asked about "cheating," on the production floor, the women acknowledged that people have been terminated for what management said was cheating. But then they asserted that CTI cheated them too because work had been known to "disappear." Women in all five departments talked about "missing work." They brought up another point: If the sheer power of the network can enable CTI to determine when it was being cheated, then surely it could find their "missing work." Nola, Shakira, Fatuma and their circles of friends all complained that CTI's management had told them it did not know where their "missing batches" disappeared to, a claim the workers did not believe. Nola, Shakira, Fatuma resented the expectation that they should have faith in a technology controlled by a management team they did not particularly trust. "Missing work" meant they did not get paid, so the women developed strategies for tracking their work. Some saved the ID numbers on their batches online. Others smuggled paper on which they recorded their batch IDs—paper was not allowed on the production floor. On the production floor at Omega one day a woman, Zamila, and another woman next to her told me that they were keeping online records of their work because they have had cases of "missing batches" and that with those saved records they could show that they did do the work. I asked rather loudly if this happened often and all the women chimed in with "yes"! One woman then pointed out to Zamila and her friend that keeping online records was a waste of time because "they look after the computers too." So, there was mutual mistrust--while the management team did not trust employees, the employees did not trust the company either. Among the employees, this mistrust was manifested in "subversive" (or at least non-sanctioned) uses of the computers, such as watching DVDs of Mexican soap operas, movies and music videos.

The management team often acknowledged the different worlds they claimed the women and their team members inhabited. In Kofi's view,

for instance, employees did not understand the larger geo-political context of the site's work. As an example he pointed out that when the
management team held an all-employees meeting and told people about
the pressures and competition in the larger outsourcing market, the
women thought they were being sold the goods so management could
get more work out of them. It was only when a department got disman-
tled and shipped out to India that people got what Kofi termed "the
wakeup call" that their jobs could go if quality and competitiveness were
not kept up by the site. Though Kofi believed he had to "walk a tight
rope," taking care not to be too blunt about the shortcomings of the job,
he nonetheless believed he had to let employees know how they fit into
the larger global market- place. Yet in departments like Delta, employees
were not told the rationale for decisions. They were simply told what to
do because management believed sharing information added to the stress
that workers felt. These different understandings and investments in the
site's performance served to highlight the differences between management and employees. Kofi's point was also taken up by the production
supervisor for Delta. Solo told me in an informal interview on the Delta
production floor that his employees are used to receiving salaries and
that at the ministries where a number of them worked as secretaries they
got paid whether or not they actually worked. Thus, for them, working at
CTI represented a cultural shift which was compounded by the incessant
pressure to keep jobs from going to India.

Differences in the understanding of certain practices were underscored by the recognition by members of the management team that they
and their employees were working at cross purposes. Management had
challenges that, according to them, the women didn't share or care about.
Kofi, for example, felt that the women wanted salaries like most Ghanaians have; the piece rate was therefore not only alien but also harsh by
their standards. Further, the unorthodox employment practices made
people feel like outsiders simply hired to do a job, not as members of a
community with a stake in the company's identity. Kofi pointed out that
while the management was under constant pressure to deliver high quality services at high volume to stave off losing jobs to India, the rank and
file employees had no sense of how competitive the outsourcing environment was and did not see their own stake in maintaining high standards
while keeping down costs. This position is not borne out by what employees had to say. Things were further complicated by the apparent
disconnect within CTI's higher and lower management ranks. On the one
hand, some low level CTI supervisors did not see themselves as managers; on the other hand, CTI's production managers were disconnected
from rank and file data processors. Disjuncture in the hierarchy, according to Kofi, led to data processors feeling like outsiders in the company
culture. Still, Kofi pointed out that "every one of us has something to lose
if CTI decides to pack up and leave Ghana. That is the one thing that

unites us all." He saw it as part of his job to frame this idea of a common ground to employees.

Though it was clear that the different groups had their own under-standing of practices at CTI, the position of the site manager had not been transparently articulated until towards the end of November as I pre-pared to exit the field. This visit with Nate Mackman turned out to be my last at CTI as he subsequently requested that his corporate bosses with-draw my access to the site. My intention had been to request an extensive interview for a later date. Nate Mackman offered me a few minutes of his time and sensing that he did not want me working there any longer, I asked the questions I had been saving for my exit interview. Even though he had said he could only spare a few minutes, we ended up talking for almost an hour. As a condition for talking to me Nate Mackman stipulat-ed that I could take notes but could not use my tape recorder. Notably, Nate Mackman did not or could not discuss questions about women's health at work. Our conversation touched on overtime work, working conditions, morale and the general mistrust of management. My field notes for November 22, 2004, paraphrased Nate Mackman's responses. I note:

> Nate Mackman acknowledged that morale is low at the site. He ac-knowledged that his predecessor, Jack Halles, broke Ghanaian labor laws. He acknowledged that the women were being made to work seven days a week repeatedly. He acknowledged that he was aware that the women work on U.S. holidays and then are asked to work on Ghanaian holidays too. He accepted that that was wrong. His explana-tion of why it happened—domestic clients (in the United States) and the managers put pressure on Ghanaian managers because all they care about is their cost, turnaround time, and keeping their customers hap-py. When they pile on the pressure, there is no one at the Ghana end ready to stand up for employees and say "Hey—these people need time off too." The managers up the pressure on the production teams and supervisors and they in turn pile it on the data processors (mainly the women rank and file employees). There is stress, and though the data processors know that their employer is breaking labor law there isn't much they can do and all this causes a lot of mistrust in the work environment.

Nate Mackman, like the rest of his management team members, pointed out that as a transnational, CTI is always under pressure and there is a lot of stress because of global competition. To him the way to deal with the stress was to balance it so that the women on the production floor wer-en't the only people living it. Nate Mackman offered a concrete example. He referred to the Muslim holiday Eid al Fitr, which fell on November 15, 2004. Since it is a lunar holiday, he had only one day's notice, but he had told his domestic managers in the United States that it was a Ghanaian holiday and therefore that they should ship work to other sites on the

company's network. He had given those non-Muslim Ghanaian employees who wanted to work the option of working, but many of the participants in the study had taken the holiday off as "it is rare that we get a day
off" according to Shakira. While Nate Mackman saw this as a gesture of
good will, the effect was undercut by something else he had done a few
days earlier. He had told employees during one of his meetings with
them that he was raising productivity at the site and adjusting their productivity rankings from 98 percent back to 99 percent unilaterally. According to the women he couched his point thus: "just as all students
with hard work could make 'As' on report cards, he expected all of them
to make the grade." As Nola put it to me, "he put the fear of the Lord into
all of us that day." Though the women saw Jack Halle's style as demean-
ing, their initial impressions of Nate Mackman suggested more of the
same.


## WHY WORK IN OUTSOURCING?: WORK, GENDER AND IDENTITY IN TWENTY-FIRST CENTURY GHANA

Women's work in outsourcing highlights changing social-cultural gender
partners. Women at CTI saw their jobs as one of the few choices they had
for employment while the women at CDN tended to see that work as a
stepping stone to something else. Some of the women at CTI, such as
Nola, were attending college in the evenings as a way to develop other
career options. Women at both sites were nevertheless thankful for the
jobs they had and frequently talked about how hard it was to find jobs in
Ghana. Ghana's high unemployment rate was not lost on them. Though
some women at CTI had diplomas and degrees, they noted that a good
education did not guarantee one a job. Women talked about having
learned a lot by working at CTI; they acknowledged that the experience
had strengthened their speed, accuracy and work ethic because of the
pressure to produce high productivity numbers. Sarah, for example, said
she had written many applications without finding work until a friend
told her about CTI and gave her books to study in order to pass the test.
Once she took the test she was fine. In her applicant pool she said there
were about eighty people and only fifteen got job offers. Sarah was proud
of having viable employment and controlling her own finances. Sarah
and her friend Toni offered typical explanations for why they worked at
CTI. Sarah and Toni were both single and in their twenties. To them
having a job wasn't out of the ordinary for Ghanaian women because
they've always had to work—at market trading, hairdressing, and similar
activities—in order to contribute to their families. Women, they told me,
have always had their own revenue stream separate from men. What
their generation of women was doing was working in offices rather than
the market. According to Sarah and Toni the women at CTI always had

money because they were paid bi-weekly. This, they noted, has given them and many of their co-workers a lot of power and control over their own lives. Toni noted that as a result there were a lot of women who "have no respect for their husbands and fiancées:" Sarah concurred with this point, noting that "there are a lot of problems with relationships" — tensions are arising because, as she put it, "women are making it." Thus, it appears, work gives these women control over their own lives but it also empowers them to re-negotiate their relationships with others. Nola and her peers often talked about how the societal assumption that men were breadwinners for families often led employers to choose male over female applicants. Women, according to this (false) assumption, were expected to be looked after by the men in their lives.

Many of the women at CTI had been trained as secretaries. However while typing is a large part of what data processors do, for some women it was not the fact that these places utilized their skills that explained their presence. Rather it was what they were trying to avoid in a workplace — sexual harassment. For example, Zita, who had taken a private computer course which had opened the door to work at CTI, claimed she liked working at CTI because she did not want to "deal with male bosses" even though she was a very competent secretary. Asked to elaborate on what she meant by this Zita noted that "in Ghana some male bosses assume that their secretaries are there to be their lovers too." Since she did not want to be in that situation, working at a female-dominated workplace like CTI suited her just fine.

Women developed practices and strategies to sustain their sense of community. Practices like singing embodied the here and now; the women sang together as they worked. In some CTI departments women sang religious songs, especially when deadlines were looming. These practices were important enough to the women that once while visiting the Gamma department on a day when they faced a looming deadline the supervisor asked the women to stop singing. Emma, a leader among them, shot back with "we can sing and work at the same time." They were not going to be told what they could or could not do. The Gamma group was under pressure — they had 426 batches to finish at 10:30 am and they had to have them all done by noon to meet their turnaround time. They sang and worked and they did meet their turnaround time. The Gamma workers treated their supervisors with respect as long as they were treated respectfully. Emma remarked that she did not like being treated like a child. Singing, Emma explained, was a way to relieve the pressure of the work place. In other departments younger women sang mainly American pop and rhythm and blues tunes. Sometimes they'd stop keying to snap their fingers. They were often told to stop this diversion, but they just simply ignored their supervisors.

Community was also sustained through the constant chatter on the production floor. Women shared stories about families, children and life generally—sometimes these sharing episodes solicited advice about intra-family problems. Weddings, births, birthdays and other social occasions provided the women with opportunities to bond outside of the workplace. Women's conversations on the production floor were often critical of the CTI leadership. Nola and Shakira, for example, often talked about leadership qualities that they felt their supervisors lacked. Communal conversations touched on having work but wanting to be respected and treated with dignity at work. A recurrent theme was that the company treated employees like children. As Shakira put it, "we are just told things. The management acts like we cannot understand complex things." Nola found that particularly offensive. Nola and her circle of friends conceded that there were some employees with "low education" backgrounds—they only finished Junior Secondary School and went on to learn how to type. According to Nola these women have no sense of what is appropriate for workplaces, (that is dress, presentation, etiquette, and expectations) and do not understand a lot about the context of the work they do. Nonetheless, Nola argued, communicating with all employees was what managers are supposed to do and they should be able to do that without alienating all employees. It was this sense of community and the natural leaders that emerged from these small groups that enabled the women to forge interventions on their own behalf.

Group solidarity provided a mechanism to challenge instances where their work "disappeared" or when they collectively confronted management on unilateral decisions on piece-rate cuts. On a number of occasions talk turned to politics—the women complained that politicians had cut deals with the transnational corporations leaving them to be exploited. They were particularly disgusted with a comment the then President Kuffour had made. He had suggested that women working in outsourcing were making more money per week than their fathers made in a month. This was, of course, a gross exaggeration of their earnings.

The focal women and their network of friends were conscious of how they were perceived by management. They often talked about feeling expendable. Zita, who sold hand-crafted jewelry and batik items as a sideline, offered this comment: "If I miss my target I will be sacked. Never mind I have worked here for three years and done all they asked me to do. I have no security . . . that is why I have a business. If I get the sack at least I will have something to fall back on." When I pointed out that the company says they get "good pay," Zita's response was "yes we get a check but this is after the management has helped itself with what they believe they should charge us for." Community permitted the women to trade stories about their work experiences at CTI which either heightened the tensions or spread the tension and stress in this work place. The employees recognized their low morale but offered each other ways of navigating their work. These positions and understandings are compelling evidence that in fact the women in the study understood a lot more than their bosses were giving them credit for.

The consensus among the women at both CTI and CDN was that data processing should not be long-term employment. Interestingly, all the women in the study at CTI said they would not let their daughters work at the company. The women's views led me to ask middle managers like Kofi if they would allow their daughters to work at CTI. Kofi said that if his daughter really wanted to, he would let her but it should not be her first choice. The women's goal they said was to protect their daughters from the monotony and physical stress of sitting in front of a computer screen for eight or more hours a day. Though they were required to take short breaks, it was still hard. Women talked about the aches and pains they felt, particularly at the beginning of their work at CTI. Pregnant women like Rosa talked about their difficult pregnancies—swollen legs, difficult deliveries and babies born with low birth weight. There were women who had had miscarriages and though they could not link these directly to their work, they blamed their jobs nonetheless. To foreground women's health issues, I will share two profiles: that of Lina who worked at Omega, and Rosa who worked at Gamma.

Lina returned to work after a couple of weeks of vacation and so I asked her if she had had a restful break. Lina told me she had spent her break seeing doctors because she was in so much pain she couldn't sleep, and couldn't sit for long periods of time. Beyond her vacation days, she had in fact taken two sick days because she just couldn't return to work. I checked with her supervisors and they confirmed that she had had to be sent home because she was ill. At her terminal Lina showed me her doctor's appointment for that day. She described feeling pains and aches particularly in her lower abdomen and lower back though she said her whole body ached. At Omega she had been working seven days a week sometimes for as much as twelve hours and pointed out that her body wasn't getting any rest. Given Lina's complaint, I asked Nola and her network of friends at Alpha about aches and pains. Nola and her peers told me they all had them. Though some people's aches and pains were debilitating, most people were able to function with them. Lina's colleagues at Omega confirmed that they had similar aches and pains. Women often told me about aches and pains but I hadn't heard about any as dramatic as Lina's. Lina's hours were rather long—she had to be up by 4:30 am so she could catch her bus for work. She worked the 6:00 am shift. Most days she didn't get home until 5:00 pm. With a family of her own, she still had to take care of her own home after her long work day at CTI.

Rosa's profile highlights issues related to reproductive health at work. Rosa worked at Gamma. She had secretarial training and left a secretarial job at a private school to work at CTI. She had had one miscarriage. At the time of fieldwork she was pregnant and was having a rather difficult time with it. Nonetheless she worked long hours, sitting for long periods as the allotted length of breaks did not alleviate the cramps she had. Her feet and hands were often swollen by the end of her shift. She had made her own arm rest to support her wrist and prevent injury as she keyed (a practice that many of the women at CTI followed). She often stretched and exercised her feet and fingers at work. As her pregnancy became more and more difficult, she planned to take all her outstanding vacation, sick days and three month maternity leave (as allowed under Ghanaian Labor Law) so she could stay away from work. Even so she was concerned about how she was going to breastfeed her baby after she returned to work. She told me it was hard for working women to breastfeed their babies after their three months leave. Her bus left CTI at 2:20 pm and she got home at 4:00 pm. Her child does not see her in the morning as she has to leave at 5:00 am to be at work to start the morning shift at 6:00 am. For Rosa, holding down a job and taking care of her family was therefore increasingly challenging.

For the women at CTI there were personal costs of working. There were broken relationships, miscarriages, and they were fatigued chronically. There was also an emotional cost to working—they had no lives outside of work. With all the overtime demanded by CTI, and their own families to look after, they were essentially juggling two full time jobs. A number of the women talked about looking after elderly relatives and their extended families, yet they saw working as being worth it because it gave them some control over their lives. As Nola told me, "going to school and working" in the official economy "is a way to gain self respect and the respect of others."

For the women at CDN there was a different understanding of the relationship between being women and opportunity. Thus Koe, an employee who worked in Selective Data Solutions Department at CDN, could say:

> Yes, I'll say it's equal opportunity. If you have it, you have it. If you have to go to school, fine. . . . If you don't have it, you don't have it and you will not get the job. If you want a job and you don't have what it takes you just have to work on it. You can go to Senior Secondary School; you can go to university. No one is saying you can't because you are a woman.

Koe's point is in effect that at least to her there is equal opportunity for women in the wage market. This is certainly a point to which some women at CTI may take exception.

## WORK, DESIRE AND THE IMAGINATION

Work at CTI and CDN was shaped by women even as it shaped their identities. At CTI for example, the culturally grounded identifier—working for a western company and doing work that others sought— "marked" employees. This identification was related to the supposed value of wages and or benefits that were represented as generous but which employees disputed. Identities constructed and shaped by work practices also paradoxically framed the dimensions of desire. Part of this re-making of desire is related to the time-space compression of postmodern industrial production and bringing the global into local workspaces. Virtual proximity created by networks also brought the outside world into the physical work space as employees sat in Ghana and solved problems related to, for instance, health care delivered to a client in Peoria, Illinois. Do women wonder what Peoria looks like or do they work on data as though they are disinterested subjects? At both CTI and CDN it was clear that women did not do their processing jobs as disinterested subjects. They did imagine the places and the lives represented in the data they processed. As with the account by Ghanaian women in the *New York Times* story, who said as they processed ordinance violation tickets, they also imagined the sites at which those violations occurred, so did the women at CTI and CDN dream of faraway places in the United States.

The virtual proximity to the United States that emanates from processing transactions at CTI and CDN stems from the enculturation that goes with the work and the manner in which it fuels and reshapes the workers' fantasies of life in the United States. Women talked repeatedly about learning the geography of the United States, learning names of cities and states, learning about the things that Americans visit health care facilities for—many of which the women themselves did not or could not have. As one woman at CTI put it, "The dream of everyone at CTI is to go to America one day." Women, with their post-industrial value-added abilities enhanced by the technologies they work with, refashioned desire— imagining the worlds they believed Americans occupy. Living these imagined lives whether in or out of the workplace situated women squarely in global cultural flows. Meanwhile the dominant economies, having created desiring subjects as a result of the casualization of labor, seal their borders in the face of mass migration—believing that their interests are best served when workers stay and work in their own communities and societies. My argument here is that a consequence of globalization is "glocalization" (see Robertson 1994, 100) that creates outsourcing communities where work has now become another "work of the imagination" as it offers "new" resources for the construction of imagined selves and imagined worlds (see Appadurai 1996, 3). What is happening in workplaces such as CTI and CDN is an example of the "massive, twofold process involving *interpenetration of the universalization of particularism and the particularization of universlism"* (Robertson 1994, 100). At CTI and CDN workplace practices are both shaped and undermined by what Crothers describes as "the emergence of a new cosmopolitan culture whose values and ideals are to a large degree determined by the demands of globalization"(2012, 30). The *New York Times* article that got me started on this research, for example, reported the following about data entry work:

> It is good work, by Ghanaian standards. The typists earn 500,000 cedis a month (almost $70—three times the Ghanaian minimum wage and more than twice the average per capita income) to type the offender's name, address, fine and offense location into a searchable database that is sent back to New York. It can then be stored electronically and used to generate payment notices, Mr. Sturcken said. (Worth 2002, A17)

A World Bank poster that hails Ghanaian participation in the knowledge economy notes that "In Accra hundreds of young men and women are involved in the knowledge economy earning $300.00 a month; that is more than ten times the average national income." The poster argues that the information revolution offers young Ghanaians a real chance to leap forward into the knowledge economy in ways that they never could have dreamt of just a decade ago. But there is a large gap between the $300 per month earnings promised by this poster and the $70 per month earned by the workers described in the *Times* article and in my study. Nonetheless, the excitement of working for a high-tech transnational firm invoked by the poster is felt by the workers.

Indeed imagination is critical to adapting to the flows and scapes of work in outsourcing communities. For example, given the relatively higher level of education of many CDN employees and the fact that besides those working in specialized areas like programming and technical writing most did not appear to be using their education directly, I often asked the women at SDSD in particular about the connections they saw between their education and work. When I asked Zoe about working at CDN, a job that did not appear to be related to her degree in Psychology, she offered the following:

> Zoe: Well, not exactly because really, with the psychologist, you are trying to understand behavior and behavioral patterns of people and I'm working with people you know. I move with people and like I said, I have to try and understand the background of the people I am working with and the people I am working for. So even though it's not directly psychology, it gives me a lot of fun because I've had training to know that not everyone is . . . you have to know how people are, you have to study people; I mean the people I work with, the people I work for, and all that. So, I believe that if they are able to relate what we are doing to the jobs that are out there and what we want to do, it will make it much easier, you go out there and you have value in you. You really know you go into the job place and you perform. Yeah, I believe

so. What I have really come to realize about the first degree is that it just prepares the mind you know. It's not so much of getting you professional training.

The imagination was also related to how women understood the location of their work and how they made sense of the fluid nature of the flows that shaped that work. Maye, whose work with clients as a programmer was highly collaborative, explained her understanding thus:

> You cannot even begin to explain what you do to people alright? Let's say you get a call while you are online working on a client's job, the client could be anywhere but between the net and the phone you can work together to find the right solution. It is kind of interesting; when you started work, and you finally find out that you are here and you know that they employed you as a programming engineer and you want to explain what you do to somebody who doesn't understand because you are talking about things and your working environment— well that too can be interesting. You know it's not like you are really meeting the people you work with online or on the phone, but in a sense you are still meeting people out there. It is only that it's different. I mean my job gives me; it affords me the opportunity to know more about what is going out there. I will say it's not really about being a college graduate; you should have an open mind and this job forces you to. You never know who you will be working for or with tomorrow.

When globalizing processes produce laborscapes like CTI and CDN in places like Ghana, they also in effect create simultaneously hybrid workplace cultures where the local and the global intersect. There was a fusion of cultural expectations at both CTI and CDN. At CTI while a version of that fusion was pushed down the hierarchy from the American site manager, the employees through their own perceptions and subjectivities seemed to internalize and enact their own brand of these hybridized/ glocalized cultures and practices. Their understanding of the culture of their workplace was different from that of the management team and neither party had found a mechanism for reaching the other. At CDN it appeared as though the management had figured out a set of practices that were "glocal" and acceptable enough that while employees wanted more in salaries and transportation services, they had by and large bought into the ethos the company projected and represented. In contrast, some of CTI practices were part of a mechanism for feminizing the workplace and the work that is done in it as I will argue in chapter 8.

I return to Nola's question "Are you going to write about us?" I did respond to Nola's question that day with a "Yes, I am going to try to. I hope I will be able to do justice to all I have learned from all of the women at CTI." That seemed to satisfy her. But the question I have now as I write these chapters is this: how do I establish what doing justice is? Whose justice? I suspect that what may constitute justice for management may be different from what may constitute justice to employees. I also suspect that what I have done here may not seem just to any of the actors in these complicated workplaces. As a researcher interested in workplace literacy my critical questions throughout fieldwork were focused on the related literacies various actors in these workplaces used. It became clear that one could not pose that question without looking at the social world in which those practices were embedded. The result is this attempt at a "thick description" of practices. The CTI and CDN networks defined work for these women and for them it was "new" work, as it was different from any work they had ever done. It was also "new" in the sense that it was globalized work enacted in material/immaterial local spaces. In this workplace there were recognizable "old" literacy practices: the employee uses of language, reading, and writing, speaking and listening were physical and tangible but there were also "new" practices and others that were intangible but important for getting work nonetheless. In the next chapter, I examine literacies in these workspaces.

Nola left a secretarial job to work at CTI because, since it was a global North company she assumed CTI would pay more, provide good benefits—such as health and life insurance—and that it would offer opportunities for skill development and career advancement. She conceded that when she began working at CTI in 2000 she did in fact make a "lot of money" but that had changed as time passed.

Nola, unlike many of her co-workers, was interested in understanding the context in which CTI operated. She used her technology skills outside of work—often using the web to research the parent company. She often gave me comparative information about Ghanaian and American workers. She knew what CTI's global North employees were given in benefits and wages and could therefore put her own compensation in a larger context. For a two week period in September 2004 Nola worked for 88.73 hours and took home 370,000 cedis. With the Bank of Ghana exchange rate pegged at 9240 cedis to the dollar at the time, Nola's wages for those two weeks were $39.99 (Appendix G). Nola notes that "When people learn I work for an American company, they think I am making a lot of money. They think I get good benefits. But for real I am suffering to make it. I can't save much and things are getting expensive all the time. My wages keep disappearing."

CTI and CDN offer evidence of how expanding markets have resulted in Marx's axiom that the bourgeois "must nestle" jobs everywhere—in this case Ghana—while connecting these jobs and the workers (women mainly) to places elsewhere *(The Communist Manifesto* 1967: 83). These dynamics offer evidence about the 'reception' of globalization (in the 'local') and in the process reveals how "globalization is 'produced' by specific agencies, institutions and actors" (Saukko 2003, 179). The study of CTI and CDN demonstrates that these processes are in fact observable.

The multiple mini laborscapes, and the flows that ran through them at CTI and CDN further highlight how literacies of practice were negotiated by the different actors. As this chapter shows women at the different sites navigated and made sense of what it meant to be an outsourcing employee in the context of their situation and location. At CTI they recognized the practices of the different levels of surveillance and managed them. They developed here and now embodiment practices to negotiate the pressures brought on by flows originating from elsewhere and thereby managed the rhythms of the workplace as human agents. At both CTI and CDN women by and large recognized and made some sense of shifting narratives about the cultural constructions of gender and the shifting literacies associated with these in the workplace. Women learned how to read their workplaces and how to act as a result. In effect work offered the women in outsourcing ways of being literate in these contexts.

## NOTES

1.  See Bukartek, Feingold, Patterson & Walker (n.d). Telecommunications and ICT Development in Ghana: Lessons Learned from Two Call Centers in Accra. Ghana Cyber Group. www.ghanacybergroup.com/research/getres.asp?MC=RE&cat=2&id=18

# SEVEN

# Literacies of Outsourcing: "Scapes" and "Flows" of "New Work"

This chapter explores the situated uses of literacy practices at CTI and CDN and investigates how the demands of "new" work are shaping how citizen/employees acquire and or adapt their literacy competencies in the workplace. As James Gee has observed, "reading and writing only make sense when studied in the context of social and cultural practices of which they are but a part" (Gee 2000, 180). Such an orientation, following Helen Nixon, requires seeing literacy as the "repertoire of practices for communicating and for getting things done in particular social and cultural contexts" (Nixon 2003, 407). For CTI and CDN, this points to taking up issues surrounding the integration of communication networks, the coordination of financial markets, and deregulation. Additionally, such an orientation situates literate practices at CTI and CDN in the materiality of local practices in ways that capture locality as a "scape" traversed by global "flows." The flows in this "laborscape" provide a context for understanding the links between the activities of reading, writing, viewing and speaking and the broader social contexts in which they are embedded—that is, examining practices in CTI and CDN can demonstrate the socially constituted and situated nature of workplace practices. Understanding globalized work at CTI and CDN can illuminate dynamics that shape work communities, the multiple literacies employees control and their socially embedded nature (Street 2001). This chapter uses two very broad data-generated thematic parameters to anchor the discussion of multiple literacies at CDN and CTI. The broad data-generated parameters are:

1.  The nature and context of literacy acquisition, its sponsors (Brandt 2001), its links to local, sub-local, and non-local practices, and the dynamics that frame negotiation, appropriation and contestation.
2.  The acquisition of knowledge, the sources and uses of that knowledge, and the textual/discursive cultures made possible by these processes. Here I am operating with Spradley's (1980) definition of "culture" as "the acquired knowledge people use to interpret experience and generate behavior."

The last part of the chapter shows how literacy practices and their ancillary discourses defined and shaped power relationships, locating employees and management in conflicted and contradictory positions.

## LITERACY, SELF-MAKING, AND THE CONSTRUCTION OF CYBER-WORKERS

In the workplaces I describe in this book, the nature of the literacy and educational experiences of participants provided the building blocks upon which cyber-work identities were constructed. Literacy and educational experiences determined what work participants did and how they did that work. Across sites, a significant theme that emerged was that the acquisition of knowledge and abilities deemed appropriate for outsourcing work were influenced by pressures originating elsewhere. Knowledge acquisition was therefore not a neutral proposition and it was not a local decision. For the focal participants across sites and their immediate networks of peers the acquisition of abilities was also linked to a generational transition toward ICTs. A key dynamic here was the pressure and competition for a limited number of jobs, the constraints on developing economies like Ghana in their ability to adequately fund education that prepares citizens for emerging ICT-related work and the shift of the responsibility for workforce preparation from the state to private citizens who then depend on the private sector educational institutions for their training. To work in outsourcing, these workers had to become entrepreneurs in self-creation, shaping their identities to fit the demands of the emerging workplace. Across sites IT related knowledge was acquired at private institutions, though CDN, unlike CTI, offered intensive on the job training (I discuss these issues further below). Since these workers went through elementary and secondary schools where IT-related instruction was not part of the curriculum, they were what Barton and Hamilton (1998, 181) termed "a transitional generation." They neither used computers in schools nor did they have them at home. Schools in Ghana did not have computers and most schools still do not have them. In fact only two CDN employees (Zoe and Maye) reported that their families bought computers around the time they went to college. Many of the women at

CTI reported first encountering computers during their secretarial training, which always occurred beyond their Junior Secondary or Senior Secondary education—the two exit points in public education in Ghana. Their previous workplaces were not computerized either; CTI was the first network environment they had worked in. Interestingly, the desire to participate in the new economy precipitated the pursuit of access as women sought ways to learn new technologies. The women's technology use at work was, however, only for purposes sanctioned by their employers. Women on the production floor at CTI did not have email access, for example. The women at CDN had yahoo, hotmail and other free email accounts and could access these at the café.

For CTI employees in particular, computer use (new technology) simply replaced the old technology of writing (typing) because the bulk of their work involved filling in data fields. Consider the case of Liza, a twenty-three year old who had worked at CTI for eight months at the time of my fieldwork. In an interview with me in August of 2004 Liza noted:

> I went to school when I was six or seven. I don't remember, but from primary, I went to JSS and from JSS I went to SSS. From SSS I went to Takoradi Polytechnic. I studied for a Diploma in Business Studies. That was when I started learning to type first on a typewriter. Then I learned to use Microsoft Word and other software. I took classes at a private technology school. After I got my diploma I did my national service at V-A-T (Spells it out: Value Added Tax), Takoradi. Then I heard of CTI and so I came here. At VAT I was performing three different jobs— secretarial duties, receptionist and then because they were not having Administrator [Office Manager], by then I was performing that function too. Here my job is a little bit different. It's like my career there (VAT) was more the secretarial aspect and here it's like it's more of data entry. If I should put it like that—data entry. The only thing that I'm using right here is my typing.

Two other women in her network recount similar experiences. Sarah and Toni, like Liza, had JSS to SSS certificates. To work at CTI they attended a private computer training school where they learned software applications. Their secretarial training secured them secretarial jobs. They left these secretarial jobs to work at CTI because they thought they would make more money working in outsourcing. Although they expected to learn new, more advanced skills while working in the high-tech environment at CTI, Sarah, Toni and Liza noted wryly that work at CTI required them to learn to key both alphabetic and numeric characters even though the alphabetic was what they were used to as secretaries. Local practices (the local isn't entirely local, of course) were clearly influenced by pressures, policies, etc. originating elsewhere. In fact some of these dynamics were tied to the structural adjustment policies discussed earlier.

This general point on the acquisition and uses of knowledge manifested itself at CDN too. For example, at the Client Computing Services Department (CCSD) department at CDN data entry entailed indexing data and offering solutions related to document imaging. Most of the data entry work in this department related to the banking industry. Employees needed typing speeds of 45–50 wpm to work in the data entry areas of the department. All the data entry women worked regular hours. They were a supportive group who helped each other and trained new employees collaboratively. The data entry employees all had Senior Secondary School certificates. Additionally they had attended either secretarial schools or had taken software classes at private schools. None had had any computer classes in school and were not sure they would have taken such classes even if they were offered. Taking into consideration the fact that Ghana's per capita income as of 2011 was according to the World Bank, $1230.00, an expansive public investment in accessible IT infrastructure for all may be difficult.

Selective Data Solutions Department (SDSD), another CDN department, provided voice-related services for Canadian, U.S., and UK companies and their subsidiaries. This department provided solutions mainly related to transcription, telemarketing, customer care, working with voice texts, and images. The SDSD work force was highly educated; all employees had either a higher national diploma in Journalism, Public Relations, or university degrees in the liberal arts or sciences. In conversations with the women in this department, many considered their liberal arts degrees or higher education curricula to be a great asset to the work they did. Interestingly, CDN valued hiring employees into SDSD who were highly educated but not necessarily good with computers or typing. The manager, Eddie, explained that they valued employees who could think, solve problems and work on teams—typing and other skill sets the employees could acquire on the job. As the women talked about their training, many acknowledged that they did not need to have all the requisite technical training. CDN put them through a rigorous six-week training regimen after they were hired. Beyond that initial training, there was on-task coaching for another ten weeks. Employees continued to get ongoing training, usually during times when they had no active projects. Eddie suggested that using such slow periods for training helped CDN maintain quality. For example over the U.S. Thanksgiving holiday SDSD employees used what they call "dummy webcasts" to hone their skills. The "dummy webcast" simulated a fourth-quarter conference call for analysts and investors for an American client. They had completed this live job a couple of days before but because it was Thanksgiving weekend in the United States, there was low activity. Employees essentially conducted retrospective analysis of their transcription processes, did error analysis on their parts of the job, looked at what the verifier of their job had isolated as "errors" and then re-transcribed the section again. Other employees were provided "new" sections of the call to transcribe. What both Eddie and employees describe as needed for work at SDSD were analytic abilities, quick thinking, active listening and reading and writing abilities. As one employee noted, these were the abilities that "a well rounded liberal arts education" provided them. For those employees at the low end at CDN who came to the workplace with some technical expertise, their knowledge had been secured through their private efforts—private schools taught them what they knew about software. The women at the low and middle strata of CDN did not see their jobs as careers. To them, these jobs were stepping stones to other experiences and many talked about going back to school.

## RECRUITING CYBER-WORKERS: AIMS, VALUES AND REALITIES OF LITERACIES IN USE

Recruiting practices at CTI and CDN were imbued with what each site valued *vis a vis* work-related literacy practices. At CTI the goal was to recruit as many employees with good typing speed and accuracy as possible. At CDN the approach was to recruit highly educated employees and then invest the resources needed onsite for training. These approaches suggested different goals, attitudes, values and realities and they produced different consequences for the sites.

Recruitment at CTI was explicitly focused on skill sets and the screening activities used suggested that these skills were discrete, measurable and transferable. CTI data processor recruiting was centralized and managed entirely by the Human Resources (HR) staff. CTI applicants were screened via three activities: a typing test (for which they needed to have 60-65 wpm—by the end of fieldwork the standard was 65 wpm), a thirty minute timed writing sample, and an aptitude test that purported to measure problem-solving abilities. The benchmark for accuracy on the typing test for prospective employees was 95 to 96 percent. Prospective employees were allowed thirty minutes for the writing test and fifteen minutes for the Aptitude Test. If applicants got through all three screening gates successfully, they were invited in for a face-to-face interview with one or two human resources personnel. The fundamental premise here was, it seems to me, that the skills these activities purported to assess could be isolated and measured and that workers who performed well on these tasks would transfer the compartmentalized decontextualized tested skills into a context of processing client data that originates from the global North—mainly the United States. At the time of fieldwork, CTI neither had to advertise for applicants nor for the dates on which it screened potential employees—a good underground network ensured that potential applicants appeared on screening days. While this may underscore the dearth of employment opportunities available, CTI's high employee turnover rate and its simultaneous capacity to attract more contracts to the Ghana site contributed to an atmosphere of a company that was constantly hiring and firing employees.

Benchmarks for recruiting were decided at the U.S. home office, often without local input but undoubtedly with local consequences. For example, in early November 2004, when the typing test cut-off was set at 65 wpm, CTI had 150 potential applicants to screen. Out of the 150 only four successfully completed the three initial screening activities. A week after that none of the twenty four applicants completed the three activities successfully. Tricia, the HR assistant who administered these activities remarked that "when they were making the decision [to raise the typing speed to 65 wpm] no one came to ask me about it." This prompted me to ask her who "they" were, to which she said the decision was made in the U.S. by the Director of International Operations. Outside standards trumped yet regulated local input but the stress of finding local bodies was borne by local personnel.

To make visible the complexity of screening activities I elaborate on the typing, writing, and reasoning tests. Though no one at CTI ever articulated this point, it is clear that keyboarding was used as the main gatekeeping mechanism because of the assumption that the Ghanaian education system while promoting alphabetic literacies did not teach typing. Further, since a major skill CTI cyber-workers needed, at least according to the management, was typing in a network environment, screening for the skill simulated this as much as possible. The typing test had three subtests and importantly required the test taker to read on-screen and follow the instructions after each section in order to be taken to the next screen. On-screen passages had space underneath each line into which test takers were to type the exact passage. Texts varied in length and complexity and the software tracked speed and accuracy as test takers typed. Successful applicants then proceeded to take the writing and aptitude tests.

For the writing and aptitude tests, Tricia put prompts face down on tables in the lunchroom and called in the prospective employees. They were told to sit at the spots with paper; often Tricia left space between test-takers to discourage "cheating." Applicants were only allowed to bring in a writing implement. Thirty minutes was allotted for the writing portion and fifteen for the aptitude. On a day in September 2004 when I observed the writing portion of the recruiting screening there were thirty-eight test takers; ten men and twenty-eight women. That day's essay prompt was: "Describe any sad incident you have witnessed in your life and state TWO lessons you gained out of that experience." The writing prompts as well as the aptitude tests were scored by Tricia alone.

The screening process at CTI was tense and stressful for both those administering the test and the test takers. For test takers their very futures hang on getting the right speed since the typing test was really for gate-keeping. During my November 2004 observation of the screening process, one woman was so nervous that she had to be sent away. To underscore the tensions and complexities of recruiting at CTI, I share the story of a young woman who also reported for screening that November morning. Hagar, as she later told me, was twenty-one and had travelled from a town in the western region of Ghana in order to take the test. She was visibly nervous and as she sat at the computer it became apparent that she knew next to nothing about how computers work. When she did not listen to Tricia and therefore could not follow her instructions, her computer froze. Hagar blamed the machine and asked to be reseated. Tricia obliged but Hagar managed to get that computer to freeze up on her as well. Hagar was given three more chances before Tricia asked her to leave. But she didn't leave. Tricia refused to let Hagar take the test. Hagar then started crying. Seeing a male CTI IT staff member, she approached him to plead her case. He took her to a computer, calmed her down, read her the instructions and got her started. She typed for about twenty minutes and her recorded speed was 66 wpm with 96 percent accuracy. I spoke with her after the typing test; she was still anxious but she wanted to take her writing and aptitude tests later that day because she couldn't afford to be in Accra for two days. I asked Hagar why she couldn't seem to get her computer to work—though she could type, she told me, she had learned to type on a typewriter not a computer. That day I noted my impressions thus:

> While Hagar's experience shows the disparities between what the State is able to offer citizens in terms of career education and what globalized work expects of would-be employees, it also points to how skills such as typing are not entirely neutral. Hagar was only able to adapt to the technology (computer) because someone had the patience to offer some coaching. The recruiting process and the literacy abilities it was based on operated with a logic of simple transfer of neutral skills from neutral technologies onto processing data generated in another culture and, more importantly, radically different discourse communities, given that CTI catered to health care and insurance clients. The recruiting process sought information on reasoning abilities, reading, writing, and typing accuracy and speed. The interface used for testing these abilities, especially the typing part, at the very least complicates transferability.

There is some paradox to this episode. The juxtaposition of Tricia's rigid, mechanical application of the testing procedures with the relative flexible intervention of Joe the IT supervisor stands as an example of a drawback of strict "Taylorist" management practices. CTI clearly operated with an assembly line structure—having different people trained narrowly to perform particular aspects of data processing. This practice was then linked to its testing philosophy. Could a flexible, more sensitive approach produce better results? Yet, in this case, Hagar seems to have cast herself into a traditional patriarchal scenario that, in effect, trumped the streamlined efficiency of the transnational work regime. Joe rescued a damsel in distress, producing a happy outcome all around. Hagar got her second chance, and CTI got an employee it nearly rejected but who turned out to be competent.

The premise for recruitment at CDN, as articulated by management personnel such as Eddie and Ms. Naku, was, according to them, in alignment with employing and maintaining a quality workforce. The management considered this goal critical to competitiveness. The central issue at CDN was therefore the fit of an employee for the department she or he was applying to work in. Department heads were actively involved in the hiring process and often screened applicants themselves with assistance of human resource personnel. For software engineers, for example, Naku insisted on hiring what she termed "only the brightest and the most confident." In a conversation on recruiting, she pointed out that her engineers, unlike other employees at CDN, had to work closely with clients. For transcribers and data entry employees Ms. Naku said the company hired applicants with good education and good command of reading and writing in English and then trained them intensively on the job to develop their typing, listening and other abilities (CDN had a phonetic laboratory). Every CDN employee, according to CDN managers (and certainly all the participants in the study fit this profile), had either a higher-level diploma or a bachelor's degree. Both CDN management and employees identified the level of education and onsite training as highly critical not only to the quality of work at the company but also to morale, confidence and professionalism at the site. Employees in different departments at CDN talked extensively about their educational backgrounds and often linked their ability to think and solve problems on the job to their educational preparation.

Here I offer a few profiles of CDN employees who had university degrees:

> Zoe: Okay. I went through Achimota (JSS and SSS) and then to Legon, that is, the University of Ghana, and I hold a degree in Psychology – B.Sc. (Psychology). Typing here is my first experience; I have never really taken any typing lessons before this my first experience typing. So, right now, I can type like 30 to 40.

> Moe: I just studied Physics, Chemistry, and Biology for two years, and then I went in for Psychology. I went to the University of Ghana. I went to SSS at Wesley Girls School at Cape Coast. I learned to type after I came here. Now I can type about 42 wpm on average—sometimes I can do more—it depends.

> Boe: I went to Aburi Girls School and then I went to the University of Ghana at Legon. There I read Geography and Philosophy. For this job

right, you need some kind of education to be able to do this. But sometimes you have to-- it has to make sense. Other times you don't even
hear what the people are saying but you have to listen intently because
of the accent. You have to make sure that what you're writing makes
sense and you need some form of education to do that. I mean in this
sense Philosophy helps you to be analytical. I guess then maybe Geography is another help. Let's see, I think Geography deals with everything.

Noe: Well I read Sociology at the University of Ghana and I graduated
last year. This is my first job after National Service.

And a similar attitude of purposefulness and self-confidence was characteristic also of CDN employees without university degrees. Here, for example, is Hawa describing her training and its effect on her work.

Hawa: Well, typing . . . I learned it on my own but here they taught us
typing here as well and right now I can do 45 and above a minute. It all
depends on the quality of the voice data I am working with. We also
have two things: we have the transcribers and we have verifiers; but
what we have to do is that we have to type. When we are done the
verifiers also work on it and the verifiers will have to go through our
information to make sure everything is okay. It is easier on their part
we just have to make sure we get things right because we work with a
turnaround time.

Data entry work was done in the CCSD department at CDN and required
typing speeds of 45-50 wpm. Data entry employees at CCSD were expected to have basic knowledge of word processing, spreadsheets, data
management and internet navigating abilities. Most of the data entry was
for the banking industry. The level of education of employees at CDN
was higher than it was at CTI but there are some questions about the
intellectual stimulation of low end work for a highly educated employee.
Bukartek, Feingold, Patterson & Walker (2007), in an examination of call
center work in Ghana, argue that to develop and sustain the BPO and
ITO sector in Ghana it will be necessary to develop higher-end and so-
phisticated-sector jobs in order to keep the many new college graduates
who work in the sector from leaving it. This was a sentiment shared by
women at CDN more so than CTI.

## SITUATED LITERACIES: CONTEXTS AND PRACTICES

Literacies at CDN and CTI were situated in these work contexts but they
were also indicative of wider social practices in which they were embedded. The social context of work in the various CDN and CTI departments
opened up different opportunities for employees to function as literate
beings and to tap into different language and literacy-related abilities.

Online and offline work precipitated creative adaptations in literate practices. Tasks were textual, digitized or in other semiotic modes and required content knowledge and expertise as employees at both sites did not only work with alphabetic texts. Depending on which department a CDN or CTI employee worked in, she/he also needed to control iconic systems such as signs, symbols, and images in addition to print.

At both sites the spaces where the actual work occurred were entirely virtual and were the conduits for flows originating elsewhere. Online spaces defined the work environment of employees. At CTI work-related literacies were enacted within the company's networked interface. Tasks required what appeared to be repetitive low-end skills—typing, reading, writing, speaking, and listening in English by workers who used English as an official second language but often negotiated work practices in their local languages. The interface required familiarity and facility with computers and network environments. Work required employees to command the situated literacies of the various interfaces. Skill in this context was therefore more complicated as it required both declarative and procedural knowledge. Declarative knowledge, in the case of CTI, was related to concepts in health care, health insurance processing discourses, facts, organization, and different "genres" of data categories. Procedural knowledge enabled workers to develop strategies and procedures for using this knowledge in context. The high level of employee turnover at CTI suggested that the assumption that abilities tested during recruiting were adequate to function at CTI might in fact be flawed. Indeed middle managers such as Kofi acknowledged a disconnect between what CTI tested and what the women actually did once they started data processing on the production floor. Some middle managers had started using a buddy system for mentoring new employees as a way around the problem. New employees were paired with experienced ones and given a six week grace period during which their errors were not penalized. Beyond that point penalties were applied and these were staggered, with the ultimate penalty being termination.

To tease out some of the situated practices at CTI I use Nola's experiences as an Alpha department employee. By the end of fieldwork Alpha was working in an online space that sent its data directly into a shared space with a U.S. point on the company's networked site. Flows into her workspace were not unidirectional. Nola's work at the beginning of fieldwork involved processing batches of dental insurance claim data using provider codes, service codes, rate codes, and others and checking for alignment of service to insurance stipulations. Sometimes Nola verified data that her colleagues had completed—a CTI internal quality control mechanism. As a verifier, her role was to check the accuracy of processed data by field and category. Since this was CTI's internal quality control, her job as a verifier was to catch errors and then fix them. Her verified work was subject to further internal audit before that data left the site.

Sometimes Nola used online tools such as calculators to double check the numbers her colleagues had assigned on claim forms. For example, I once sat with Nola as she worked on a sample that had six pages of supporting documents. The content of the documents were not all alpha numeric: There were shots of receipts, Rx prescriptions with the standard "doctor" hand-writing, and "images" of x-rays. To work with multiple documents of various lengths Nola had to have a strategy for reading online. In some instances Nola had to manipulate images of documents on screen in order to have a good "reading" of them. Sometimes she zoomed in on images or rotated them. Text-heavy processing jobs took her long periods of time to work through in order to avoid errors. Nola's workplace literacy demands changed often as client needs changed and those changes also affected the processes of sense-making for Nola and her colleagues. The changing technologies of work have brought new texts to the workplace—manuals, operating procedures, visuals, charts, symbols, tables, etc., (see table of examples of dental terms used at Alpha). Nola had to master these to get work done, to be part of the workplace culture, to identify with and to belong to Alpha and CTI. Again, the impact of transnational players on local actors in this workplace is apparent. Literacy activity in this local workplace shows how texts originate, circulate and spill across boundaries of space and time and what can be learned from the process.

CDN offered multiple online spaces where employees enacted literacies related to a range of tasks. Employee practices ranged from low-end routinized work to sophisticated software programming. CDN had mini communities where different dimensions of literacy work were embedded. At CDN employees communicated with various groups on the job, they gathered information for projects, they solved day-to-day work-related problems, and they had to be comfortable with various web-based technologies. However departments such as CCSD and QOSD at CDN clearly demanded additional sophisticated specialized knowledge. The uses of AutoCAD for 2D and 3D design and drafting at CCSD, for example, meant employees needed specific AutoCAD related abilities. Drawing lines using Cartesian coordinates, offsetting objects and creating sophisticated 3D figures/objects were routine for some CCSD employees. These employees created solutions such as after-sales support for replacement parts and parts numbers; they created and maintained service manuals for transnational companies and their subsidiaries. In addition, CCSD employees often reviewed parts, managed proofs of part listings, and created image mappings of these to part numbers for clients. Another solution CCSD offered was the review of client service manuals for language/grammar, and readability. In offering these solutions CCSD employees brought together their content knowledge and technical writing abilities. Web-based client maintenance solutions allowed service provider and client to collaborate extensively during the "composing" process. Employees read, wrote, and used content knowledge to create solutions for clients. Though most of this work was content-knowledge-related, online reading and writing and collaborative problem solving facilitated the work. Using AutoCAD, for example, employees created, manipulated and "read" images, figures and diagrams. An essential ability required for work in these online spaces was collaboration. Often CCSD employees shared work in progress with clients in online communities or through synchronous chats as problems were "talked" through and resolved.

Selective Data Solutions Department (SDSD) provided voice-related solutions such as transcription, telemarketing, customer care, and work with voice data and images for Canadian, American and UK companies and their subsidiaries. It required slightly different sets of practices from employees. The women here read widely and deeply about clients as a lead-in to the transcribing work they did. Voice data transfer/transcription work usually had a turnaround time of four hours. But before they ever started working on the voice data itself, the women read extensively for background information on the client. Part of this necessitated researching names of executives and their responsibilities; researching and learning the names of analysts and the financial press that covered the sector in which the prospective client conducted business. For my discussion I use "Zibba," a transnational food-processing conglomerate as an example. To transcribe Zibba material, the women working in SDSD conducted strategic online research looking for information on Zibba. They evaluated the source of the material they found and, given the time they had, decided on how best to "read" for the information they needed. The employees also decided how to store information online for ready access should they need to refer back during the transcribing process. Conducting effective and efficient research online for deep background knowledge was a critical skill for the women at SDSD because for accurate transcription they had to recognize names of executives at Zibba as well as the places where Zibba plants were located. They had to have fairly good working knowledge of Zibba product lines. Since Zibba is a food processing concern this inevitably meant understanding American food choices and the cultural significance of these choices as well as Zibba product promotions. For example, when Zibba offered promotions related to Thanksgiving, the women had to understand the significance of these promotions in order to transcribe Zibba's quarterly press report accurately and efficiently. They had to have an understanding of the larger industry, its trends and market pressures. In other words they had to have business and cultural background knowledge. Indeed this is precisely what Zoe addresses here.

> Zoe: Basically so that it helps us in our work because there are some brand names that you might not know. You might hear it but the

spelling might not be right; you might not get the spelling right. Things like that, so we just make sure that we have the right thing. They are the ones we work with, okay? So, okay we've had some training in American culture, we had someone come from the States come and teach us about American culture and how they are, how they talk, how different they are from us and all that.

Online work involving voice transcription required macro-knowledge as well as minutiae such as brand names, product types etc. For the women deep background work made their jobs easier.

Listening actively was a critical ability that women at SDSD needed to get their work done. Listening actively was in fact an ability all areas of CDN depended on. Moe discusses the abilities related to her job as a transcriber thus:

> Moe: So, I have to really learn all these cultural things—sometimes I memorize and some stay. I don't have to keep anything in my head if I don't want to. I do my research and I save stuff on my computer to easy reference. If we think or are told we're going to be getting light job from TT&Z and that it will come in at one o'clock, we come in the morning and we start doing your research online. I make sure I cover any recent activity such as any acquisitions. I see if they have lost people or had something filed against whomever—just anything. This is so that I am prepared. I just have an idea of what is going on, so that that's even why when I can't really be sure what is being said, I know that, okay, this is supposed to be this so I can fill in for what I did not hear. I have to listen constantly and carefully. I mean especially companies where they have you know people of Asian descent and whatever other people. We try to train our ears. Yes we train our ears to the different accents because in America alone, the Americans themselves have different accents. It's not that easy but we try.

On another occasion Moe spoke about the content knowledge needed for the work she does. On this day she had been working on voice texts from a webcast for an American company.

> Moe: Well, actually, I have no idea whatsoever about you know finance and what goes on, what really goes on in the companies. But I come to work; I do my bit by listening carefully and doing my best. If I get it wrong because I don't understand finance, you know this kind of thing just does not make me feel at home; so this is what the top people do. We just see them moving about and they come out to give us feedback on our work and that kind of thing. So working here has just given me an idea about investment in general. I think it's something that will add value to me as well because it will give me knowledge. Wherever I am and people are talking about business and finance I'll be able to make a contribution if I find it interesting. I have no background in finance from school whatsoever apart from Mark (a co-worker) I know no other people who have any financial background so financial education is very interesting to me.

Another transcriber, Abigail, talked about background knowledge and active listening as abilities needed for her job at SDSD:

> Abigail: You have a lot of exposure through the different kinds of con-ference calls that you do. For me, I didn't have any financial back-ground so it helps my cultural learning. My only problem is the differ-ent accents. You don't really get to hear everything simply because there is only your part of the whole call for you to work on. But you know I'm comparing you (meaning Americans) with me. We don't have different accents here or maybe that is because Ghanaians were colonized by the British so their English is what we know and that may affect how we understand. I don't want to say they (Americans) are speeding when they speak but that happens. You have to be very atten-tive to catch everything.

Active listening on the job was always on the minds of transcribers at SDSD and the women were sensitive to issues that complicated their capacity to hear clearly on the job. Early during fieldwork Koe shared her strategy for tackling difficult parts of her work. Her strategy demon-strates the kinds of independent creative problem-solving and adaptation I noted above.

> Koe: Maybe the CEO of the company spoke very nicely and you think I got it and you are able to type so fast but then when it comes to the analyst's side, it's so hard—different analysts speak and sometimes they don't identify themselves. You have to listen carefully to know who is who and what is what. Sometimes you don't know what to do so you try to make sense of the analyst's side by going to the analyst's section on old jobs so you can compare the names that have been listed to the one that you are hearing. You have to do some detective work. All work is connected to other work. If you think about it that way it makes sense.

Each employee at SDSD would get ten-minute voice text which usually took about one hour to transcribe. On listening Koe noted that "it is hard when you really have to strain, it naturally makes you exhausted when the recording is bad. It slows your pace and it takes you so much longer. Sometimes I go to old recordings for the same company and then go through the analysts." Such consultation has to happen within the allot-ted time and this often means that employees have to make strategic decisions about where to go without losing too much time. There is pres-sure but there is also fascination—getting all the elements of the puzzle in place is what enables problems to be resolved.

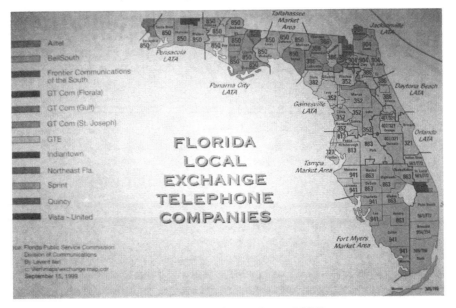

**Figure 7.1. A non-print work aid for voice workers at CDN**

Reading in the various digitized spaces at CDN had some common characteristics. A lot of that reading was in fact browsing, scanning, and keyword spotting. That reading was non-linear and in many ways selective; it was not in-depth reading and for many employees it was the kind of reading one did once and was done with it. At a number of the departments at CDN I asked employees about reading on-and-off-line. Audrey, for example, self-consciously described the difference between online and offline reading and suggested that the speed of the technologies (bandwidth) at work had a lot to do with how fast she could read to get her work done.

> Audrey: Well, for online reading, it's like you have to really grasp it; but with print, you can easily go back, maybe, you have it printed. With transcribing the system is not all that fast. It slows down your research activity more than the printed one. And that is where the disadvantage comes in. The online one where you have a slow net to work with and your whole research activity is slow—that can be a problem.

Perhaps even more importantly, women often shared how doing work at CDN had forced them into learning about global financial markets; something of no interest to them before taking jobs there.

> Zoe: Oh the reading I do now is quite different. Reading before was quite traditional. Now I don't think I read to see if I can assimilate it. What I do right now is I read the recent proposals by companies. It is financial and very different from what I am used to doing. What I have

found out is I try to understand it without understanding the whole financial world. I have to have some basic understanding of what companies are doing. So I do what it takes to retain words which for me is constantly listening, picking up the words, and finding out their meanings. So that when in transcription, you basically have some understanding to try and make some sense as you type a document. So we just listen, we learn and we go onto the Web, we find out what we can about a company before we start to work.

Like the women at the various CDN departments, the women at CTI had to enter online spaces suffused with discourses for which they were outsiders. At CTI the women entered American health care in order to process data successfully. Understanding these discourses was also critical to developing strategies for engaging and using them effectively. For example, processing U.S. physician health care claims required medical, dental, vision, hearing and sometimes pharmaceutical knowledge as well as familiarity with the culturally specific practices of American health care as background information. Consider as an example, the many digitized images of hand written correspondence that were attached to claims where the legibility of physician writing alone could be a challenge. Processing transactions therefore immersed readers in discourses for which they were, at the very least, outsiders but for which they had to develop processing strategies in order to use their reading, writing and typing skills efficiently. They read to locate essential data, to understand, and to evaluate this information in order to process texts as required by clients. There are practices that we easily recognize as "old" literacies. There are real bodies working in real time using abilities we can recognize as reading, writing and computing (Hull 1997; Luke 2003). However, there are also practices that are "new" to these workers. Watching the women at work online suggested that there were all sorts of cultural background knowledges that they needed for their work. Any idea that they simply processed transactions didn't really capture what they brought to that task. American medical, dental, vision etc. transactions are really culturally specific to the United States. For accurate processing, the women needed to understand what the terms meant. Shortly after Hagar began working, I watched as she tried to differentiate between a personal identification number (PIN#) and a 1-800- number. Going on her past experience that a particular field captured PINs she had assumed the 800 number was in fact a PIN number. She processed the data as such but was having second thoughts so she asked a colleague if she was correct. Hagar's colleague told her 1-800 . . . was in fact a phone number. Now recall that these employees are charged for any errors they make. Hagar went back and reprocessed the transaction. Clearly she took a chance by going with what her colleague told her. But Hagar's decision was actually strategic; she asked a knowledgeable peer because she recognized that there was situated sub-local knowledge that she was being socialized into.

Another example of on-task problem solving, creative adaptation and, perhaps, risk-taking is evident in the account of Liza. Liza had worked at CTI for eight months at the time of fieldwork, and she shared another dimension to data processing thus:

> You know something? I have a little problem. The only thing is that sometimes we have a claim we are keying and you see some words being spelt very badly. You see, we were British colonized. We see some spelling to us it is wrong instead of us correcting it, they are saying you key as you see. So the only thing that I am using over here is my knowledge in computer and then the typing. And the English as well because sometimes you have to reason. And if you don't understand what they've written there, sometimes, you can't key it because you can't figure out. And there are some writings, when I was in school they taught these different types of handwriting. Sometimes the manuscript it's very difficult to read yeah. But sometimes because of my background I can figure out. You see personally, when I'm keying, I used to read a lot. It's like when I start from field one, I just memorize. I just see, look at the figures while I read them; then I key. But if you read it like you'll be. . . . I don't know what to say but you'll not be faster.

Interestingly, the women at CTI insisted that typing was the skill they used most on the job. Though the women mainly used numeric keys, there were times when their work required alphabetic keys. As an observer however, I saw pacing, dexterity, facility with the interface, and reading quickly yet accurately as essential to the practices of data processing. There was dexterity with which women worked out of multiple windows while holding vital data in short term memory. At one point, Gifty, an employee in Omega, was working out of nine windows simultaneously. Her desktop was arranged so that her main data task took about a third of the space horizontally, then there was another inch and half horizontally with minimized windows— she had five of these. She also had the entry field area where she was keying in data. The data fields were color coded and she knew what the various colors signified almost instinctively. At one point she had seven colors on her screen. Her tool bar provided her with nine options.

Examining the work women like Gifty did at Omega provides a window into the complexities of skill. Omega dealt with correspondence—all the patient letters and pre-treatment letters, etc., that physicians write. Omega had about fifty different form types to process and the women had to know them all and be able to identify them and key them correctly. The work at Omega was therefore heavily textual. The women did a good amount of online searching and reading to locate "categories" they needed to key. In this department, processors had to think and they had to make decisions. Also a fair amount of the correspondence was hand-generated. This meant that Gifty had to read and understand the peculiar writings of physicians, pharmacists, and patients, plus make sense of the cultural contexts in which the texts they processed were produced. Gifty talked about making sense of unfamiliar names and script styles and getting charged for errors in wages when her "readings" did not match what was in fact required. According to CTI management, Omega was the only department of its kind outside a U.S.-based CTI office. Unlike the other departments therefore, Omega employees could not count on other sites to share the work load. Because the text-based work they did took longer to process (it took as much as thirty minutes to do one form with all its extensions) and because there was only the Ghana site, Omega employees always had a heavy workload. The heavy work-loads in turn obligated the department's employees to provide 24/7 coverage. To mini-mize errors the employees helped each other with their "reading." For example, on one visit I watched as Gifty and a co-worker processed a scanned hand-written entry. The collaborative effort resulted in what they thought was the correct reading of all items except for one. Unsure of what that item was, they flagged it. But Gifty then told me that if another Omega employee (those employees who verify initial entries for quality control, for example) happened to read it correctly, then the origi-nal keyer would be charged with an error and docked pay accordingly. In other words employees like Gifty and her friend had to make decisions about what things meant but they could not make mistakes. Working in and out of all these windows required far more than rudimentary typing and certainly more than some neutral skill set that we may label reading and writing. These were "new" practices for these women, and these practices defined the women as literate in these contexts.

Data processing required transacting with visuals for meaning mak-ing. Indeed visual literacy enabled the employees to develop the rhetoric of the digitized claim. Cynthia Selfe (2004, 69) describes visual literacy as "the ability to read, understand, value, and learn from visual materials (still photographs, videos, films, animations, still images, pictures, draw-ings, graphics)—especially as these are combined to create a text—as well as the ability to create, combine, and use visual elements (e.g., colors, forms, lines, images) and messages for the purposes of communicating." For data processors at CTI it was the visual appearance of alphabetic texts—their formatting, their lay out, their spatial representation of infor-mation, that provided processing templates for deciding which features to privilege. The fields the women enter data into provide instructions that have to be read and followed. So, for example, in order to reject a piece the keyer accessed the reject codes—this brought up a menu with multiple numbers with embedded texts. The keyer decided on the cate-gory that best matches the case and entered it. Reading, quick decision-making and technological fluency converge on the production floor. These events also required using digital texts in an integrated way: there were alphabetic literacies, as well as numeric ones. Different domains of this workplace required different practices creating microcosms of discourse communities within the larger CTI community.

A "new" dimension to "reading" practice at CTI is exemplified in the fact that some of the texts processed were not textual—women also "read" and processed graphic displays and images. The women described their online reading practices in ways that can only be construed as flexible and complex. Successful reading and data processing required background knowledge that helped women construct strategies and expectations so that violations became signals for errors. Online reading comprised scrolling, scanning and skimming for information, relying on visual rhetoric to locate sought-after information in texts. When their expectations were violated workers read with heightened attention to detail. In such cases workers had to identify the problem, know where to access the information needed to solve the problem, collaborate with coworkers on solving the problem, or decide whether to call in a supervisor. These modes of reading therefore incorporated abilities such as problem solving, reasoning, decision making and team work. Working as part of a team in turn required interpersonal skills. There was a dimension to online reading that was "new" to the women. Online reading, in whatever form it took, involved non-linear processing. The non-linearity related to working out of multiple windows at a time while holding text processed in short term memory in order to use that information in another screen environment.

The nature of literacy practices changed or were adjusted frequently through informal learning and sense making, particularly when clients changed their practices. Practices were therefore not static. CTI's clients stipulated and updated the standards by which their transactions were to be processed. Sometimes these updates were communicated to employees orally first before the updates and manuals were archived online, and in some cases employees were provided with print manuals. At departments such as Delta, employees had to take online tests each time the client changed processing codes and standards. On the production floor at CTI therefore workplace literacy was supported by a range of textual and interpersonal resources that were context-specific as client desires shaped department practices.

As Tusting (2000) argued, the constitutive multiplicity of the social practices of literacy cannot be directly observed simply because events are dynamic and changing. In fact the situated nature of practices requires them to change as situations change. This appears to be the case at CTI. Take Regina's work on a typical day. Her job required considerable on-screen reading. On one particular day she was sifting through provider and insurance correspondence that was part of the claims she was processing. She used the different pieces of correspondence as her data for processing the claims. The text-heavy correspondence was full of medical terminology, insurance terms and state statutes that govern medical coverage in the particular U.S. state. Regina read them all in order to know what to capture for the processing of the claims. There were instances where she called her Team Leader and ran her thoughts by him. In all the cases she discussed, the Team Leader agreed with her choices. Even online then, work at CTI appears to privilege alphabetic literacy, though in a rather layered fashion. While I sat by Regina, she worked on a batch that had twenty-five claims in it. Sometimes it took her an hour or more to do a batch. Most times she had to compare fields in two or three places in order to make sure she was right. Some correspondence was hand written and Regina had to take extra time decipher it. On some level CTI's assembly-line operating procedures while appearing deskilling is more accurately skilled routinization. Women had to learn how to be skilled even while their work was routinized.

## OFFLINE LITERACIES AT WORK

At CTI offline reading was print-based and such texts had various functions in this workspace. Employees mainly read texts generated by management in the form of memos, supervisor directives, corporate newsletters and other publications. Some reading was hybrid—workers who were encountering difficulties read aloud bits of text to others in order to collaborate on processing or solving problems. The workers were mainly recipients rather than generators of texts. Management-generated texts were posted on bulletin boards, on walls in the employee break room, and throughout the workplace. Supervisors often read these aloud to employees before posting them. Texts were mainly instructions, declarations, warnings, and were predominantly informational. Texts defined and regulated behavior as well, providing a mechanism to control employees. Often texts had no identifying human agents.

The rhetoric of memos to employees at CTI caught my attention almost immediately. My first encounter was with a curious memo signed by "Jack Halle." It was the only memo to employees with an identified human agent and it was posted in the lunch room. The memo said in part, "Ladies, we ask you to keep bathrooms clean and to pick up and dispose of used sanitary towels. Thank you, Jack Halle." Other memos did not have any human agents—they were signed "Management" or "Human Resources." Another memo began thus: "It has come to the attention of management that some employees have been sleeping in the room on the second floor. You are asked not to use this area for such purposes." It was signed "Human Resources." The absence of human agents rhetorically constructed management as a collective power. In the case of Jack Halle's restroom memo, the request implied that the women lacked the knowledge to make appropriate choices on disposing of used sanitary supplies. The appearance of the hygiene memo prompted me to check out the women's restrooms on each floor and I did so once a week. None ever had bathroom tissues; some had soap some of the time. Baffled by the absence of toilet tissue in the restrooms, I asked the women. They informed me that they carried their own supplies. Rita in an interview remarked that "the company is so interested in profits that it will not provide us with even toilet tissue for bathrooms. When people asked them they said if they buy it people will abuse it." Other women said the same. Talking to Kofi I asked about the women's assertions. He acknowledged that CTI had stopped putting tissues in the restroom because they were misused. As he put it "it is difficult to supply so many women with toilet roll." This may seem trivial but to the women it was more evidence that CTI did not value its employees and this perception contributed to the mistrust and suspicion that pervaded the workplace.

In contrast to CTI, the washrooms at CDN were clean, dry, and throughout my visits always had toilet tissue. Washrooms also had detergent in the wall mounted dispensers. There was a clean roll of cloth towels for wiping hands and the blow dryer worked. In the washrooms at CDN there were notices reminding employees not to leave the washrooms without washing their hands.

Working at CTI required knowing and navigating bureaucratic literacies. There was a considerable amount of offline reading, writing, speaking, and listening among employees at work. Work-related writing included requests for vacation, for other benefits, for transfers, for filing complaints and for arguing one's case for erroneous charges and deductions from wages. These required writing letters and or memos to supervisors and human resources personnel. Workers also engaged in non-work-related writing: writing that maintained social relationships and networks such as the sharing of cards and notes. While this was not officially related to work, it nonetheless enabled the construction of a social climate that enhanced the working conditions of employees. The women used their literacy abilities to gain and maintain employment as well as create and maintain social relationships at work.

English was the language officially sanctioned by CTI and it mediated practices in its workspaces. The mini sites, the scapes and the flows of CTI were officially mediated through English. However, Ghanaian languages were also used to mediate work practices among employees and in the process hybrids of language mediated practices became part of being literate in these particular contexts. Like many Ghanaians, CTI employees spoke multiple Ghanaian languages and often collaborated and solved work-related problems in those languages. Workers switched codes and practices back and forth seamlessly between English and Ghanaian languages, notably Twi, Ga, and Ewe. For example, employees would speak to coworkers in Ghanaian languages to describe processing-related challenges. The co-workers, having listened to a description of the problem, would then offer possible solutions in the Ghanaian language.

If the solution seemed acceptable, the worker translated the information into processing the onscreen data which was in English. Often, these exchanges were neither entirely in English nor a Ghanaian language— there was a mixture with technical health care terms retained in English mixed in with the Ghanaian language rendition of problems. In this way, it appears that these local literacies positively supplemented the uses of official literacies at CTI. They enabled abstract procedures to be translated into practices that were meaningful to those who did work on the production floor.

## LITERACIES AND THE NEGOTIATION OF ASYMMETRICAL POWER RELATIONS

Work communities such as CTI and CDN epitomize the kind of complex interdependence of power and knowledge conceptualized by Michel Foucault. For Foucault, both power and knowledge are relative social/ rhetorical forces. Power is not merely controlled by the dominant subject; power is unstable and to some extent decentralized. The dominant subject must have a subordinate subject in order to exercise power. Likewise, knowledge is unstable and to some extent decentralized. "Truth" must be constantly re-constituted in the face of the potential of it being disregarded. Different groups negotiate, appropriate or contest these power-knowledge dynamics to construct and or to represent their roles. Applying Foucault's power-knowledge insight, we can see how literacy practices located employees and managers in different power constellations and relations at CTI and CDN. While I make general observations based on my data analyses, I also focus on Nola's practices, contestations, and appropriations of this power-knowledge tension to illuminate how power works in this outsourcing site. In addition to Nola's experiences, I also use interviews with Kofi, the middle management employee, to understand how worker's abilities are represented.

At the point of recruiting, the two outsourcing sites presented prospective employees with different power-knowledge narratives and in effect promised different employer/employee relationships. For prospective employees, CDN's strategy of foregrounding its claim of training employees in-house projected an ethos of investing in employees. In its recruitment appeals the company explicitly assumed the role of a "sponsor" of workplace literacy development (Brandt 2001). This stance meant that CDN effectively erased the fact that it depended on the entrepreneurial self-making of would-be employees—after all the company depended on the women having some higher education as a foundation for recruiting and training them. Yet that education and the discursive spaces and practices it enabled also meant that the negotiation of the power-knowledge dynamic at work was more nuanced and more complex than it would have been had the company downplayed its training role and acknowledged its dependence on the employees' prior education. I will return to this point below.

There was variability in literacy sponsorship and how this mapped onto the two sites. CTI's approach of using control over discrete measurable skill sets as conditions for employment and the very nature of what data processing at CTI entailed presented employees with a different narrative on power-knowledge and also constructed an ethos that was somewhat different from the "sponsor of literacy development" ethos that CDN presented. These differential constructions of workplaces linked employee agency with literate practices with divergent effects. Corporate culture at CTI, at least as it was represented by site management and the parent company, might be called "American" only because it was different from what the women recognized as "local." The company proffered a narrative of going "above and beyond" for customers in order to stay competitive, a situation that translated into expectations for high productivity and perfect quality targets. The employees, however, made their own sense of this narrative. To Nola and her peers "going above and beyond" simply meant being pushed too hard, and this push was underscored by the management practice of writing up employees for errors and terminating them on their third infringement rather than investing in and retraining employees. The fact that the company was always firing, then hiring and training new recruits left veteran employees with little doubt about CTI's lack of concern for the professional development of its employees. The practice is however congruent to the narrative presented to prospective employees at recruiting—CTI was in fact not interested in "sponsoring" work-related literacy development for employees and that position created a culture of soft coercion.

At CTI the control of work-related knowledge was intimately linked to the pace of work which was also linked to wages. In other words control of situated knowledge was connected to reward and punishment. Literacy was a mechanism for getting things done but it was also the mechanism for exercising the systemic power of those in the higher ranks of CTI. Literacy was a means of disciplining rank and file employees into complying with how the systemic power of others was exercised. The rhetoric of memos to employees, as I noted above, was one example of how literacy events at CTI became mechanisms for the exertion of the collective power of management. The absence of human agents inscribed management as omnipresent. Power was further exercised through the regime of layers of surveillance that I have already alluded to. Though the women often spoke about the ubiquitous management and their representatives, the women mastered and used work-related knowledge and the literate practices associated with them both in ways that CTI sanctioned as well as in ways that subverted what was sanctioned. For example, the women bonded around illicit watching of Mexican soap operas on the production floor. These soap operas then became the focus of conversations that inevitably led to communal problem solving with older women offering advice to younger women with relationship trouble advice. These practices were in fact acts of resistance but they are also acts of here and now embodiment that women enacted as a way to talk back to official power. They demonstrate the ways in which flows other than the ones officially underwritten by CTI influenced the pool of flows and thus the culture of the workplace.

Some management personnel at CTI understood acquisition of knowledge through the lens of social class and this affected how work-related literacies were constructed and represented. To highlight this facet of CTI I use interviews with Kofi. In one of my conversations with him, Kofi remarked that the management was trying to weed out as many unqualified people as they could, though they were not always successful. Considering how the company positions skill in recruiting, I asked about education and its relationship to the work done at the site. Kofi noted that their goal has been to seek and "hire highly qualified, educated people." Unfortunately for CTI because "the work is so low-skill and monotonous, most of those people do not find that work stimulating" and therefore leave. Further, in his view there was "a cultural element" to this. According to Kofi,

> In Ghana certain types of people go to secretarial schools. And there is a vast difference in the secretarial schools. When we have been fortunate to get people from government secretarial, they have been really good. Government secretarial graduates have access to good jobs and they often do not take our data entry jobs because of that.

I asked Kofi to explain what he meant by "certain kinds of people"—he noted that there is clearly "a social class element"—secretarial schools are considered vocational and the people who go there are often either unable to get into Senior Secondary School (SSS) because of poor grades or cannot afford to pay for an SSS education. Private secretarial schools "do not have much of a standard—they take anybody who can pay the tuition." The government secretarial schools have entry requirements. Since class has a lot to do with access to education, Kofi argued, many people who end up working as data entry clerks may come from "low class backgrounds." In fact Kofi used the term "ignorant" to describe the women who fell in this category. In spite of his characterization of the work of data entry as not stimulating, low skill and monotonous he nonetheless talked about "the cultural knowledge" that employees needed to have in order to read and make sense of names, streets, apartments, medical discourse, etc., and, he acknowledged, this was hard for people who have very little interaction with print. As he put it, "They don't have a reading culture. Even some of our managers are not readers." In Kofi's view many of the CTI employees lacked the gravitas and cultural sophistication that comes with what he perceived as good education. Kofi's position here shows that as a management representative he did not grasp the complexities of the literacies and practices that women controlled at CTI. His point about reading is quite remarkable considering what the data processors did and how.

Visual and print texts facilitated how instructions were given. For Nola and her peers in the Alpha department the visual dominated the "literacies in use" and "meanings in use" that were prevalent, valued and that defined a worker as competent. Nola not only controlled Alpha contextual knowledge per the quality and pace of her work, but it was clear that both her supervisors and peers considered her to be knowledgeable. Nola's group leader described her as follows:

> She is one of our best—hard working and respectful most of the time. She can have opinions but she is good and helpful. The other women respect her too—sometimes maybe they listen to her too much because she is with the employee welfare people. You see, some people want some changes here. I think she is one of them—I don't know. She is good. Good education, knows the job, and helps the new people.

In several interviews, Nola talked about her understanding of her location as a data processor at CTI. Nola obviously understood that being a data processor meant she was at the low end of the hierarchy at work. She clearly understood the power relationships at her workplace. Nonetheless she created her own spaces for asserting her agency. For example, she was actively involved in the Employee Welfare Association and complained that management had high-jacked it by micro-managing its agenda and by always putting forward its own agenda items so that employees hardly got the time to discuss issues that were important to their well-being at work. Alpha never had any air-conditioning during my entire time at the site. CTI had purchased giant fans but they only blew hot air. Nola and the other fifty-seven women worked in a room that had fifty-seven computers and a number of servers generating heat in a tropical climate. While observing Alpha one day Nola asked me this pointed question: "Would a white person work in this heat?" My honest answer was I didn't think so. Here I note that though Nola asked about a "white person" that descriptor captures something else: it registers the fact that the only non-Ghanaian at the site was the manager, an American who happens to have been white and whose work area had a functioning air conditioner. The significance of this was not lost on Nola.

Nola used her new-found technology expertise as well as her work-related literacies to enhance her knowledge and to create viable alternative spheres of power for herself and her peers: She often researched CTI's parent company. She knew the company's stock price, its quarterly earnings and would always "read" the actions of the site management as ways to maximize profit for stock holders. To Nola, CTI's penchant for lean operations and what she perceived as maximum profit-making translated into a state of affairs where her wages and benefits were always in flux. To Nola, reducing or cutting what employees were given seemed a fairly straight forward way for management to control costs. Nola described her workplace as full of pressure and stress. In numerous conversations on the production floor Nola often returned to the issue of heat in her department; asserting that the heat affected their productivity. To the management, however, heat induced by a malfunctioning cooling system was irrelevant—errors were errors and the women lost wages because of them.

In one instance, Nola and the other women at Alpha refused to work after CTI unilaterally cut their piece/batch rate. After their immediate supervisors tried and failed in convincing them to work, a member of the management team was summoned. The management representative provided assurances that they would reverse the cut before the women started work. Such overt challenges to the power-knowledge dynamic, though rare at CTI during my time there, exemplify the ways in which Nola and her peers constructed and represented their own interventions as human agents. When I asked Nola how they had decided on this action, she explained that the night shift employees were the first to get the news and they coordinated their response using cell phone text messaging. A few leaders discussed possible responses and then as a group they came to a consensus that the day-time shift will play out their plan since management was available at the site during the regular 8:00 am to 5:00 pm workday. Once they agreed on the work stoppage strategy each member of the department got a text message informing her or him of the impending action. Employees arrived at work and put their plan in motion.

If globalizing processes and their attendant fusion of cultures, values and images created both a material and discursive CTI, it is clear that the different categories of its workers internalized different versions and that these were always under contestation and negotiation. The scapes and flows of CTI created literate practices that were intricately woven into these material and discursive constructions and representations and literacies were intimately implicated in these processes. Technology convergence has been an incipient catalyst to workforce skill consolidation. Whether one worked at CTI doing health care related transactional processing or at CDN doing data entry, indexing, transcribing, call center customer servicing, etc. employees spent their work time similarly; in front of computer terminals with keyboards and other accoutrements doing essentially the same thing. Even in the global South therefore, computer-related skills are now generic skills required for just about all white collar jobs even if employees required many ancillary abilities beyond those basic computer skills. On some level even though ICT-related skills are creating new kinds of work for many workers offshore the control of these skills also simultaneously makes workers fairly dispensable as others with similar skills can be found to replace them. These conflicting dynamics were especially apparent at CTI, where employees had new work opportunities because of the private investments they had made in acquiring skills but where opportunity was narrowly constrained.

The foregoing discussion has foregrounded the nature and context of literacy acquisition, its sponsors, the links among local, sub-local, and non-local practices, and the dynamics that frame the ways various actors negotiated, appropriated and contested them. It has also demonstrated how citizens acquired knowledge as well as the sources and uses of that knowledge in textual/discursive cultures shaped by non-local pressures. The discussion here supports Brandt and Clinton's proposition that we examine how literacy ability "travels, integrates and endures" in new spaces (2002, 347). It also suggests how we may look at what is localizing and what is globalizing about local practices that characterize these sites. At both CTI and CDN literacy events and practices were localized as much globalized. In some ways practices were simultaneously local and global (glocal), the contours of their intersections could be mapped, and their "transcontextualized and transcontextualizing potentials" (2002, 347) were visible. These workspaces were translocal, transnational and contested.

# EIGHT

## The "New" World of Work: Women and Workplace Literacy Practices

Offshore outsourcing transcends nation-states even as it concurrently inhabits physical national boundaries. Offshore work, in its various permutations, is therefore, a localization of globalized dynamics. The local offers an encasement of the global (Sassen 2007, 80) and in places like CTI and CDN these global/local articulations occur in both material and virtual spaces. Indeed as has been demonstrated throughout this book, virtual workspaces are now significant domains of contemporary globalization *vis a vis* labor. It is apparent that situated gender-focused analyses of specific "global/local" workspaces highlight the impact of globalizing processes on particular women in particular workspaces. These analyses make obvious what Brandt and Clinton term the "transcontextualized and transcontextualizing potentials" of local literacy practices (2002, 347). But, at best, the local is in fact a shorthand metaphor because there is no essentialized local practice that traverses all scapes and all sites. The local is hard to pin down. The foregoing analyses illuminate the intersections of globalization, gender, and literate practices in outsourcing at the two sites and illustrate how those supposedly excluded from the benefits of globalization, particularly women, are reframing the terms of their work. As the analyses of practices at CTI and CDN demonstrate, there is reciprocity between the gendering of labor practices at these sites and the globalizing processes out of which the locus of work is constituted. These gendering dynamics have feminized labor practices in both the physical and virtual workspaces that the employees (most of whom are women) inhabit. The net result is a complex interplay between benefits and costs of globalization. For local communities in these arrangements to balance costs and consequences—for communities to reap some positive outcomes—it is necessary to disaggregate the multiple sub-issues, articulate how they map on to each other and how they intersect. A critical nexus, in my view, is the one bundled around education, literacy learning, knowledge and work and how that bundling maps onto gender.

The rhetoric on workplace literacies in the Knowledge Economy is dominated by managerial philosophies that assert that the literacy demands have changed as workplace hierarchies have become flatter. The boundaries between management and rank and file employees, according to these philosophies, are increasingly blurred. A corollary of this discourse on this new work environment is that many workers lack the needed skills to function effectively in knowledge-saturated workplaces. Systems that educate workers have therefore come under intense scrutiny as politicians, business leaders, community leaders, organizations, and parents all argue for what they believe to be the solution to the perceived education crises and their resultant workplace literacy crises. While research (Billett 2007; Chappel, Scheeres, and Solomon 2007; Gee et al. 1996) has indeed documented the changing demands of work, it has also documented the need for new kinds of workers with different types of education and training. This body of research points to rethinking education and training in ways that are different from the programs currently espoused by reform movements associated with donor programs. Gee et al.'s work in a Silicon Valley electronics assembly plant, for example, documents how realities of these workplaces tend not to square with the rhetoric of managerial philosophies about new work. They show that far from "empowering" workers, many of the new literacy practices workers encountered were in fact disempowering. Other research has corroborated these points (Butterwick, Jubas, and Zhu 2007; Farrell 2009; Mirchandani and Maitra 2007). And indeed evidence from the current study also supports these claims.

In this last chapter I highlight the significant issues that the study foregrounds, how they intersect with other research on workplaces, and the contributions that this project makes. Lastly, I discuss the implications of globalization for work in places like Ghana and what conclusions, if any, can be drawn.

## EDUCATION, KNOWLEDGE AND WORK

As Ghana positions itself as an IT hub of Sub-Saharan Africa, it has had to concomitantly create a workforce capable of providing IT-related expertise to employers. On the surface, a critical site for producing this globally skilled workforce is the education system. As previous chapters show, part of the Economic Reform Program mandated education reform. The reform process aims to provide a version of education deemed appropriate for competing in the global economy. The reconfiguration of education, as per World Bank (2003) propositions, has also meant a realign-

ment of the very social, cultural and pedagogic assumptions that under-
gird approaches to educating young people. A byproduct of the reform
process has been the state's active participation in reconfiguring the relationship between students and teachers, parents and children, as well as
the place of the individual (Farrell and Fenwick 2007). In the case of
Ghana the reform blueprint moved teachers away from transmission
models to more hands-on and interactive practices. Interactive pedagogies are generally credited with producing flexibility, creativity and critical thinking among students; qualities generally associated with globalized work. Interactive pedagogies are also generally seen as pedagogies
of empowerment. But these pedagogic assumptions ran counter to traditional codes of social interaction among adults, teachers and authority
figures and the young in Ghanaian society. Therefore, the extent to which
these shifts have affected the authority of teachers in classrooms, for example, is certainly worth examining. For my purposes here I will only
note that such reconfiguration of interactions also ultimately reframes the
relationship between employees and their employers. As previous chapters show, at both CDN and CTI employer-employee relationships,
though demarcated by differential power relations, were fairly fluid and
constantly under negotiation. Women such as Nola and Emma understood these power/authority demarcations but carved out spaces within
which to function as human agents and from within which they resisted
or subverted their superiors. At CTI acts of resistance contested the various disciplinary surveillance regimes operative in the workplace.

Education reform proposals in general and arguments for literacy acquisition in particular imply that an educated or literate workforce or
citizenry is a solution to the persistent social problems that plague less
developed societies like Ghana. As some authors have already noted
(Farrell & Fenwick 2007; Lauder, Brown, Dillabough & Halsey 2006) such
positions not only conflate economic and social well being and education,
they also mask the complex intractable disparities between groups and
among subgroups within particular nation states. For example, though
access to education has improved for girls and women in Ghana, it is
clear that there is still a disparity in access to secondary and tertiary
education—but these are the levels of educational attainment that could
transform work options the most (UNESCO Global Education Digest).
Thus, any agenda to significantly improve the educational outcomes for
girls and women does need to confront access to higher education and
career preparation but it has to frame the process rather self-consciously
so that it does not leave low-end work as the best option.

A significant challenge in the forgoing discussion is discerning the
layers of the processes of feminization and how women navigated these
processes. Understanding these processes will be critical to ensuring that
girls and women are not left with low-end work as the only viable entry
point into the wage labor market. As preceding chapters make clear,

outsourced work at CTI and CDN was by and large feminized. The work was low-end, labor-intensive, repetitive, stressful and boring. The conditions under which the work was done were also feminized. The manner in which labor practices and conditions in the form of rules and regulations operated at CTI and to a lesser extent CDN demonstrate this. Women were the majority of employees at both sites but the key point is that the low-end work they did would not be taken by men unless, of course, those men were desperate and had no other options. The few men who worked in data processing made it very clear that they were looking for better options. The non-data processing men at both sites were in positions of authority or they did high-end work and were paid accordingly. While the women worked for low wages, at CTI at least, the management could also actively work against union organizing. Furthermore, wage labor was in addition to the roles women had as mothers, care providers and homemakers. A number of the women at CTI in particular were still expected to fulfill these roles even as the new job openings that globalization was bringing into their communities beckoned them. That said, women like Fatuma and Shakira were using work outside the home to renegotiate their relationships and obligations at home. Yet they also noted the difficulty of being independent and having one's own money. As Shakira put it "they [Ghanaian men] don't want liberated women." Shakira pointed out that the traditional Ghanaian view is "that women belong in the kitchen." But Shakira and a few of the other married women said their spouses see them more as partners than as wives they had to control and look after. The presence of so many women in workplaces like CTI and CDN is serving as a catalyst for the re-writing of gender relations for both the women and the other people in their lives. Their presence is providing a heuristic of sorts for negotiating and learning new gender-related literacies. If nation building and contribution to it is gendered—then more importantly, the women at CTI and CDN saw wage work as their contribution to national development. Again, how some of these women read their work re-writes what it means to be part of a national development agenda.

Another layer of the processes of feminization relates to the offshore location of the work itself. In discourses on globalization, the North has traditionally taken on the markers of masculinity while the South has tended to be feminized. This raises the larger question of the relationship between globalized work and the feminization of labor. As Manuh has noted, gender activism—activism on behalf of women's full economic and social participation—in Ghana has been almost exclusively "women's work" and as a result gender activism has been indigenized in order to chart a course for social and political transformation (2007). In Ghana as in other regions of the world, globalization has not changed the gender division of labor; it has only widened gender disparities and amplified the feminization of poverty (Hawkesworth 2006). The lowest-paying jobs continue to be assigned to women and for poor women existing inequalities and insecurities have only deepened. These unequal labor conditions leave women and girls vulnerable and the vulnerabilities of a feminized workforce are further accentuated by the inability or the unwillingness of the government to enforce its own labor laws and regulations. In the case of the women at CTI it appears that despite the government's laudable move of establishing a cabinet level portfolio to oversee issues affecting women and children, transnational entities employed Ghanaian women under conditions that broke labor laws and other legal protections but employees had little or no recourse for intervention.

Another vital issue highlighted by the study is the place of the individual in society or her/his community. The data clearly suggest an apparent shift of the responsibilities for training citizens from the state, or the collective, to the individual, or the worker. This shift, a core principle of neoliberalism, is a direct outcome of structural adjustment and economic reform programs. It is apparent from the current data that work-related training for the employees working at CTI and, to a lesser extent, CDN was almost always acquired through ingenuity, initiative and resourcefulness in the free marketplace. For the women at CTI and CDN, the absence of state funded technology-related training and their desire to enter the wage labor market meant being individually responsible for funding their access to technology-related skills that they then adapted for the work they ended up doing in CTI and CDN. This is a critical point considering the levels of unemployment, the traditional patriarchal structure of Ghanaian society and the tendency to assign low-end skill work to women. For the women, securing technology skills was a significant pathway to the wage market. But such free market entrepreneurship is dependent on financial sacrifice that leaves behind people who cannot muster the resources for training. The CDN practice of offering intensive on the job technical training at least assumes cost-sharing between employer and employees. But that was of course contingent on employees making sizeable initial investments in higher education.

Technological innovation and distribution makes offshore work possible. Outsourced BPO work such as that done by the women at CTI and CDN in Ghana is thus representative of work in the emerging Knowledge Economy. Knowledge work, according to Farrell, operates with the assumption of "literate engagement on a global scale" (2009, 181) even as it simultaneously acknowledges reliance on local practices. This assumption implicitly assigns to the education system the responsibility of career preparation. However the experiences of the women at CTI and CDN underscore the conventionally accepted axiom among literacy studies researchers that literate practices are always embedded in some social context. In these workplaces, workers adapted or developed specialized practices that were tied to their local histories, politics and economics (Farrell 2009, 181). Indeed the de-contextualized skills that employees controlled as they came into the workplace had to be adapted to the context of work rather quickly if employees were to survive and meet production targets—particularly at CTI. While English was the dominant language through which practices were mediated, local languages were extensively in play. The results were complex conversations and negotiations between local and globally instigated literate practices. These points support Farrell's contention that the field ought to do more to understand the specific contours of literate practices in the emerging economy. Farrell notes, "In much of the debate around the globalisation of work and the Knowledge Economy the centrality of literate practice is acknowledged as important, but conceptually unproblematic, and the debate moves on" (2009, 182). The current study foregrounds the extent to which literate practices are complex and conceptually problematic to pin down at these sites.

A critical dimension to knowledge work at CTI and CDN is knowledge translation and transfer. For Farrell & Fenwick (2007) the level at which knowledge work is done—research and development, techno-scientific work, knowledge mobilization and transfer and so on require different ability sets and levels of abstractions. For the rank and file employees at both CTI and CDN, work required making sense of processes and procedures that came down through the hierarchy. First, those "above" at both sites "imported" or developed and translated complex practices, processes and procedures from their levels of abstraction into useful knowledge and information for employees. The level of abstraction was often linked to the non-local origin of practices and procedures—for example, adherence to HIPPA. Second, the "translation" process required middle management to factor in local culture, capabilities, sensibilities, tools, values and resources. As Farrell and Fenwick (2007, 3–4) note, it is out of these negotiations that "common knowledge"—what one may call localized knowledge—is created, internalized and used to inform the many micro-processes that employees use at particular work sites, at particular moments. At CTI it was this translation—or rather the inability to recognize this translation as necessary for the work the women did— that, I believe, informed the practice of withholding critical information from employees. As middle management personnel failed to translate knowledge into a form that would be useful to rank and file employees, often assuming things were too complex for them, they also in the process closed off opportunities to authorize employees to assume ownership of the knowledge they used or created on the job. Instead of creating incentives and a culture of support, withholding what management saw as complex knowledge undercut the potential bonds that could have developed among employees and between employees and their supervisors. It also, I believe, undercut or limited the identities that employees negotiated or could negotiate around work. At CTI in particular, it created a mistrustful and stressful work environment. What management at

CTI saw as lack of effort or understanding was for the women a set of strategies to work without being invested in what one did. The system of punishing employees for errors was a significant disincentive to productive knowledge creation on the job at CTI.

Communication played a critical role in getting work done and in solving problems as production leaders and supervisors worked with employees on production floors. These localized qualities and the languages used to negotiate/mediate them were not skill sets that could be taught outside the social context of the work environments into which they were to be used. Furthermore, even though these women did "knowledge" work, this work involved a good deal of physical effort in the form of sitting at terminals for long periods using alpha numeric keys. The speed at which they worked while paying attention to accuracy and the repetitive nature of most of what they did made any clear distinction between physical and mental labor hard to maintain. Employees created knowledge on the job, albeit localized knowledge—a localized hybrid. At particular sites the knowledge needed to do specific departmental work, such as that done at Alpha at CTI, was different from what was needed for another department such as Delta at the same site. And the knowledge base needed for work at CTI was different from CDN. Yet the learning that women did on the job was always in the context of the larger outsourcing market. On a general level, the women's work involved fairly complex detective work. Talk happened around literacy events instigated by digitized texts. But these complexities were jarringly contradictory when juxtaposed with the hardship of the struggles of making one's way home after work at CDN and at CTI (when women worked overtime).

If management assumptions and practices constrained identity negotiation around work, they also simultaneously opened up possibilities because, as I have demonstrated, work and its attendant literacy practices also created spaces where women constructed working identities. While women at CTI in particular entered the workplace touting their typing skills, their uses of technologies added a post-industrial "value" to those skills. But the technologies of work for the most part made that work boring, repetitive, alienating, and stressful. The women at CDN on the other hand came into the workplace often without typing skills because their employer valued other qualities but provided typing training and support on the job. The orientation of the employer at CDN—the conscious decision to hire employees with higher education backgrounds rather than those with typing skills—seems to have created a different set of expectations at CDN. That may also perhaps be related to the kinds of services provided. On some level then, the literacy practices needed to get work done at both CTI and CDN go beyond mere neutral skills. Labor and literate practices at CTI and CDN therefore have implications for policy debates on job creation, and the fashioning of genuinely equitable working conditions for workers in societies such as Ghana, especially as more and more of these societies become hubs on the global communication network.

*Implications of Networks*

Technology has had dramatic impact on work arrangements. In these workspaces, technologies and their attendant networks were the architecture for fashioning specific scapes at the different sites. The network was the conduit of flows originating elsewhere. For the women at these sites, technology not only brought on changes to life at work, it also highlighted the dramatic impact these technologies—and the flows they pool—have on low-end workers. It is tempting to operate as though the effects of networks on work are gender-neutral, but I will contend that they are not. The few women in positions of authority at CDN pointed out the dearth of women and girls who enroll to study the natural sciences, computer sciences and engineering in Ghana—one might say this fits into the global trend. But they also pointed out the fact that apart from upper income households, access to computers and the internet is not a common phenomenon. Indeed with a per capita income of $1230.00 in 2010 (World Bank), technology purchase requires significant resource outlay. It is not surprising then that by and large, few women are producers of information technology, either as internet content providers, programmers, designers or fixers of computers and other technologies. Therefore, women are conspicuously absent in the decision-making structures in relation to IT policy. A series of factors, including those of education, language, time, costs, geographical location of facilities and social and cultural norms constrain women's access to ICTs. Consequently large numbers of women are concentrated in the end-user; low-skilled segment of IT jobs related to word processing, data entry and other low-end IT enabled sectors.

ICTs had a somewhat complex effect on the women who worked at CTI and CDN. The ICTs that enabled globalized work at CTI and CDN were underwritten by state supported investment in infrastructure—an investment that is part of the commitment by the state to be a player in the knowledge economy. That strategy has clearly paid off as it has created viable employment for the many women and men who work in outsourcing in Ghana. Nonetheless, it is clear that Ghana and in effect the women and men who work at CTI and CDN do not have much political or economic leverage in the larger global economy. This explains the location of high volume low-end feminized work there. It also helps explain why labor practices that break local labor laws persisted, particularly at CTI.

The gender divide as far as technology is concerned is underscored by efforts such as the Group of Eight (G 8) digital task force that was set up after the Okinawa summit of 2000 to work on ways to eliminate this divide. Globally the United Nations considers access to IT as the third most important issue facing women after poverty and violence (UN 2000). As Pande (2005) and Huws (2000) have noted, ICT use at work reproduces the gender division of labor in the home. The development of both simple and sophisticated but secure interfaces allows companies like CTI and CDN to monitor work, keep records of the number of key strokes per minute, find error rates or the number of processed items, track the duration of breaks and compare productivity of one group of employees against another (Pande, 59). In short, networks enabled by ICTs make the domination of employees easy. Sophisticated networks with powerful surveillance capabilities permit companies to control employees' time on the job. At CTI, for example, that control was linked directly to productivity, and I'd argue that this had a lot to do with the women's perceptions about the quality of their lives at work and beyond. The network's capabilities highlighted the limited control the women had over their lives at work, particularly at CTI. As Huws (2000) has noted, autonomy and control over work processes contribute to a sense of well-being and job satisfaction at work. Inversely, lack of control over one's time at work contributes to stress-related disorders. Conflicts at CTI were centrally connected to time and thus to ultimately the quality of life of employees. As a number of the research participants noted, these jobs were transient. CTI is only in Ghana for as long as the global labor conditions sustain them.

The transient nature of work at CTI and CDN underscores the fact that in these arrangements, it is the work that is mobile. Indeed a component of the intense pressure in these workspaces relates to the pressure brought on by the network which is itself a conduit for the pressures inherent in the highly competitive global circuit of outsourced work. While the network makes the location of work in Ghana possible, it also highlights the mobility of the work itself. If conditions were no longer favorable to a company like CTI, it could relocate work somewhere else on its global network. Because CTI had a global presence and moved jobs on its worldwide network, its operations were standardized so that all employees followed the same procedures and protocols. This also made the shifting and the flows of work across borders practically effortless and unproblematic. Yet as chapters 6 and 7 demonstrate, standardization does not erase locally influenced practices, nor does it preclude attempts at creating hybridized versions of the "standard." The women who worked at both CTI and CDN brought their ideas, history, and problems into their workplace and it is from these locations that they negotiated their understandings of what company policy required of them. Labor practices at CTI were not homogenized—rather they were hybridized as employees negotiated practices proffered by their employers from their local cultural location.

The other question virtual work at CTI and CDN raises is of course where work is located. When women were asked where they worked, they often named their material locations as the place of work. However when I pointed out the fact that the network was in a way placeless, interesting discussions about place ensued. Indeed placelessness underscores the contingent and de-localizable nature of this stage of globalized work and the ways in which it creates geography without distance, and history without time—even for those who do low-end work. The work the women did in the network happened in a placeless environment—an environment that was de-local or perhaps a-local. Clients could download their completed tasks from anywhere—geography, as physical space between clients and the women who did the work—was irrelevant. The network also obliterated any notion of time between client and worker across physical space.

Despite of all the barriers and hardships, women were proud of the fact that they worked outside their homes and in the official economy. Additionally, globalized work and the attendant technology-related abilities that women learned to control were useful to women outside the workplace. Most of the women maintained online lives outside the workplace even though none owned computers. They patronized cybercafés, maintained email addresses, and used most of their online times to email, chat and surf. CDN women used the in-house cybercafé and many of the CTI women were frequent patrons of cybercafés. The online lives of women outside of work were in fact, extensions of the lives the women navigated online at work.

## WORK AND THE IMAGINATION: OF "SCAPES" AND "FLOWS"

The content that made up work at CTI and CDN originated outside the workers' local communities and, as earlier chapters demonstrate, doing this work necessitated a level of enculturation. Depending on where they worked, women learned the names of U.S. states, cities and towns. They learned zip codes, medical terminology, and the discursive practices of U.S. medical and health care industries. They learned what Americans go to health care providers for. They learned about U.S. banking, Wall Street quarterly reports, stocks, and customer service among other things. They learned about American sports teams, weather, food, holidays, etc. In effect, work was a specific site for multiple levels of sense-making and the acquisition of the literacies that went with these. That sense-making, I would argue, also engaged the imagination. Outsourcing work of the kind the women did at both CTI and CDN inserted workers into different spheres of experience. These spheres—whether health-related or finance-related, simultaneously invited imaginative work on the part of workers. Indeed, women talked repeatedly about how much U.S. geography they knew as a result of their jobs. They talked about how they wanted to travel to the United States because of what they now know as a result of their jobs. The use of their technology-aided skills in cybercafés further opened up access to flows of global media, images and other content. Their use of cybercafés, their consumption of U.S. media products, and the DVDs they watched illicitly on the job all complicated and layered what was imagined about other places and other lives. Work therefore offered material, discursive and virtual spaces in which to imagine not only places but also to negotiate identities. As I have argued elsewhere (Quarshie Smith 2005), this imaginative work is in many ways a precursor to migration. Imaginative work makes "virtual immigrant[s]" (Mathews) of people at the very least. A level of imaginative work relates to the America or American that women imagined. In fact it wasn't wanting to be American so much as wanting to be their imaginary construct; a construct that they had created. Work offered women a way to imagine places and faraway alternative lives, and the constant "I want to visit America" verbalized how one might turn the imagined into reality.

## IS GLOBALIZED WORK EMPOWERING FOR THESE GHANAIAN WOMEN?

Debates about outsourcing inevitably turn to questions of justice and empowerment. And the question of who defines justice and empowerment and in what context is generally not straightforward. My approach here is to draw on Held and McGrew (2007) and specifically Pogge (2007, 213) to attempt to address the issue. At a minimum an empowering "good life" for women who work in places like CTI and CDN should be that work should not make their condition any worse and should bring them no more harm than they would face without that work—a standard Pogge (2007) uses to judge the benefits of globalization for the poor. In other words an argument that the women at least have jobs—and in fact just about all of them were grateful to have jobs—should not in itself be seen as a benefit just as, as Pogge (2007) notes, we will not accept an argument that the husband who now beats his wife less frequently is somehow benefiting the wife. At some point then we have to accept some standard of social justice that, at the minimum, is designed to honor the human rights of employees and earn them wages that take them over the World Bank poverty standard benchmark of $2.00 a day. Further, I'd argue, rights at work are in fact part of what makes work just. To explore this minimal standard I use Nola's experience. Nola's wages for a two week period of 09/01/2004 to 09/15/2004 was ¢369,542.84; with the then exchange rate of ¢9,240 = US$1.00 she made $39.99. Since she worked 7 days a week to make up for leaving at 2:00 pm daily for her college classes, her daily wage, including her overtime hours was $2.86. By the

World Bank benchmark this globalized job was at best a double-edged sword—it offered Nola an entrance into wage work and provided her with independent income. However, without some state enforcement of labor laws, without wages that took her and other people beyond $2.86 a day, this work could not be labeled "empowering." Indeed, it is only by "reading" this workspace as gendered that one can unmask the harm this work was doing to these women—the "reading" is contrary to what the World Bank professes and is contrary to what advocates of the position that globalization is easing the plight of the poor want us to believe. In effect we have to consider the extent to which globalization advances or constrains advancement towards particular ideals of the "good life" or how globalizing processes hinder different "ways of life" for particular communities at particular moments. For, after all, Nola did say when she first started at CTI she made "good money." As CTI externalized the costs of doing business in Ghana onto employees (as in the penalties for errors, for example) Nola's wages declined and will only continue to decline. As long as CTI continues to actively work against employees organizing for collective representation and as long as the state proves unable to enforce its labor laws, Nola will continue to work under unjust conditions.

Nonetheless, work empowered Nola to seek other avenues to self-improvement. Work provided both a motivation and the means to seek a baccalaureate education. The opportunity to train, to work outside the domestic sphere, and to contribute to community was clearly positive for Nola's sense of self and well being. Having an independent income enabled Nola to define a self-identity that navigated the boundaries of social mores—she was single, she was young, she was an independent working woman, yet she lived at home. Her work and her leadership abilities also garnered her respect both at work and in her church community. The abilities she used at CTI were important for supporting groups such as the choir at her church. Nola had been her church's secretary the previous year and was involved in leadership activities. Thus, while CTI offered tenuous economic empowerment, the work offered Nola other intangibles. Some of these intangibles demanded the investment of time, something Nola often did not have. There was therefore a tension between what globalized work offered and what Nola could do with it.

## LINKS TO POLICY AND PRACTICE: SOME IMPLICATIONS AND RECOMMENDATIONS

A significant discursive trope for the exportation of tedious low-end work offshore has been print-related English literacy; skill-based print-related literacy to be exact. It is often said that low-end work such as that performed at sites like CTI and CDN is sent off-shore because on-shore workers make too many mistakes or are too expensive. For developing economies the outsourced work is accompanied by reform programs and incentive packages meant to attract as many of these jobs as possible. However, reforms have not translated into better education and career prospects for women and girls, nor have they resulted in better enforcement of legal protections in workplaces. Indeed, despite educational reform, many of the women at CTI and CDN went through schools where the literacies of slate, chalk, paper, pencil and print technologies were the only options offered. To gain a foothold in the new workplaces, many women had to finance their own access to new technologies. For the career prospects of women and girls to improve, there needs to be a re-commitment of resources by the state to education and particularly to the new literacies related to the effective use of information and communication. There need to be public policy initiatives that go beyond mere ICT adoption and narrow skills-oriented approaches to nurturing complex, situated and nuanced literacy achievement among all citizens. Considering the dearth of female enrollment in Science, Technology, Engineering and Mathematics (STEM) education, it is not surprising that there are few women contributing to policy initiatives in these areas. While women's groups have been working to encourage more girls to enter these fields, it is critical that the State and its agents develop long-term strategies to attract, mentor and place women in STEM.

Offshore work is creating conditions for hybridizing gender/sexual politics and both women and men have to learn the literacies related to such politics. As I learned at CDN, when women work in programming, they are often minorities in a male-dominated environment. Women in such work situations need technical education as well as education on harassment. Their male co-workers also need education on harassment so as to stop labeling harassing behaviors as "joking." A male programmer at CDN confidently told me, "In Ghana we do not have harassment at work; we don't have a word for this in our local languages. Some women just copy that from outside"—he said this even while he conceded that just about every one of his male counterparts has had a conversation with Ms. Naku (the supervisor) over inappropriate behavior towards the only female programmer in their midst. Additionally, workplaces also need to enforce protections. The enforcement of legal protections for all workers will ensure women's well-being in the workplace.

## CONTRIBUTIONS OF THE PROJECT

The foregoing discussion contributes to the field on two levels: on the level of methodology and on the level of theory. On the level of methodology, using a multi-sited design that drew on Saukko's (2003) reading of Appadurai (1997) and Marcuse (1998a), the project enacts an examination of how what being literate in offshore outsourcing practices looks like from different perspectives and from different locations (Saukko, 195–196). The sites in the study each had different mini-sites within them. These mini-sites offered sub-local contexts within which to examine the nature and complexities of flows and how these affected practices. Further, this approach to design located offshore outsourcing within wider local/global contexts opens up for examination the connections and disconnections between the foci of the study and other social processes framing the experiences of the women at the sites. The idea of scapes and flows contributes analytic tools to connect the spheres that layer reality in CTI and CDN. Thus one could trace labor and literate practices, images, policy, emotions, embodiment strategies, etc., within sites as well as across them and thereby make it possible to foreground the multiplicity of cultures at CTI and CDN.

Another methodological contribution is adaptation to the participant observer role in the face of the access limits to proprietary spaces. The shift to the observant participant stance was supplemented with verbal-in-process-talk-me-through interviews that helped me to learn what the women did. As more proprietary spaces become the location of work, and as owners set limits on where researchers may go, adaptations to canonical practices will become increasingly necessary. There is a need to anticipate how research can function in these sites productively. I return to this point below.

For feminist practice, this project documents various mechanisms of feminization and proletarianization at a particular place and at a particular time. It foregrounds the dynamics of the literacies that particular women have to negotiate in relation to gender and sexual politics as pools of flows enter the scapes and spheres of their work and social worlds. It demonstrates the effects of globalizing processes on particular women and it therefore contributes to what we already know about the gendered effects of globalization.

A clear area of contention within literacy studies, specifically within conceptions of literacy as social practice (New Literacy Studies)[1] has been how to adequately explore contexts (local) and at the same time account for the non-local flows that influence situated local practices. I have touched on this issue above but will explore it more here. Reder and Davila, for example, argue that there has been no systematic articulation of "what makes a context 'local'"(179). They question the spatial and the temporal boundaries of contexts and then offer Barton and Hamilton's notion of "textually mediated social worlds" as a possible resolution of this theoretical tension. In documenting work at CTI and CDN, it is clear the entities for which I used the terms "local," "context" and "local context" are actually complex, layered, fluid, non-essentialized, unstable, non-static, digitized-textually mediated work worlds. The same short-hand descriptor applies to my uses of the term global. And it too is fluid.

For Street these terms are heuristics or metaphors that help us to describe sets of practices (2010, 187). I would argue that the analytic tools offered by the concepts of flows, sites, and scapes make it possible to map non-local influences on the specific practices that women at CTI and CDN negotiated in their work worlds. These analytic tools make it possible to document these local-global practices in dialog. The hybrid practices that resulted from these negotiations were neither local nor global—they were observable hybrids that changed as the pools of flows instigated shifts in practices. For example, as I describe in chapter 7, Nola's practices in her work world shifted in the course of fieldwork. What prompted that shift was traceable and it was non-local; it originated elsewhere. When those demands entered her work world, Nola reoriented her practices and adapted accordingly; she absorbed the new demands into what she already knew and did.

## UNFINISHED BUSINESS: WORKPLACE LITERACY AND GLOBALIZATION

Global economic, political, social, and cultural changes, and, particularly, economic competition, have caused rapid changes in what we now deem appropriate literacy acquisition. Developments in literacy, no matter the context, have been driven by the rather fast-paced evolution of technologies. Efficient uses of emerging technologies for effective communication and an adroit determination of the value of information require us to examine workplace literacies in the contexts in which they are practiced. Looking at workplace literate behaviors as social practice and looking at the situated nature of practices has enabled the field to advocate for practices based on research. The new workplaces emerging offshore and the manner in which most of these straddle the material and the immaterial pose difficult challenges. As I note above, work in the locations demands creative adaptations of research approaches. Researchers must take up interdisciplinary conversations and begin to grapple with understanding how offshore workers negotiate their local, school-based and employer-sponsored literacies to get other peoples' work done, often on terms set elsewhere. Complicating matters further are the limits of conducting research in proprietary spaces where owners set the terms of how spaces may be accessed and under what conditions. All this requires us to wrestle with questions about the intersections of literacy, workplace practice, research, and policy. These issues are the unfinished business that I hope this project has foregrounded.

## REPRESENTATION AND LEGITIMIZATION: NOLA'S QUESTION

To conclude this last chapter, I return to Nola's question—"Are you going to write about us?" This book has been about Nola and the many women who work in outsourcing at CTI and CDN. In writing the book, I have been acutely aware of my academic interests. After all, I stand to gain professionally from this project. However, I also hope that this book achieves far more than enhancing my professional credentials. Ultimately, I hope it starts conversations that contribute to the well-being of the women who work in the outsourcing industry in Ghana and in places like Ghana around the world. Have I been just? I leave that to readers and to Nola and her friends to decide. But I return to a point I made in chapter 4—that a gender-focused exploration of the intersections of globalization, knowledge, literate practices and "new" work in outsourcing in Ghana sheds light on how the supposedly inconsequential actors in the "global now," particularly women, are rewriting the terms of their "exclusion." Nola and her peers as human agents collectively re-wrote the terms on which those shaping the dominant narratives of globalization may see them as inconsequential actors in the "global now," and the story of how they did and continue to do so belongs to them.

## NOTES

1.  See Brandt and Clinton (2002), Collins and Blot (2003), Reder and Davila (2005), Street (2003), and Street and Lefstein (2010).

# Appendix A

RESEARCH QUESTIONS

- In what ways and for what purposes do women in process outsourcing use digital and information communications technologies in their literacy practices in the workplace?
- In what ways and for what purposes do women enact gender and culturally specific literacy practices in their online and offline workspaces?
- How are constructions of gender implicated in the women's technology-mediated literacy practices within their online work communities?
- How do the local and the global intersect? That is to say, what are the global economic conditions that make this arrangement proliferate for outsourcing companies?
- What are the current and potential future political implications of such arrangements? How are these economic and political issues perceived by Ghanaian workers?

# Appendix B

*I. Background questions*

1. How long have you worked at _____?
2. What is your educational background?
3. How are your uses of reading, writing, listening and speaking at work different from what you use these abilities for outside work?
4. How did you find out about the work you do here?
5. How difficult is it to find this kind of work in Ghana?
6. How many hours do you work every week?

*II. Workplace Practices-related questions*

1. What technologies do you use as part of your work?
2. What do you use them for?
3. How would you describe your training in using these technologies?
4. Do you use these technologies outside work? If so where and for what purposes?
5. Are there ways in which your uses of these technologies at work is different from the ways in which men use them or might use them in this workplace?
6. How much of your work is done online?
7. How much is done via the Internet?
8. What literacy abilities do you use online?
9. How different are these from those you use outside this online environment?
10. Are there any behaviors that you would characterize as Ghanaian in this environment? How? And why?
11. What is the nature of the contacts you have with the employees of the overseas companies for whom you work?
12. Why do you think you are doing work for these companies?
13. What benefits do you see? What disadvantages do you see?
14. What are the current and potential future political implications of such arrangements?
15. How are these economic and political issues perceived by Ghanaian workers?

# Appendix C

Dear _____,

I am writing to you as a faculty member of Illinois State University's College of Education who is planning to conduct research at _____. The purpose of this letter is to inform you about the research project and to ask that you consider participating in it. The research project seeks to investigate the ways in which women who work in outsourcing use literacy both online and offline. It also seeks to understand the dynamics that affect outsourcing work that women do.

This will be an ethnographic study, though it pushes the boundary of what we have traditionally labeled ethnographic because it will examine experiences in hybrid environments. The design will explore the question of what form ethnography takes when it is no longer about physical space. The design calls for my immersion in the multiple environments in which women work as I gather data from the contexts that shape their work experiences. I will take a participant observer stance during the data gathering process.

Data will be collected over a six-month period—from June 2004 to December 2004. During this time, I will be present in the physical work place each work day. I will also participate in online environments for which I gain access. I especially expect to use online data gathering tools after December 2004. Data will include field notes from formal and informal interviews with women, some of them face-to-face, and others online. Field notes from informal interviews with management will enable me to get the perspective of managers on the nature of the work that women do. Other sources of data will be work-related discussions that occur both on and offline, online documents, artifacts such as websites, email, and other online practices that shape the women's work environment.

Additionally, three focal informants will be chosen after the first couple months of field work. For the three focal women there will be more extensive data collection that will involve out-of-the work place visits and informal interviews to gather data on work and out work practices that shape the women's work environment. The data will be coded and analyzed inductively and recursively so that the researcher can use such data as a backdrop for ongoing investigation, deeper exploration and clarification as necessary.

I hope you will participate in my research as I hope what I learn and share may be useful.

Sincerely,


Beatrice Quarshie Smith
  Associate Professor,
  Illinois State University,
  Normal, IL

# Appendix D

CONSENT FORM

BEATRICE QUARSHIE-SMITH, CURRICULUM AND INSTRUCTION

Title of Study: Stories from the Trenches of Information Technology Process Outsourcing: An Ethnographic Study of the Literacies of Women in "Cyber Sweatshops" in Ghana

Purpose of Study: This is an investigation into the effects that the Internet and global connectivity is having on the literacy practices of women who work in process outsourcing in Ghana. It seeks to understand the political economy of Information Communication Technologies and their relationship to gender and to workplace literacy practices.

Nature of Participation: The researcher will be at your work place daily for a period of about six months. Further, the researcher will maintain contact with women employees via email after she returns to the United States in order to keep collecting data on the work place. Ongoing interviews will provide the researcher with opportunities to evaluate impact of technologies on literacy practices in the outsourcing work that women do in Ghana. Managers will also be interviewed to get their perspective on the nature of work in the workplace. Participation will involve semi-structured interviews to gather information on their perspective on the work that women do.

Risk: The risks of this study are minimal though I acknowledge that the presence of a researcher in a workplace might affect its dynamics. Your privacy may also be affected. Questions about participant literacy histories, practices and work performance may reveal private information about you. However, the data that is collected will be confidential and you will have your identity protected by the use of codes in any report or publication that is based on this project. All data will be stored in secured files and will only be available to the researcher or their authorized research assistants.

<u>Possible Benefits:</u> This study will contribute to our understanding of how ICTs are changing the literacy practices that researchers have traditionally seen as related to work. It will also help us see how ICTs are being adopted and integrated into workplaces outside the west.

<u>Opportunities to Question:</u> If you have questions about the study, please contact Dr. Beatrice Quarshie Smith at (309) 438-3008 or via email at bbsmith@ilstu.edu. Any questions about your rights as a participant may be directed to Nancy Latham in Research and Sponsored Programs, (309) 438-2520 or via email at nilatha@ilstu.edu.

<u>Opportunity to Withdraw:</u> If you decide now or at any point to withdraw this consent or stop participating, you are free to do so at no penalty to you. You are also free to skip particular questions during interviews and continue to participate in the study without penalty.

<u>Sharing Results:</u> The results of this will be shared with the professional community. The real names of participants will not be used in any publications or presentations. No references will be made to individuals in ways that divulge their identities. If any images of you are going to be used in any publication or presentation, I will seek separate written permission from you.

I have read and understand the above statements and voluntarily sign this form.

I grant permission to Beatrice Quarshie Smith to record interviews with me as part of their investigation of the literacy practices of women who work in process outsourcing in Ghana.

Name:_____ Date:

Signature:_____

Please return this form in the enclosed return addressed envelope by 5/30/04. Thank you!

# Appendix E

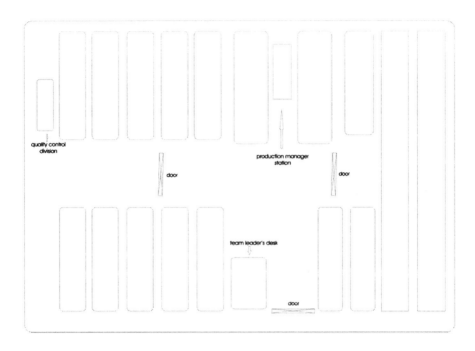

# Appendix F

ORTHO KEYWORDS

If any of the following keywords are present within the description of the billing detail section of the claim, then it should be classified as an Orthodontic claim and keyed as such with only one detail line. You will still use the keywords present on the keying rules to determine if it is Ortho, i.e., 8000 procedure codes, etc.

*If the description automatically fills in one of these keywords due to the procedure code that is keyed, this will not make it an Ortho claim.*

Active ortho tx
Appl
Applian
Appliance
Arch wire
Band
Banding
Banding fee
Bands
Bonding
Bonding fee
Brace
Braces
Bracket
Brackets
Class l
CL l
Class ll
CL ll
Class lll
CL lll
Continuing ortho tx
Debanding
Debonding
Exam/ortho
Initial payment
Month

Months
Monthly
Monthly adj.
Monthly adjustment
Monthly adjustments
Monthly amount
Monthly billing
Monthly fee
Monthly orth
Monthly ortho
Monthly payment
Orth
Ortho
Orthodontia
Orthodontic
Orthodontics
Interceptive TX
Periodic ortho
Pre-orth
Pre-ortho
Pre-orthodontics
Quarterly
Quarterly billing
Quarterly orth
Quarterly ortho
Quarterly payment
Ret.
Retainer
Retainers
Transitional TX
Appliance adjustment
Appliance insertion
Initial banding
Initial fee
Initial appliance fee
Initial placement
Initial placement fee
Continuation of TX
Continuation of treatment
Continuing treatment
Continuing TX
Continuing monthly
Monthly orthodontics billing
Monthly TX
Monthly treatment

Monthly visit
Orthodontic records
Orthodontic treat
Periodic treatment
Periodic TX
Periodic visit-car
Ortho adj
Total case fee
Quarterly TX
Quarterly treatment

# Appendix G

CTI GHANA LIMITED
CTI TOWERS
RETIREMENT ROAD, ACCRA.

Pay Slip of the period: 16/06/2004 to 30/06/2004

**Name:** SHAKIRA
**Job Title:** DATA PROCESSING ASST
**Regular Hours:** 72.85

**SS Number:** 1236789    **ID:** A00000012
**SBU.:** ATDA    **Shift:** Morning
**Overtime Hours:** 1.69    **Team:** 1ST SHIFT

### *Earnings Detail*

| | |
|---|---|
| 111 WORK SHORTAGE | ¢11,094.00 |
| 122 OVERTIME 1.5 PIECE RATE | ¢4,522.48 |
| 150 PIECE RATE | ¢387,847.22 |

### *Deductions Detail*

| | |
|---|---|
| 201 INCOME TAX | ¢35,652.50 |
| 202 EMPLOYEE SHARE OF SSF 5 | ¢19,947.06 |
| 211 ASSOCIATION DUES | ¢5,000.00 |

**Total Earnings:** ¢403,463.70

**Total Deductions:** ¢60,599.56

**Net Pay:** ¢342,864.14

*Employer's Share SSF: 12.50%* ¢49,867.65

---

CTI GHANA LIMITED
CTI TOWERS
RETIREMENT ROAD, ACCRA.

Pay Slip of the period: 01/09/2004 to 15/09/2004

**Name:** NOLA ADDY
**Job Title:** DATA PROCESSING ASST
**Regular Hours:** 88.73

**SS Number:** 2348910    **ID:** A00123456
**SBU.:** ATD    **Shift:** Morning
**Overtime Hours:** 5.22    **Team:** 1ST SHIFT

### *Earnings Detail*

| | |
|---|---|
| 114 MEETING | ¢11,094.00 |
| 122 OVERTIME 1.5 PIECE RATE | ¢11,788.25 |
| 150 PIECE RATE | ¢413,237.67 |

### *Deductions Detail*

| | |
|---|---|
| 201 INCOME TAX | ¢40,360.50 |
| 202 EMPLOYEE SHARE OF SSF 5 | ¢21,216.58 |
| 211 ASSOCIATION DUES | ¢5,000.00 |

**Total Earnings:** ¢436,119.92

**Total Deductions:** ¢66,577.08

**Net Pay:** ¢369,542.84

*Employer's Share SSF: 12.50%* ¢53,041.46

183

# Bibliography

Agar, Michael. *Language shock: Understanding the Culture of Conversation*. New York: William Morrow& Co, 1994.

Agar, Michael. *The Professional Stranger: An Informal Introduction to Ethnography*. 2nd ed. San Diego: Academic Press, 1996.

Agyeman-Duah, Ivor, Christine Kelly, eds. *An Economic History of Ghana: Reflections on a Half-Century of Challenges and Progress*. London: Turnaround Publisher Services, 2008.

Allah-Mensah, B. "Women and Politics in Ghana, 1993–2003." 251–279 in *Ghana: One Decade of the Liberal State*, edited by Kwame Boafo-Arthur. New York: Palgrave Macmillan, 2007.

American Association of University Women. *Tech-savvy: Educating Girls in the New Computer Age*. Washington, D.C.: Author, 2000.

Apffel-Marglin, F.and Loyda Sanchez. "Developmentalist Feminism and Neocolonialism in Andean Communities."159–180 in *Feminist Post-Development Thought: Rethinking Modernity, Postcolonialism, and Representation*, edited by Kriemild Saunders. London: Zed Books Ltd, 2002.

Appadurai, Arjun. "Disjuncture and Difference in the Global Cultural Economy." 295–310 in *Global Culture* edited by Mike Featherstone. London: Sage Publications, 1990.

Appadurai, Arjun. *Modernity at Large: Cultural Dimensions of Globalization*. Minneapolis: University of Minnesota Press, 1997.

Appadurai, Arjun. "Grassroots Globalization and the Research Imagination." 1–21 in *Globalization*, edited by Arjun Appadurai. Durham, NC: Duke Press, 2001.

Appadurai, A. "Deep Democracy: Urban Governmentality and the Horizon of Politics." *Public Culture, 14*, no. 1 (Winter 2002): 21–47.

Appiah, Kwame Anthony. "The Case for Contamination." *The New York Times Magazine*. www.nytimes.com/2006/01/01/magazine/01cosmopolitan.html?_r=1&scp=3& sq=Kwame%20Anthony%20Appiah&st=cse&oref=slogin. (January 1, 2006). Accessed September 26, 2008.

Apusigah, Agnes, A. "Gender Mainstreaming the Ghana Poverty Reduction Strategy or Is It?" *Women in Action 2*, (August, 2004): 83–91.

Asante, E. "Review: Engendering Development through Gender Equality in Rights and Resources, A World Bank Policy Research Report." *Canadian Journal of Sociology* 27, no. 2 (2002): 293.

Athanases, Steven, Z. and Shirley Brice Heath. "Ethnography in the Study of the Teaching of English." *Research in the Teaching of English, 29* no. 3 (October 1995): 263–87.

Avgerou, Chrisanthi . *Information Systems and Global Diversity*. Oxford, UK: Oxford University Press, 2002.

Balden, Sally, Cathy Green, Naana Otoo-Oyortey, and Tessa Peasgood. *Background Paper on Gender Issues in Ghana*. Institute of Development Studies, Brighton, UK: Bridge Reports no 19, 1994.

Baldoz, Rick, Charles Koeber, and Philip Kraft., eds. *A critical study of work: labor, technology and global production*. Philadelphia: Temple University Press, 2001.

Barlow, Tani. "Picture More at Variance: Of Desire and Development in the People's Republic of China." 146–58 in *Feminist Post-Development Thought: Rethinking Moder-*

*nity, Postcolonialism, & Representation*, edited by Kriemild Saunders London: Zed Books Ltd, 2002.

Barton, David and Mary Hamilton. *Local literacies: Reading and Writing in One Community*. London: Routledge, 1998.

Barton, David, Mary Hamilton and Roz Ivanic, eds. *Situated Literacies: Reading and Writing in Context*. London: Routledge, 2000.

Baynham, Mike and Mastin Prinsloo. *In The Future of Literacy Studies*. London: Palgrave Macmillan, 2009.

Beck, Ulrich. *What is Globalization?* Translated by Patrick Camiller, Malden, MA: Blackwell Publishers, 2000.

Behar, Ruth. *Translated Woman: Crossing the Border with Esprenza's Story.* Boston: Beacon Press, 1993.

Behar, Ruth and Deborah A. Gordon, eds. *Women Writing Culture.* Berkeley: University of California Press, 1995.

Bell, David. *An Introduction to Cybercultures.* London: Routledge, 2001.

Belfiore, Mary Ellen, Tracy A. Defoe, Sue Folinsbee, Judy Hunter and Nancy S. Jackson. *Reading work: Literacies in the new workplace.* Mahwah, NJ: Lawrence Erlbaum Associates, 2004.

Benefo, Kofi D. and Vijayan K. Pillai. "Determinants of Women's Non-family Work in Ghana and Zimbabwe." *Canadian Studies in Population,* 30, no. 2 (2003): 389–406.

Berger, Arthur. *Media and Communication Research Methods: An Introduction to Qualitative and Quantitative Approaches.* Thousand Oaks, CA: Sage Publications, 2000.

Berger, Iris and Frances E. White. *Women in sub-Saharan Africa: Restoring Women to History.* Bloomington, IN: Indiana University Press, 1999.

Berry, La Verle, ed. *Ghana: A Country Study.* Washington, D.C.: Federal Research Division, Library of Congress, 1995.

Bhabha, Homi, K. *The Location of Culture.* London: Routledge, 1994.

Billett, Stephen. "Negotiating Self thorough Changing Work." *Educating the Global Workforce: Knowledge, Knowledge Work, and Knowledge Workers,* edited by Lesley Farrell and Tara Fenwick. New York: Routledge, 189–99, 2007.

Blunch, Niels-Hugo and Dorte Verner. *Is functional literacy a prerequisite for entering the labor market? An analysis of the determinants of adult literacy and earnings in Ghana.* Denmark: Centre for Labour Market and Social Research, 2000.

Boafo-Arthur, Kofi. "A Decade of Liberalism in Perspective." 1–20 in *Ghana: One Decade of the Liberal State,* edited by Kofi. Boafo-Arthur New York: Palgrave Macmillan, 2007.

Boafo-Arthur, Kofi. "The Liberal Ghanaian State and Foreign Policy: The Dynamics of Change and Continuity." 227–50 in *Ghana: One Decade of the Liberal State,* edited by Kofi. Boafo-Arthur New York: Palgrave Macmillan, 2007.

Boateng, Kwabia. *Youth and ICT skills in African Labor Markets,* 2006. www.un.org/esa/socdev/unyin/documents/tc_addis06_2_ict_education.pdf. Retrieved September 26, 2008.

Bogdan, Robert C. and Sara K. Biklen. *Qualitative Research for Education: An Introduction to Theories and Methods.* 4th ed. Boston, MA: Pearson Group, 2003.

Borris, Eileen. "Gender After Africa!" 191–204 in *Africa After Gender,* edited by Catherine. M. Cole, Takyiwaa Manuh, and Stephan F. Miescher. Bloomington, IN: Indiana University Press, 2007.

Boyle, Mary-Ellen. *The New Schoolhouse: Literacy, Managers, and Belief.* Westport, CT: Praeger Publishers, 2001.

Brandt, Deborah. *Literacy in American Lives.* Cambridge, UK: Cambridge University Press, 2001.

Brandt, Deborah and Clinton, Katie. "Limits of the Local: Expanding Perspectives on Literacy as a Social Practice." *Journal of Literacy Research,* 34(3), 337–56.

Bretton Woods Project. *SAPRIN Findings overwhelming, but Wolfensohn tells NGOs to "Change their Tune,"* 2002. www.brettonwoodsproject.org/art.shtml?x=15863. Retrieved February 24, 2009.

Brooke, James. "Ghana, Once 'Hopeless,' Gets at Least the Look of Success." *New York Times,* January 3, 1989. query.nytimes.com/gst/full-page.html?res=950DE3D7163AF930A35752C0A96F948260&n=Top/News/World/Countries%20and%20Territories/Ghana&scp=2&sq=Ghana%20World%20bank%20model&st=cse. Accessed February 23, 2009.

Bruce, Bertram C. "Critical issues. Literacy and Technology: What Stance Should we Take?" *Journal of Literacy Research,* 29, no. 2 (June 1997): 289–309.

Bruce, Bertram C. "Speaking the Unspeakable about 21st Century Technologies." 221–28 in *Passions, pedagogies and 21st century technologies,* edited by Gail Hawisher and Cynthia Selfe. Logan, UT: Utah State University Press, 1999.

Buah , F. K. *A Short History of Ghana.* London: Macmillan, 1998.

Burawoy, Micheal. "Manufacturing the Global." Introduction to a Special Issue of *Ethnography* 2, no. 2 (June 2001): 147–59.

Burbules, Nicholas and Thomas Callister. *Watch IT: The Risky Promises and Promising Risks of New Information Technologies in Education.* Boulder, CO: Westview Press, 2000.

Burgess, Robert G. *In the Field: An Introduction to Research.* London: Allen & Unwin,1984.

Burkatek, Justin, Ron Feingold, Ryan Patterson and Joshua Walker. "Telecommunications and ICT Development in Ghana: Lessons from Two Call Centers in Accra." n.d. www.ghanacybergroup.com/get-file.asp?file=120729147531_Ghana_call_Centre.pdf. Retrieved January 20, 2008.

Butterwick, Shuana, Kaela Jubas, and Hong Zhu. "Gender Matters in IT: Skills Hierarchies and Women's on-the-job Learning." 278–88 in *Educating the Global Workforce: Knowledge, Knowledge Work, and Knowledge Workers,* edited by Lesley Farrell and Tara Fenwick. New York: Routledge, 2007.

Carspecken, Phil F. *Critical Ethnography in Educational Research: A Theoretical and Practical Guide.* New York: Routledge, 1996.

Castells, Manuel. *The Rise of the Network Society.* Oxford: Blackwell, 1996.

Castells, Manuel. *The Power of Identity.* Malden, MA: Blackwell, 1997.

Castells, Manuel. *End of Millennium.* Malden, MA: Blackwell, 1998.

Castleton, Geraldine. "Workplace Literacy as a Contested Site of Educational Activity." *Journal of Adolescent & Adult Literacy* 45, no.7 (April 2002): 556–66.

Central Intelligence Agency. (n.d.). *The World Fact Book.* www.cia.gov/cia/publications/factbook/geos/gh.html. Retrieved February 10, 2005.

Chandler-Olcott, Kelly and Donna Mahar. ""Tech-Savviness" Meets Multiliteracies: Exploring Adolescent Girls' Technology-related Literacy Practices." *Reading Research Quarterly* 38, no. 3 (July, August, September 2003): 356–85.

Chatterjee, Piya. "Ethnographic Acts: Writing Women and Other Political Fields." 243–62 in *Feminist Post-Development Thought: Rethinking Modernity, Postcolonialism, and Representation ,* edited by Kriemild Saunders. London: Zed Books Ltd, 2002.

Chappell, Clive, Hermine Scheeres and Nicky Solomon. "Working on Identities." 167–77 in *Educating the Global Workforce: Knowledge, Knowledge Work, and Knowledge Workers,* edited by Lesley Farrell and Tara Fenwick. New York: Routledge, 2007.

Clifford, James. "Spatial Practices: Fieldwork, Travel, and the Disciplining of Anthropology." 185-222 in *Anthropological Locations,* edited by Akhil Gupta and James Ferguson. Berkeley: University of California Press, 1997.

Clifford, James. "Traveling Cultures." 96–116 in *Cultural Studies,* edited by Larry Grossberg, Cary Nelson, and Paula A. Treichler. London: Routledge, 1992.

Clifford, James and George E. Marcus., eds. *Writing Culture: The Poetics and Politics of Ethnography.* Berkeley: University of California Press, 1986.

Cole, Catherine M. "'Give her a Slap to Warm her Up': Post-gender Theory and Ghana's Popular Culture." 270–84 in *Africa After Gender,* edited by Catherine. M. Cole, Takyiwaa Manuh, and Stephan F. Miescher. Bloomington, IN: Indiana University Press, 2007.

Collins, James and Richard Blot. *Literacy and literacies: texts, power, and identity.* Cambridge and New York: Cambridge University Press, 2003.

Cope, Bill and Mary Kalantzis. *Multiliteracies: Literacy Learning and the Design of Social Futures.* London: Routledge, 2000.

Crothers, Lane. *Globalization and American Popular Culture.* 2nd edition. Lanham, MD.: Rowan & Littlefield, 2010.

Darrah, Charles N. "Workplace Skills in Context." *Human Organization* 51, no. 3 (Fall 1992): 264–73.

Darrah, Charles N. "Complicating the Concept of Skill Requirements: Scenes from a Workplace." 249–72 in *Changing Work, Changing Workers: Critical Perspectives on Language, Literacy and Skills,* edited by Glynda Hull. Albany, NY: State University of New York Press, 1997

De Beauvoir, Simone. *The Second Sex.* New York: Vintage Books, 1973.

Denzin, Norman K. and Yvonna S. Lincoln., eds. *The Landscape of Qualitative Research: Theories and Issues.* 2nd ed. Thousand Oaks, CA: Sage Publications, 2003.

Dobbert, Marion L. *Ethnographic Research: Theory and Application for Modern Schools and Societies.* New York: Praeger, 1984.

Dolphyne, Florence Abena. *The Emancipation of Women: An African Perspective.* Accra, Ghana: Ghana Universities Press, 1991.

Duran, Jane. *Worlds of Knowing: Global Feminist Epistemologies.* London: Routledge, 2001.

Editorial. "An African Success Story." *The New York Times,* January 8, 2001.

Economist Intelligence Unit (European Union). *Country Reports: Ghana.* London: EIU, 1998.

Economist Intelligence Unit (European Union). *Country Reports: Ghana.* London: EIU, 1999.

Nicoll, Kathy and Richard Edwards. "The Ghost in the Network: Globalization and Workplace Learning." 300–10 in *Educating the Global Workforce: Knowledge, Knowledge Work, and Knowledge Workers, edited by* Lesley Farrell and Tara Fenwick. New York: Routledge, 2007.

El-Ojeili, Chamsy and Patrick Hayden. *Critical Theories of Globalization.* New York: Palgrave Macmillan, 2006.

Ellen, R. F., ed. *Ethnographic Research: A Guide to General Conduct.* Orlando, FL: Academic Press, 1984.

English, Leona M. "Third-space Practitioners: Women Educating for Justice in the Global South." *Adult Education Quarterly,* 55 no. 2 (February 2005):85–100.

Erickson, Frederick. "On the Evolution of Qualitative Approaches in Educational Research: From Adam's Task to Eve's." *Australian Educational Researcher,* 23 no. 2 (August 1996): 1–15.

Facer, Keri and Ruth Furlong. "Beyond the Myth of the "Cyberkid": Young People at the Margins of the Information Revolution." *Journal of Youth Studies,* 4, no. 4 (December 2001): 451–69.

Farrell, Lesley. "Ways of Doing, Ways of Being: Language, Education and 'Working' Identities." *Language and Education,* 14 no. 1 (March 2000):18–36.

Farrell, Lesley. *Making Knowledge Common: Literacy and Knowledge at Work.* New York: Peter Lang and Co, 2006.

Farrell, Lesley. "Texting the Future: Work, Literacies, and Economies." In *The Future of Literacy Studies,* edited by Mike Baynham and Mastin Prinsloo. 181–98. London: Palgrave Macmillan, 2009.

Farrell, Lesley and Tara Fenwick. "Introduction." 1–10 in *Educating the Global Workforce: Knowledge, Knowledge Work, and Knowledge Workers,* edited by Lesley Farrell and Tara Fenwick. New York: Routledge, 2007.

Farrell, Lesley and Tara Fenwick. "Educating a Global Workforce?" 13–26 in *Educating the Global Workforce: Knowledge, Knowledge Work, and Knowledge Workers,* edited by Lesley Farrell and Tara Fenwick. New York: Routledge, 2007.

Feenberg, Andrew. *Transforming Technology: A Critical Theory Revisited*. New York: Oxford University Press, 2002.

Firestone, Shulamith. *The Dialectic of Sex: The Case for Feminist Revolution*. New York: Morrow, 1970.

Fischer, Maria Clara Bueno and Clair Ribeiro Ziebell. "Women and their Knowledge Managing the 'Other Economy.'" 289–99 in *Educating the Global Workforce: Knowledge, Knowledge Work, and Knowledge Workers*, edited by Lesley Farrell and Tara Fenwick. New York: Routledge, 2007.

Florio-Ruane, Susan and Mary McVee. "Ethnographic Approaches to Literacy Research." 77–86 in *Methods of Literacy Research* edited by Michael L. Kamil, Peter B. Mosenthal, P. David Pearson and Rebecca Barr. Mahwah, NJ: Lawrence Erlbaum, 2002.

Foucault, Michel . *The Archaeology of Knowledge*. Trans. A. M. Sheridan Smith. London and New York: Routledge, 2002.

Fredric Jameson and Masao Miyoshi. *The Cultures of Globalization*. Durham: Duke University Press, 1999.

Friedman, Thomas L. *The World is Flat*. New York: Farrer Straus and Giroux, 2006.

Gee, James, Glynda A. Hull, and Colin Lankshear. *The New Work Order*. Boulder, CO: Westview Press, 1996.

Gee, James. "New People in New Worlds: Networks, the New Capitalism and Schools." 43–68 in *Multiliteracies: Literacy Learning and the Design of Social Futures*, edited by Brian Cope and Mary Kalantzis. New York: Routledge, 2000.

Geertz, Clifford. *The Interpretation of Cultures*. New York: Basic Books, 1973.

Ghanaweb.com. http://www.ghanaweb.com/. Accessed November 18, 2011.

Giddens, Anthony. *The Consequences of Modernity*. Cambridge: Polity Press, 1990.

Goad, Tom W. *Information Literacy and Workplace Performance*. Westport, CT: Quorum Books, 2002.

Goldin, Ian and Reinert, Kenneth, A. *Globalization for Development: Trade, Finance, Aid, Migration, and Policy*. 2nd ed. Washington, DC: World Bank Publications, 2007.

Gowen, Sherly. *The Politics of Workplace Literacy: A Case Study*. New York: Teachers College Press, 1992.

Green, Judith L. Carol N. Dixon and Amy Zaharlick. "Ethnography as a Logic of Inquiry." 201–24 in *Handbook of Research on Teaching the English Language Arts*, 2nd ed. edited by James Flood, Diane Lapp, James R. Squire and Julie M. Jensen. Mahwah. NJ: Lawrence Erlbaum, 2003.

Greenstreet, Miranda. "The Woman Wage Earner in Ghana." 18–30 in *Manpower supply and utilization in Ghana, Nigeria and Sierra Leone*, edited by Ukandi Damachi and Kodwo Ewusi. Geneva: International Institute of Labor Studies, 1979.

Grubb, W. Norton. "Dick and Jane at Work." 249–72 in *Changing Work, Changing Workers: Critical Perspectives on Language, Literacy and Skills*, edited by Glynda Hull. Albany, NY: State University of New York Press, 1997.

Hagood, Margaret. C. "New Media and Online Literacies: No Age Left Behind" *Reading Research Quarterly* 38, no. 3 (July, August, and September 2003): 388–413.

Hale, Briony. "In Search of Africa's Silicon Valley." news.bbc.co.uk/2/hi/business/3000004.stm June 23, 2003. Retrieved January 25, 2009.

Hale, Briony. "Ghana Enters Telesales Era." news.bbc.co.uk/2/hi/business/3039355.stm May, 20, 2003. Retrieved January 25, 2009.

Hardt, Michael and Antonio Negri. *Empire*. Cambridge: Harvard University Press, 2000.

Harvey, David. *The Condition of Postmodernity*. Oxford: Blackwell, 1989.

Hawisher, Gail E. and Selfe, Cynthia L. *Global Literacies and the World-wide Web*. New York: Routledge, 2000.

Hawkesworth, Mary E. "Confounding Gender." *Signs: Journal of Women in Culture and Society* 22, no. 3 (January 1997):649–85.

Hawkesworth, Mary E. *Globalization and Feminist Activism*. Lanham, MD: Rowman and Littlefield Publishers, 2006.

Heath, Shirley Brice. *Ways with Words: Language, Life and Work in Communities and Classrooms.* Cambridge, UK: Cambridge University Press, 1983.

Held, David and Anthony McGrew, eds. *Globalization Theory: Approaches and Controversies.* Malden, MA: Polity Press, 2007.

Held, David and Anthony McGrew. "Introduction: Globalization at Risk?" 1–14 in *Globalization Theory: Approaches and Controversies* edited by David Held and Anthony McGrew. Malden, MA: Polity Press, 2007.

Herbert, Pat and Clinton Robinson. "Another Language, Another literacy?: Practices in Northern Ghana." 121–36 in *Literacy and Development: Ethnographic Perspectives* edited by Brian Street. New York: Routledge, 2001.

Hine, Christine. *Virtual Ethnography.* Thousand Oaks, CA: SAGE Publications, 2000.

Hodson, Randy. *Analyzing Documentary Accounts.* Thousand Oaks, CA: SAGE Publications, 1999.

Hodson, Randy. *Dignity at Work.* Cambridge: Cambridge University Press, 2001.

Hodson, Randy and Sullivan, Teresa A. *The Social Organization of Work.* 4th ed. Florence, KY: Thomson Wadsworth, 2007.

Hoggart, R. *The Uses of Literacy* . London: Penguin, 1958.

Holkner, Bernard. "Social Technologies at Work." 239–50 in *Educating the Global Workforce: Knowledge, Knowledge Work, and Knowledge Workers,* edited by Lesley Farrell and Tara Fenwick. New York: Routledge, 2007.

Holmes, Douglas R. and George E. Marcus. "Refunctioning Ethnography: The Challenge of an Anthropology of the Contemporary." 519–37 in *The Landscape of Qualitative Research: Theories and Issues,* 3rd ed. Edited by Norman Denzin K. Norman and Yvonna S. Lincoln. Thousand Oaks, CA: Sage Publications, 2008.

Howell, Sharon L., Vicki K. Carter and Fred M. Schied. "Gender and Women's Experience at Work: A Critical and Feminist Perspective on Human Resource Development." *Adult Education Quarterly* 52 no. 2 (May 2002): 112–27.

Hull, Glynda. "Critical Literacy at Work." *Journal of Adolescent & Adult Literacy,* 43 no. 7 (May 2002): 648–52.

Hull, Glynda and Norton W. Grubb. "Literacy, Skills, and Work." 311–417 in *Literacy: An International Handbook,* edited by Daniel Wagner, Richard L. Venezky and Brian Street. Boulder, CO: Westview Press, 1999.

Hull, Glynda and Jessica Zacher. "Identity Formation and Literacy Development within Vocational Education and Work." 330–48 in *Educating the Global Workforce: Knowledge, Knowledge Work, and Knowledge Workers* edited by Lesley Farrell and Tara Fenwick. New York: Routledge, 2007.

Huws, Ursula. *The Making of a Cybertariat: Virtual Work in a Real World.* New York: Monthly Review Press, 2003.

Huws, Ursula. "What Will We Do?: The Destruction of Occupational Identities in the 'Knowledge-Based Economy.'" www.monthlyreview.org/0106huws.htm, January 2006. Retrieved November 10, 2009.

Huws, Ursula. "Fixed, Footloose, or Fractured: Work, Identity, and the Spatial Division of Labor in the Twenty-First Century." www.monthlyreview.org/0306huws.php, March 2006. Retrieved November 10, 2009

Hymes, Dell. "Models of Interaction of Language and Social Life." 35–71 in *Directions in Sociolinguistics: The Ethnography of Communication* edited by John Gumperz and Dell Hymes New York: Holt, 1972.

Hymes, Dell. *Foundations of Sociolinguistics.* Philadelphia: University of Pennsylvania Press, 1974.

Hymes, Dell. "What is ethnography?" 21–32 in *Children in and out of School: Ethnography and Education,* edited by Perry Gilmore and Allan A. Glathorn. Washington: Center for Applied Linguistics, 1982.

Ikezi, Eri and Evaristus Mainsah. "Is Ghana an Attractive Proposition for IT Services and Business Process Outsourcing?" *Chazen Web Journal of International Business,* (Spring, 2004) www2.gsb.columbia.edu/chazenjournal/article.cfm?pub=849. Retrieved January 19, 2005.

International Business Publications. Ghana Country Guide, 4th Edition, Washington, DC: 2012.

Jacob, Evelyn. "Combining Ethnographic and Quantitative Approaches: Suggestions and Examples from a Study in Puerto Rico." Pp. 124–47 in *Children in and out of School: Ethnography and Education*, edited by Perry Gilmore and Allan A. Glathorn. Washington: Center for Applied Linguistics, 1982.

Johnston, William B. and Arnold E. Packer. *Workforce 2000: Work and Workers for the 21st Century*. Indianapolis, IN: Hudson Institute, 1987.

Jorgensen, Danny L. *Participant Observation: A Methodology for Human Studies*. Newbury Park, CA: SAGE Publications, 1989.

Kellner, Douglas. "New Technologies/New Literacies: Reconstructing Education for the New Millennium." *Teacher Education* 11, no.3 (December 2000): 245–65.

Kleinman, Sherryl. *Feminist Fieldwork Analysis*. Thousand Oaks, CA: SAGE Publications, 2007.

Kleinman, Sherryl and Martha A. Copp. *Emotions and Fieldwork*. Newbury Park, CA: SAGE Publications, 1993.

Komer, Robert W. Memorandum From Robert W. Komer of the National Security Council Staff to the President's Special Assistant for National Security Affairs (Bundy). Robert W. Komer files: National Security File, Country File, Ghana, Vol. II, Cables, 3/64–2/66. Johnson Library. www.lbjlib.utexas.edu/johnson/archives.hom/ .../presiden.asp, (Washington, May 27, 1965).

Konadu-Agyemang, Kwadwo, ed. *IMF and World Bank Sponsored Structural Adjustment Programs in Africa: Ghana's Experience 1983–1999*. Burlington, VT: Ashgate Publishing Company, 2001.

Konadu-Agyemang, Kwadwo. "Africa under World Bank/IMF Management: The Best of Times and the Worst of Times." 427–34 in *IMF and World Bank sponsored structural adjustment programs in Africa: Ghana's experience 1983–1999*, edited by Kwadwo Konadu-Agyemang. Burlington, VT: Ashgate Publishing Company, 2001.

Konadu-Agyemang, Kwadwo and Takyi Baffour Kwaku. "Structural Adjustment Programs and the Political Economy of Development and Underdevelopment in Ghana." 17–40 in *IMF and World Bank Sponsored Structural Adjustment Programs in Africa: Ghana's Experience 1983–1999* , edited by Kwadwo Konadu-Agyemang. Burlington, VT: Ashgate Publishing Company, 2001.

Konadu-Agyemang, Kwadwo. "Structural Adjustment Programs and Housing Affordability in Accra, Ghana." *Canadian Geographer* 45, no. 4 (2001): 528–44.

Kwapong, Olivia Adwoa Tiwaah Frimpong. Widening Access to Tertiary Education for Women in Ghana through Distance Education. *Turkish Online Journal of Distance Education* 8, no. 2 (2007): 65–79.

Lacey, Marc. "Accents of Africa: A New Outsourcing Frontier." *The New York Times*. Accessed February 2, 2011, www.nytimes.com/2005/02/02/business/worldbusiness/ 02outsource.html?scp=1& sq=%E2%80%9CAccents%20of%20Africa:%20A%20New%20Outsourcing%20Fronti er.%E2%80%9D%20&st=cs.

Lankshear, Colin, James P. Gee, Michele Knobel, and Chris Searle. *Changing Literacies* . Buckingham, England: Open University Press, 1997.

Lauder, Hugh, Brown, Phillip, Dillabough, Jo-Anne and A.H.Halsey. (Editors), *Education, Globalization and Social Change*, Oxford University Press, 2006.

Leander, Kevin M. "Writing Travelers' Tales on New Literacyscapes." *Reading Research Quarterly 38*, no.3 (July, August and September 2003): 392–97.

Lechner, Frankand and John Boli. *The Globalization Reader*. 2nd ed. Malden, MA: Blackwell, 2004.

Lincoln, Yvonna and Egon Guba. "Paradigmatic Controversies, Contradictions, and Emerging Confluences." 253–91 in The Landscape of Qualitative Research: Theories and Issues, 2nd ed. edited by Norman Denzin and Yvonna Lincoln. Thousand Oaks, CA: Sage Publications, 2003.

Luke, Carmen. "Cyber-schooling and Technological Change: Multiliteracies for New Times." 69–91 in *Multiliteracies: Literacy Learning and the Design of Social Futures*, edited by Brian Cope and Mary Kalantzis. London: Routledge, 2000.

Luke, Carmen. "Pedagogy, Connectivity, Multimodality, and Interdisciplinarity." *Reading Research Quarterly* 38 no. 3 (July, August and September 2003): 397–403.

Mackey, Margaret. "Researching New Forms of Literacy." *Reading Research Quarterly* 38, no. 3 (July, August and September 2003): 403–7.

Manuh, Takyiwaa. "Doing Gender Work in Ghana." 125–49 in *Africa After Gender*, edited by Catherine. M. Cole, Takyiwaa Manuh, and Stephan F. Miescher. Bloomington, IN: Indiana University Press, 2007.

Manuh, Takyiwaa. "Women and their organizations during the Convention People's Party period." 101–27 in *The Life and Work of Kwame Nkrumah*, edited by Kwame Arhin, Sedco: Accra, 1991.

Manuh, Takyiwaa. "Women, the state and society under the PNDC." 176–95 in *Ghana under PNDC Rule*, edited by E. Gyimah-Boadi, CODESRIA: Dakar, 1993.

Marcus, George. E., ed. *Connected: Engagements with Media*. Chicago: University of Chicago Press, 1996.

Marcus, George. E. *Ethnography through Thick and Thin*. Princeton, NJ: Princeton University Press, 1998a.

Marx, Karl and Friedrich Engels. *The Communist Manifesto With an Introdution by AJP Taylor*. Great Britain: Cox and Wynan Ltd, 1967.

Matthew, Annu. "*The Virtual Immigrant.*" Accessed February 23, 2009, www.annumatthew.com/Portfolios/virtual%20immigrant/ta_Virtual%20Immigrants.htm.

Mazawi, André Elias. "'Knowledge Society' or Work as 'Spectacle'? Education for Work and the Prospects of Social Transformation in Arab Societies." 251–67 in *Educating the Global Workforce: Knowledge, Knowledge Work, and Knowledge Workers*, edited by Lesley Farrell and Tara Fenwick. New York: Routledge, 2007.

McDermott, John. The Culture of Experience. New York University Press, 1976.

Mensah, Rose Kutin. "Women Prepare to Make their Mark in Elections." Accessed February 25, 2009, www.peacewomen.org/news/Ghana/October03).

Mhone, Guy. "The Impact of Structural Adjustment on the Urban Informal Sector in Zimbabwe." Geneva: ILO, 1995.

Miescher, Stephan F. "Becoming an Opanyin: Elders, Gender, and Masculinities in Ghana since the Nineteenth Century." 253–69 in *Africa After Gender*, edited by Catherine. M. Cole, Takyiwaa Manuh, and. Miescher. Bloomington, IN: Indiana University Press, 2007.

Miescher, Stephan F., Takyiwaa Manuh and Catherine M. Cole. "Introduction: When was Gender?" 1–16 in *Africa After Gender*, edited by Catherine. M. Cole, Takyiwaa Manuh, and. Miescher. Bloomington, IN: Indiana University Press, 2007.

Ministry of Women and Children. "Domestic Violence Act of 2007." Accessed February 26, 2009, www.mowacghana.net/files/dva.pdf.

Mirchandani, Kiran and Srabani Maitra. "Learning Imperialism through Training in Transnational Call Centres." 154–64 in *Educating the Global Workforce: Knowledge, Knowledge Work, and Knowledge Workers* edited by Lesley Farrell and Tara Fenwick. New York: Routledge, 2007.

Moghadam, Valentine. *Globalizing Women: Transnational Feminist Networks*. Baltimore: Johns Hopkins University Press, 2005.

Moser, Caroline, O .N . "Gender Planning in the Third World : Meeting Practical and Strategic Gender Needs." *World Development* 8 no.11 (1989) :1799–1825.

Mosley, Layna. "The Political Economy of Globalization." 106–25 in *Globalization Theory: Approaches and Controversies*, edited by David Held and A. McGrew. Malden, MA: Polity Press, 2007.

Moss, Beverly. J. "Ethnography and Composition: Studying Language at Home." Pp. 153–71 in *Methods and methodology in composition research*, edited by Gesa Kirschand Patricia Sullivan. Carbondale, IL: Southern Illinois University Press, 1992.

New London Group. "A Pedagogy of Multiliteracies: Designing Social Futures." *Harvard Educational Review* 66, no.1 (Spring 1996):60–92.

Newfield, Christopher. *Unmaking the Public University: The Forty-year Assault on the Middle Class.* Cambridge, MA: Harvard University Press, 2008.

Ninsin, Kwame A. "Markets and Liberal Democracy." 86–105 in *Ghana: One Decade of the Liberal State,* edited by Kwame Boafo-Arthur. New York: Palgrave Macmillan, 2007.

Nixon, Helen. "New Research Literacies for Contemporary Research into Literacy and New Media?" *Reading Research Quarterly* 38, no.3 ( July August and September 2003): 407–13.

OECD. *Education at a Glance 2005.* OECD Education, 2005.

Ogbu, John U. *The Next Generation: An Ethnography of Education in an Urban Neighborhood.* New York: Academic Press, 1974.

Ogbu, John U. *Minority Education and Caste: The American System in Cross-cultural Perspective.* New York: Academic Press, 1978.

Ogbu, John U. "Cultural Discontinuities and Schooling." *Anthropology and Education Quarterly* 13, no. 4 (Winter 1982): 290–307.

Okedara, J. "Literacy in English-speaking Africa." 410–13 in *Literacy: An International Handbook,* edited by David Wagner, Richard Venezky and Brian Street. Boulder, CO: Westview Press, 1999.

Ó Riain, Sean. "Net-working for a Living: Irish Software Developers in the Global Workplace." 258–78 in *A Critical Study of Work: Labor, Technology and Global Production,* edited by Rick Baldoz, Charles Koeber and Philip Kraft. Philadelphia: Temple University Press, 2001.

Otoo-Oyortey, Naana., and Sonita Pobi. "Early Marriage and Poverty: Exploring Links and Key Policy Issues." Gender and Development 11, no. 2 (July 2003):42–51.

Panford, Kwamina. "Structural Adjustment Programs, Human Resources and Organizational Challenges Facing Labor and Policy Makers in Ghana." 219–39 in *IMF and World Bank Sponsored Structural Adjustment Programs in Africa: Ghana's Experience 1983–1999,* edited by Kwadwo Konadu-Agyemang. Burlington, VT: Ashgate Publishing Company, 2001.

Panford, Kwamina. *African Labor Relations and Workers' Rights.* Westport, Connecticut: Greenwood Press, 1994.

Panford, Kwamina. *IMF-World Bank and Labor's Burdens in Africa: Ghana's Experience.* Westport, Connecticut: Greenwood Press, 2001.

Parpart, Jane. "Lessons from the Field: Rethinking Empowerment, Gender, and Development from a Post-(Post-?) Development Perspective." 41–56 in *Feminist Post-Development Thought: Rethinking Modernity, Postcolonialism, & Representation,* edited by Kriemild Saunders. London: Zed Books Ltd, 2002.

Parpart, Janel L., and Staudt, Kathleen A. eds. *Women and the state in Africa.* Boulder, Col. : L. Rienner Publishers, 1989.

Penley, Constance and Ross, Andrew. *Technoculture.* Minneapolis: University of Minnesota Press, 1992.

Pennycook, Alastair. *Language as a Local Practice.* New York: Routledge, 2010.

Pogge, Thomas. "Reframing Global Economic Security and Justice." Pp. 207–24 in *Globalization Theory: Approaches and Controversies,* edited by David Held and Anthony McGrew. Malden, MA: Polity Press, 2007.

Polgreen, Lydia. "Ghana's Unlikely Democrat Finds Vindication in Vote." *The New York Times.* Accessed February 24, 2009, www.nytimes.com/2009/01/10/world/africa/10rawlings.html?_r=1&scp=1&sq=Rawlings%20Ghana%20democracy&st=cs.

Powell, Walter W., and Snellman, Kasia. "The Knowledge Economy." *Annual Review of Sociology* 30, no.1 ( August 2004): 199–220.

Probert, Belinda and Wilson, Bruce W. eds. *Pink Collar Blues: Work, Gender, and Technology.* Carlton, Victoria: Melbourne University Press, 1993.

Quarshie Smith, Beatrice. "Outsourcing and Digitized Work spaces: Some Implications of the Intersections of Globalization, Development and Work Practices." *Journal of Adolescent and Adult Literacy* 48, no. 7 (April 2007): 596–607.

Reder, Stephen and Erica Davila. "Context and literacy," *Annual Review of Applied Linguistics*. 25, 170–87, 2005.

Reich, Robert. *The Work of Nations: Preparing Ourselves for 21st Century Capitalism*. London: Simon and Schuster, 1991.

Reiner, Erik S. ed.*Globalization, Economic Development, and Inequality: An Alternative Perspective*.Cheltenham, UK: Edward Elgar Publishing, 2004.

Riemer, Frances. "Becoming Literate, Being Human: Adult Literacy and Moral Reconstruction in Botswana." Anthropology and Education Quarterly 39, no.4 (December 2008): 444–64.

Robertson, Ronald. *Globalization: Social Theory and Global Culture*. London: Sage, 1992.

Robertson, Ronald. "Glocalization: Space, Time and Social Theory." *Journal of International Communication* 1, no. 1, 1994.

Rothchild, Donald, ed. *Ghana: The political Economy of Recovery*. Boulder, CO: Lynne Rienner Publishers, 1991.

Rist, Ray. "Blitzkrieg Ethnography: On the Transformation of a Method into a Movement." *Educational Researcher* 9, no.2 (February 1980): 8–10.

Ross, Andrew. *Real Love: In Pursuit of Cultural Justice*. London: Routledge, 1998.

Sacks, Nancy. E. and Catherine Marrone, eds. *Gender and Work in Today's World: A Reader*. Cambridge, MA: Westview Press, 2004.

SAPRIN. Structural Adjustment Participatory Review International Network. *World Economy*, May, 20:285–305, 1997.

SAPRIN. SAPRIN in Ghana. *Structural Adjustment Participatory Review Initiative*. August 22. www.worldbank.org/research/sapri/ghana.htm.

Sassen, Saskia. "Counter-geographies of Globalization: Feminization of Survival." 89–104 in *Feminist Post-Development Thought: Rethinking Modernity, Postcolonialism, and Representation*, edited by Kriemild Saunders. London: Zed Books Ltd. (2002).

Sassen, Saskia. "The Places and Spaces of the Global: An Expanded Analytic Terrain." 79–105 in *Globalization Theory: Approaches and Controversies* David Held and Andrew McGrew. Malden, MA: Polity Press, 2007.

Saukko, Paula. *Doing Research in Cultural Studies: An Introduction to Classical and New Methodological Approaches*. Thousand Oaks, California: SAGE Publications, 2003.

Saunders, Kriemild, ed. *Feminist post-development thought: Rethinking modernity, postcolonialism, and representation*. London: Zed Books, 2002.

Sawchuk, Peter H. "Work and the Labour Process: 'Use-value' and the Rethinking of Skills and Learning." 54–64 in *Educating the Global Workforce: Knowledge, Knowledge Work, and Knowledge Workers*, edited by Lesley Farrell and Tara Fenwick. New York: Routledge, 2007.

Schultz, Katherine. "Discourses of Workplace Education: A Challenge to the New Orthodoxy." 249–72 in *Changing work, changing workers: Critical perspectives on language, literacy and skills*, edited by Glynda Hull. Albany, NY: State University of New York Press, 1997.

Scott, Joan. "Gender: A Useful Category for Historical Analysis." *American Historical Review* 91, (December 1986):1053–1075.

Selfe, Cynthia. L. *Technology and Literacy in the 21 st century: The Importance of Paying Attention*. Carbondale, IL: Southern Illinois University Press, 1999.

Shami, Seteney. "Studying your Own: The Complexities of a Shared Culture." 115–38 in *Arab Women in the Field*, edited by Soraya Altorki and Camilla Fawzi El-Solh. Syracuse: Syracuse University Press, 1988.

Shkedi, Asher. "Narrative Survey: A Methodology for Studying Multiple Populations." *Narrative inquiry* 14, no.1 (2004): 87–112.

Slayter, Ellen. Company Hopes to Take Outsourcing to a New Level: Africa. *Washington Post*. E05. (November 29 2004,).

Smith, Beatrice. "Researching Hybrid Literacies: Methodological Explorations of "Ethnography" and the Practices of the 'Cybertariat.'" 127–49 in *Digital writing research: Technologies, methodologies, and ethical issues*, edited by Danielle DeVoss and Heidi Mckee. Cresskill, NJ: Hampton Press, 2007

Smith, Cynthia R. "Click on Me! An Example of how a Toddler Used Technology in Play." *Journal of early childhood literacy 2*, no.1 (2002): 5–20.

Spradley, James P. *Participant Observation*. New York: Holt, Rinehart and Winston, 1980.

Steger, Manfred B. *Globalization: A Very Short Introduction*. New York: Oxford University Press, 2003.

Street, Brian. "The Meanings of Literacy." 311–417 in *Literacy: An International Handbook*, edited by David Wagner, Richard Venezky and Brian Street. Boulder, CO: Westview Press, 1999.

Street, Brian. *Literacy and Development: Ethnographic Perspectives*. New York: Routledge, 2001.

Street, Brian. "What's 'new' in New Literacy Studies? Critical approaches to literacy in theory and practice." *Current Issues in Contemporary Education*, 5 (2), 77–91, 2003.

Street, Brian and Adam Lefstein. *Literacy: An advanced resource book*. New York: Routledge, 2010.

Stiglitz, Joseph E. *Making Globalization Work: The Next Step to Global Justice*. New York: W.W. Norton and Company, 2007.

Sweetman, Caroline. *Gender, Development and Marriage*. Oxford: Oxfam, 2003.

The Associated Press. "Switzerland: A Step Forward for Domestic Workers." *The New York Times*. Accessed October 24, 2011, www.nytimes.com/2011/06/17/world/europe/17briefs-Switzerland.html

Terry, Jennifer and Melodie Calvert., eds. *Processed Lives: Gender and Technology in Everyday Life*. New York: Routledge, 1997.

Tikly, L. "Globalization and Education in the Postcolonial World: Towards a Conceptual Framework." *Comparative Education 37*, no.22 (2001):151–71.

Tsikata, Kwaku G. "Challenges of Economic Growth in a Liberal Economy." 49–85 in *Ghana: One Decade of the Liberal State*, edited by Kwame Boafo-Arthur. New York: Palgrave Macmillan, 2007.

United Nations Commission on Science and Technology for Development (UNCSTD), 1997

United Nations Commission on Science and Technology. Accessed September 12, 2008, www.unctad.org/Templates/Page.asp?intItemID=4452&lang=1,

United Nations Development Plan. Accessed February10, 2005, hdr.undp.org/statistics/data/cty/ctyfGHA.html, n.d.

United Nations Education and Scientific Organization (UNESCO), Institute for Statistics. Accessed March 12, 2010, stats.uis.unesco.org/unesco/TableViewer/tableView.aspx.

United Nations Education and Scientific Organization (UNESCO), Institute for Statistics. Accessed December 26, 2011, stats.uis.unesco.org/unesco/TableViewer/tableView.aspx.

United Nations Education and Scientific Organization (UNESCO). *Global Education Digest*. Accessed December 26, 2011, www.uis.unesco.org/Library/Documents/global_education_digest_2011_en.pdf.

United States Census Bureau, 2000 Census. Accessed March 10, 2010, www.census.gov/main/www/cen2000.html.

Volti, Rudi. *An Introduction to the Sociology of Work and Occupations*. Los Angeles: Pine Forge Press, 2008.

Wangari, Esther. "Reproductive Technologies: A Third World Feminist Perspective." 298–312 in *Feminist Post-Development Thought: Rethinking Modernity, Postcolonialism, & Representation*, edited by Kriemild Saunders. London: Zed Books Ltd, 2002.

Warriner, Doris. "Transnational Literacies: Examing global flows through the Lens of Social Practice." *In The Future of Literacy Studies*, edited by Mike Baynham and Mastin Prinsloo. 160–80. London: Palgrave Macmillan, 2009.

Waters, Malcolm. *Globalization.* 2nd ed. New York: Routledge, 2001.

Wichterich, Christa. *The Globalized Woman: Reports from a Future of Inequality.* London: Zed Books, 2000.

Windborne, Janice. "Literacy Groups in Ghana: Liberation with Limitation." *Women's Studies Quarterly 32*, no. ½ (2004): 59–73.

Windham, Douglas. "Literacy and Economic Development." 342–47 in *Literacy: An International Handbook,* edited by David Wagner, Richard Venezky, and Brian Street. Boulder, CO: Westview Press, 1999.

Wolf, Martin. *Why Globalization Works.* New Haven: Yale Nota Bene, 2005.

Women's Empowerment Research Project Consortium (WE RPC). Accessed February 26, 2009, http:/pathwaysghana.blogspot.com/.

World Bank. "Gender, Growth and Poverty Reduction." *Technical Report No. 428: Special Program Assistance for Africa: 1998 Status Report on Poverty in Sub-Saharan Africa.* Washington, D.C.: World Bank, 1999.

World Bank. *Lifelong Learning in the Global Knowledge Economy: Challenges for Developing Countries: a World Bank Report.* Washington, D.C.: World Bank, 2003.

World Bank. "Ghana Meeting the Challenge of Accelerated and Shared Growth Country Economic Memorandum." Accessed January 14, 2009, siteresources.worldbank.org/INTGHANA/Resources/CEM_synthesis.pdf.

World Bank. "Ghana, Data and Statistics." Accessed February 6, 2009. web.worldbank.org/WBSITE/EXTERNAL/COUNTRIES/AFRICAEXT/GHANAEXTN/0,,menuPK:351978~pagePK:141132~piPK:141109~theSitePK:351952,00.html.

World Bank. "Ghana, Data and Statistics." Accessed October 24, 2011, data.worldbank.org/country/ghana.

Worth, Robert. L. "In New York tickets, Ghana Sees Orderly City." *The New York Times,* A1, A17, (2002, July 22).

Wright, Joanne. "Deconstructing Development Theory: Feminism, the Public/Private Dichotomy and the Mexican Maquiladoras," *The Canadian Review of Sociology and Anthropology 34*, no. 34 (February 1997): 71–91.

"Youth at United Nations." Accessed March 6, 2010. www.un.org/esa/socdev/unyin/.

Zaharkick, Amy and Judith Green. "Ethnographic Research." 205–25 in *Handbook of Research in Teaching the English Language Arts,* edited by James Flood. New York: Macmillan, 1991.

# Index

# About the Author

Beatrice Quarshie Smith is an associate professor of Literacy Studies in the Department of Humanities at Michigan Technological University where she is also the Director of the Intensive English as a Second Language Program. Her research interests include explorations of the relationships among globalization, gender, English language literacies, and work-related practices.

CPSIA information can be obtained at www.ICGtesting.com
Printed in the USA
BVOW071521060612

291785BV00002B/5/P